PRAISE FOR *THE FIRST BOOK OF INVESTING*

"Here's a book to read before you begin investing, before you know anything about the market, possibly even before you have the money to invest."

**—Michael Pellecchia,
syndicated financial columnist**

"This is the book I wish had been available when I first started hacking my way through the confusing jungle of financial jargon."

**—Robert Acker,
investment analyst,
editor of *The Acker Letter***

"A very good book . . . written in language just about anyone can understand."

—*Syracuse Post-Standard*

THE FIRST BOOK
OF INVESTING

THE FIRST BOOK OF INVESTING

The Absolute Beginner's Guide to Building Wealth Safely

SAMUEL CASE

Fully Revised 3rd Edition

Prima Publishing

PRIMA PUBLISHING and colophon are registered trademarks of Prima Communications, Inc.

Library of Congress Cataloging-in-Publication Data
Case, Samuel.
    The first book of investing : the absolute beginner's guide to building wealth safely / Samuel Case. — Fully rev. 3rd ed.
        p.   cm.
    Includes index.
    ISBN 0-7615-2133-X
    1. Investments—United States. 2. Investment analysis.
I. Title.
HG4910.C355 1999
332.6—dc21   99-37477
                                                                        CIP

99 00 01 02 03 AA 10 9 8 7 6 5 4 3 2 1
Printed in the United States of America

How to Order

Single copies may be ordered from Prima Publishing, P.O. Box 1260BK, Rocklin, CA 95677; telephone (916) 632-4400. Quantity discounts are also available. On your letterhead, include information concerning the intended use of the books and the number of books you wish to purchase.

Visit us online at www.primalifestyles.com

CONTENTS

Part 3: High-Risk Investing   323

ACKNOWLEDGMENTS

Although there are many people who contribute to the making of a book, there are even more who contribute to the making of a writer. Some people have given me general help and encouragement, others have given help specific to this book. A few have done both and I would like to acknowledge and thank them all.

First of all, both my mother and father, Josephine and Everett, always supported my writing. And the fact that both are published writers gave me models to work with from an early age.

My sister Josephine and brother Jim have not only given encouragement but have, on occasion, lent houses to write in. The interest and enthusiasm of my brother John for the early drafts of this book were crucial to an author starting out. John, who has written several books on business and economics, also contributed the chapter on starting your own business, and gave much valuable advice.

One of the earliest fans of my writing and story-telling was my daughter, Syrena. She has continued her interest and support as I shifted from children's stories to investing.

And finally, the one who has lived with me through the various trials and vicissitudes of the last few years:

my wonderful wife, Judy Aizuss. Judy not only gave much support, she also did all the initial editing on the manuscript. If the reader finds that the strange ways of the World of Investment are explained in an understandable fashion, he or she owes much to Judy's editing.

Over the years, I have always been supported in my writing by my friends. In particular, I want to thank Dan Drasin, Judith Edmonds, and Betty and Don Stone for all their interest and encouragement.

I'm grateful to Dan Geiger and Susanna Moore at the Vanguard Foundation for their insights and information about socially responsible investing.

My thanks to Joanne Handfield of Conscious Times for her initial formatting and design. Although I eventually decided not to publish the book myself, Joanne's work was a very important step in the progression of the manuscript to book form.

My heartfelt thanks go to Michael Le Page for all his invaluable counseling. Jennifer Basye Sander, my editor at Prima Publishing, has provided ongoing support and information about the publishing process. Jennifer Boynton and Melanie Field at Bookman Productions, and copy editor Anne Montague have worked hard with me on the final manuscript. And Gary Morgan gave of his time and talent very generously in preparing the fine illustrations that adorn the pages of this book.

So many people! It reminds me of the story of Leo Durocher, who, upon being congratulated for managing the New York Giants to another pennant, declared grandly: "I couldna done it without the team!" Like Leo, I couldna done it either without a wonderful team of helpers, supporters, and cheerleaders behind me. Thanks are not enough. I only hope that I can be as supportive of their endeavors as they have been of mine.

Sam Case

Fairfax, California

The First Book
of Investing

INTRODUCTION

The purpose of this book is to help you make money. It will tell you the first things you need to know about investing in the various financial markets. This book is meant to be read before you do anything else.

If you have already tried to read some investment books, you may be aware that most of the authors expect you to know certain basic things. This book makes no such assumptions. If you do know a few basic things, you're that much ahead; you can still learn from this material. If you need to start from scratch, then this is truly your book. This is the book I wish I had had when I started learning about investing. I hope it will save you as much time and money as it could have saved me.

The traditional way of learning about investing has been the trial-and-error method. Most new investors try various markets, lose money, and finally acquire some knowledge through bitter experience. This is roughly analogous to learning how to drive by having a series of accidents. Others try to avoid such painful lessons by immediately giving their assets to a financial manager, before they have learned how to choose a good one. This can be another prescription for disaster.

Experience can indeed be useful, but there is no reason you can't start out a winner. With a little care and the knowledge you will gain from this book, you can set up a program that will preserve and increase your money while you continue to learn about investing.

Many people have had bad experiences not just with math, but with anything to do with math—and that includes investments. This can lead to a negative state of mind and a firm belief that you are incapable of really grasping any concept involving numbers. If this has been a problem for you, you should know that this book was written with you in mind. The small amount of arithmetic employed is only the simplest, most basic kind and is clarified with true-to-life examples. I have tried out various chapters on people with extremely high math-anxiety quotients, and have made revisions in response to their suggestions.

My hope is not only that you will easily understand everything in this book, but that this understanding will give you a new, positive feeling about yourself in relation to such things as math and investments—in short, that you will feel empowered. For those to whom math is a snap, I hope you will feel empowered just by learning about a fascinating new field.

When you undertake a foreign language, it's easy to get overwhelmed by the sheer amount of things to learn. The authors of the language texts are aware of this problem, however, and present a step-by-step approach, starting with the most basic, most important things first.

For new investors trying to learn the language of the marketplace, however, there has been no such comforting text to turn to. You are presented not only with a bewildering array of books, newsletters, and advertisements, but also with a large number of individuals who purport to have the kind of information you can't live without. Some of this material may be useful, but you have to be aware that the people giving it out are salespeople who stand to benefit from your investment with them. Before dealing with the marketplaces and the people working in them, the new investor needs to know a few basic things, as well as the best places to look for more detailed information.

One of the purposes of this book is to help you decide which areas of investment you want to pursue, or simply learn more about. These kinds of decisions need to include more than just financial considerations. For example, some people enjoy owning rental property and dealing with tenants; others are temperamentally unsuited to this task. In this book, we ask you to consider more than just the bottom line in choosing where to place your money and your energy.

You will find more sections on the stock market than on any other topic because this has been the preferred market for the majority of investors, particularly new investors. This historical preference should not keep you from pursuing other areas, however. What's most important is what feels right to you.

To help you pursue the areas that interest you, you will find at the end of many chapters a list of sources for further information on the chapter topic. These books, newsletters, tapes, and courses of instruction were chosen not just for their authors' knowledge of their fields, but also for their ability to communicate in a clear, interesting manner—a skill sometimes lacking in the World of Investment.

The problem in this field is not in finding information, but in finding quality information. I have included only a few recommendations for further research, but they are the best. By keeping down the sheer volume of material I hope to prevent the dangerous I-don't-want-to-hear-another-word-about-30-year-zero-coupon-bonds-EVER! syndrome.

These days, the place with the greatest quantity of investment information is the Internet—and, therefore, the place where the new investor is most likely to be overwhelmed. Getting online can be an important step in managing your investments, but you need to know what you're getting into. To this end, I have created a new chapter in this edition which will explain how to use the Internet to your benefit and guide you to the best online investing sites.

It may be that after reading this book and a few others, you'll decide that you're not really interested in the difference between T-bills and zero-coupon bonds, and that what you really want is an expert to do it for you. That's fine. Some people find investing an absorbing occupation or an interesting sideline; others treat it more like a business. But there are always some who view it simply as an unpleasant task.

It's important to have some knowledge of investments, however, so you can choose a good investment manager and keep tabs on your portfolio ("portfolio" means simply your combined investments of various kinds). Later in the book, we will talk about the ways to choose the best investment advisers and managers.

I am reminded, in this regard, of Richard Bach, the author of *Jonathan Livingston Seagull,* who took the considerable royalties from this best seller and gave them to a friend, who happened to be an investment manager. As he recounts in a subsequent book, Bach then went off to fly his airplanes and date beautiful women, depending on his friend to send him a check whenever he needed it. After a few years of this, he got a call saying that the money was gone—all of it. And the Internal Revenue Service was demanding a million dollars in back taxes by the next week.

So you can see, perhaps, that some knowledge and interest in your money is a good thing, whether or not you plan to manage it yourself.

How This Book Is Arranged

This book is meant not just as an introduction to the World of Investment, but as a manual to get you started. Part I—the first 11 chapters—covers the first things a new investor needs to know about this world.

In Part II, we will begin to apply what we've learned and discuss more advanced methods of investing. Part III includes the high-risk investments—what to watch out for as well as what might look interesting as you become more experienced.

This book is arranged so that you, as a new investor, will know what is most important to consider first. The amount of material in this field has been overwhelming to many people, leading them to throw up their hands and go back to the trial-and-error method. Too many investment books add to this confusion by simply presenting an entire mass of information without emphasizing which are the primary, most basic things you need to know.

It may surprise you to see how quickly you will learn your way around once you know these basics. The World of Investment has its own language, but otherwise it is much like the rest of the world—governed partly by rational thinking, partly by emotions. As you learn what to expect, you will able to set up your own investments so that they—and you—will be able to handle the ups and downs of the markets.

PART 1

AN OVERVIEW FOR BEGINNERS

CHAPTER 1

THE WORLD OF INVESTMENT

So . . . what do you want from investing? High adventure in strange and exotic places, roller-coaster rides, thrills and chills? Or perhaps a steadier trip on a comfortable train or a sedate cruise ship?

If you prefer the first, you may be a trader or a speculator rather than an investor. Traders concentrate on price, buying, and selling over a short period, often on the same day. Investors concentrate on long-term value, ignoring day-to-day price fluctuations.

For example, a trader might buy shares of IBM because he or she believes the price of the stock is about to go up sharply. If it does go up, the trader will sell and take a profit. An investor would buy IBM because the company looks good over the next few years. The investor is looking for long-term appreciation or a steady income, or both.

It's important for the new investor to realize that many advertisements for "investments" are actually ads for risky speculations. The information and sources presented in this book, on the other hand, are for *investors:* those people who are interested in a safe and reasonable appreciation of their capital over a period of years.

If You Can't Stand the Heat, Stay Out of the Kitchen . . .

At the beginning of each section dealing with a specific kind of investment, you will find risk-reward thermometers.

    Risk and reward are almost always on opposite ends of a teeter-totter. As one goes up, the other goes down. The story of speculation is the story of trying to find exceptions to this rule. Investors, on the other hand, accept it as a given rule and work with it.

    But even as an investor, you will still have to choose between different degrees of risk. It's your job to decide how adventurous you want to be. It's our job in this book to prepare you to choose intelligently.

    The first thing that any new investor needs to know is that there are no sure things in the World of Investment. It is a place of shifting sands. A method of investing that has worked wonderfully in the past may suddenly fail without warning due to a whole new set of circumstances.

    Some Investment advisers speak with such authority that they seem to have all the answers. But it never ceases to astonish me how three different analysts presented with the same set of statistics will come up with three different predictions on the direction of any given market or company. And these are not just differences in emphasis—these are radical disagreements.

A method of investing that has worked wonderfully in the past may suddenly fail without warning due to a whole new set of circumstances.

In the colorful parlance of the marketplace, an analyst who believes a market is on the rise is called a *bull,* whereas one who predicts that the same market is headed south is termed a *bear.* For example, you might say that an analyst is "bullish" on stocks, but "bearish" on bonds. Most analysts will switch from bullish to bearish depending on where they think a market is headed. A few, however—especially in the stock market—seem to be genetically predisposed to optimism and become known as perpetual bulls, while others, with bearish genes, will continually tell you that another 1929-type crash is just around the corner.

Some advisers are better than others, particularly when it comes to individual stocks. In this book, we will direct you to a few and tell you how to find others. *But it is important that you give up any search for certainty before you set out.* Certainty is one commodity in very

short supply in the World of Investing. A market may proceed in an orderly and seemingly predictable fashion for a time and then suddenly stand on its head, leaving the investor in a not-too-pleasant Wonderland that bears some similarities to Alice's.

Three Ways of Dealing with Money

There are essentially three ways of dealing with money (besides spending it all, or hiding it in a mattress). You can invest it, speculate with it, or gamble. There are important differences among the three.

Investors have expectations that the place they put their money is reasonably safe and that they will realize a fair—if conservative—return. Investors are usually willing to leave their money in the same place for a number of years.

Speculators are open to more risk. They are generally people who are knowledgeable about a certain market and hope to use this knowledge to realize profits, usually over a short period of time—days, weeks, or months.

Gamblers essentially throw themselves at the mercy of the fates. We are all acquainted with casino gambling, but investing in a risky market with little knowledge of that market is also gambling.

What would be speculation to a knowledgeable person is gambling to the novice—and with odds worse than those offered by the casinos.

The reason the odds are worse is that unlike most games of chance, speculation involves some skill, and the novice is up against experienced traders in a zero-sum game. Someone is going to win and someone is going to lose and, if you really want to gamble, you know which one to bet on. . . .

> **Don't fall into the trap of thinking that because you are very successful at your work, you will just naturally be successful at investing.**

Do you remember the Latin inscription on the archway or main building of your school? "Knowledge Is Power," it said, or perhaps "The Truth Shall Set You Free." Over the entrance to the World of Investment is inscribed the disclaimer required by government regulators on all investment advice: "Past Performance Is No Guarantee of Future Success."

But if certainty is a scarce commodity, there are certainly ways of minimizing your risk. The goal is to get a good return on your money and still sleep soundly at night. We're going to show you how to do that. Onward!

Even at this early stage, it's not too soon to start thinking about what kind of investor you will be. Conservative? Very conservative? Or are you drawn more to small Australian gold-mining operations? (Let me tell you about this amazing outfit that my cousin Jack is part owner of. . . .) What kind of investing will you be happy and comfortable with?

And it's never too early to start thinking about what you want to focus on with your investments. Retirement? College education? Achieving financial independence? Or simply getting a good, safe return on your money?

Most of us are used to employing our skills to make money. Investing, however, involves using money to make money—and doing this almost always requires a different set of skills than the ones we have developed at our jobs. Don't fall into the trap of thinking that because you are very successful at your work, you will just naturally be successful at investing. You built up your professional skills over time with much training and diligence; learning to invest will also take some time and effort.

Investing money for the greatest possible return can be a most interesting and exciting endeavor. Before getting into it, though, you may need to deal with some emotions connected with how you got the money. Waiting a few months, giving yourself time to work things out and get used to your new situation, learning all you can about investing before risking any money—all this will leave you in a much better position to be a successful investor.

Resources

American Association of Individual Investors, (800)735-0700. Membership: $49/year. Includes subscription to the AAII Journal, published monthly. Log onto <www.aaii.com> for a free two-week trial membership.

This organization can be a very useful source for the new investor. A membership gives you an automatic subscription to its monthly journal. The articles deal mostly with stocks and bonds; you won't find much about real estate or other forms of investments.

In joining the association, you open yourself up to a whole range of information and activities. Magazines, books, video instruction courses, CD-ROMs, web sites, and seminars are all available to members.

Once you're a member, you can subscribe to another newsletter for $30 that deals with computerized investing—an excellent resource for online investors.

The association will also put you in touch with their local chapters. If you're interested, you can go to meetings, seminars, or join an investment club. I have been to some very interesting dinner lectures by various investment professionals. All in all, a good resource for a new investor—especially if you want contact with other investors.

Dictionary of Finance and Investment Terms, by John Downes and Jordan Elliot Goodman. Barron's Educational Series, 1995 (updated every few years). $11.95 (paperback).

I try to define as many investment terms as possible, but as you go further, you will inevitably come upon many more unfamiliar words and phrases. This book does a great job in clarifying jargon and concepts from the World of Investment.

CHAPTER 2

DEALING WITH MONEY
CONSCIOUSLY

Investors are, more often than not, treated as a single entity. The emphasis is placed on where you want to go with your investments. Where you might be coming *from*, however, is just as important, because it can strongly affect your attitude toward money.

This is an issue for us in this book because how you invest your money should be determined as much as possible by your immediate and long-term financial needs. But if your personal history strongly colors your feelings about money, what you do with it may reflect your subconscious emotional needs more than practical considerations.

The manner in which you come into money can also affect how you feel about it. So in this chapter we're going to talk about inheriting and winning lotteries, in addition to family background and personal psychology.

FAMILIES

Whether you are from a wealthy, middle-income, or low-income background, you have probably absorbed certain ideas about money and about yourself in relation to money. It can be extremely useful to look at these ideas—and to realize that you are not alone in having them.

Money has been a very guarded subject in our society. I have heard people from all backgrounds complain that their family neither talked about it nor gave them any help in learning how to deal with it. Schools teach an enormous amount about the economy, but very little about personal economics.

Wealthy people are often embarrassed about having more than others. People on the low end of the scale are embarrassed and often angry about not having as much as most people. But, until recently, very few people talked about these feelings. Now, at last, along with other taboo topics, such as sex, money is beginning to be discussed more openly. Whatever your background may be, I encourage you to look closely at your own feelings and attitudes.

MEN

Men are born knowing how to invest. They have an innate feel for the markets and can jump into a situation they know almost nothing about and make a killing. The most successful men are those who aren't afraid to risk a lot of money on a chancy venture.

If you believe all this, then maybe I can interest you in my cousin Jack's latest venture, which is developing a line of chickens with teeth. . . .

It would be funny, except that a lot of men do take these ideas as gospel and feel they have failed if they

> **If you believe all this, then maybe I can interest you in my cousin Jack's latest venture, which is developing a line of chickens with teeth. . . .**

don't match up to such fantasies. Overconfidence seems to occur in men as often as underconfidence does in women. Add to this a tendency to use money as a way of competing with other men and you have a situation to watch out for.

This is another area where you are much more likely to hear the success stories than the failures. Would *you* volunteer that you'd lost $50,000 on a Caribbean treasure-hunting venture? On the other hand, if a guy had actually found the treasure ship, you can bet that everyone within earshot would know about it.

This is the kind of skewed information process that leads men to think that others are making it big without much trouble, so why shouldn't they? The trouble is that they're hearing only about the ones who make a big splash; the ones who jump in to find there's no water in the pool don't get reported.

They are also not hearing about the amount of time and energy that goes into successful ventures. In war, it is said that battles are won before they actually occur. The same is true of investments: The real successes almost always result from careful planning.

WOMEN

We seem to have raised numbers of men in this country who have an inflated idea of their abilities. And this, sadly, seems to be matched by the number of women with low opinions of their powers. It's ironic, then, that a number of recent surveys have shown that in almost every professional field they have entered, women's performance has either been equal to or better than that of their male counterparts.

In a recent poll, 58% of the people questioned said they didn't know how to invest. This figure went up to 71% of only the women questioned; only 9% of women said they were confident about investing. In this field, too, however, these figures are misleading. Another survey, taken by the National Association of Investors Corporation, showed that all-female investor clubs do better than all-male or mixed clubs.

Louis Rukeyser, the star of *Wall Street Week*, television's first investment talk show, believes the reason for this better performance is that "women tend to go into the market with clearer objectives and to see money for what it is—a tool."

As in many other areas in this society, women operate at a disadvantage in the world of investment. For starters, it is often assumed that men will manage the investments. Too often, in families and in schools, girls are not encouraged to learn money management, beyond running a household. And, for whatever reason, more girls than boys seem to get turned off to arithmetic at an early age.

There are other issues, too, that can make dealing with money more difficult for women. Some men feel threatened and resentful if their wives earn more money than they do—or simply *have* more, as with an inheritance. That a

"Women tend to go into the market with clearer objectives and to see money for what it is—a tool."

woman could be successful managing investments may also be threatening to some men.

Attitudes are changing in this area, as in so many others, but slowly. Many women still believe they are unable to learn about investing, and simply give up control of their money to their husbands or investment managers.

Women, Money, and Power

At this point, I want to make a clear distinction between a passive giving up of control and a conscious, considered decision to let someone else manage your money.

Many people—both women and men—discover that they have little interest in day-to-day financial dealings. For these people, a spouse who is willing and competent to manage investments can be a real blessing. Or an informed choice of an investment manager may be the route to go.

The ones who are taken advantage of, however (and too often these are women) are those who give up their power by default, because they don't feel qualified to handle their own money. Underconfidence can be just as damaging as overconfidence. But underconfidence, though it may sometimes be indicative of a deeper lack of self-esteem, can often be corrected simply by learning about a field and beginning to feel competent in it.

I would urge the women reading this book to give investing a try. At the end of this chapter, you will find listed some organizations whose specific purpose is to encourage and instruct women who want to handle their own investments. I encourage you to pursue this kind of learning—and for more than just practical reasons. Money is a kind of power, and learning to manage your own money is a way of claiming your own power.

Then, even if you later decide to hire a financial manager, the decision will be a confident, informed one, not a passin giving up of power. More than likely, the adviser will find that he or she has a client who is curious, assertive, and sure of what she wants—someone who wants to work *with* the adviser.

INHERITING

The issues raised by inheriting money are, of course, not just emotional and philosophical. Later on, we will talk about the best ways to invest. Before we get to the actual investing, however, there are a few things you can do to make life a whole lot easier for yourself.

If you have just inherited, you are probably getting lots of advice—and this advice may come from people who are experienced in investing. These may be family and friends—people who have your best interests at heart, so their advice may be hard to resist.

Difficult as it may seem, the best thing you can do with your assets at this time is essentially nothing. If you have inherited cash, put it in an insured money market account at your bank and just leave it alone for a while.

There are good reasons for this. If you have inherited money or received a life insurance settlement from somebody dear to you, you are probably grieving. Grieving takes its own time—it should not be rushed. While you need to do what's necessary to keep your life going, it's not the best moment to embark on ambitious new ventures like investing. You can learn about investing, but it's a good idea to put off important decisions until you can give them your full attention.

Make a will, or alter your will to include your new assets. Different states have different laws about where your money will go if you have no will. There's a very good chance that you will disagree with these laws, but your heirs will have no recourse without a will.

ear), but you would be sacrificing any chance for future growth. Without growth, inflation will eat away steadily at your yearly income. (At present rates of inflation, your purchasing power will effectively be cut in two in about twenty years.)

The above percentages and the income they yield may change from year to year, but they should give you a general idea of how much income you can expect to get.

If you're willing to forgo the income for a while and invest the money for growth, it will increase pretty quickly. Depending on how aggressively you invest it, and on the performance of the markets, you should be able to double the amount in five to ten years.

So you have three choices: income only, income *and* growth, or growth only. Your choice will depend partly on where you are in your life: a retired person, for example, might opt for more income while a younger person with a good salary would probably go for growth. You do have a fourth choice, of course, which is to spend it all, like the prodigal son in the Bible. Perhaps if he had heard of mutual funds, he wouldn't have been such a trial to his father. . . .

If you immediately buy a boat with part of your inheritance, there will be that much less capital to invest for growth or income. If, on the other hand, you wait for a year, you may earn enough from your investments to buy the boat while retaining all your capital. Next year, you could buy another boat, or perhaps redo the kitchen.

The trick is to hold onto your capital. This is the goose that lays the golden egg. Spend the capital and you kill the goose.

These days, you can get some excellent support in dealing with all the issues raised by inheriting. At the

Nothing can eat up money fast
stay or some other disaster. You ne
you have enough health insurance an
on your auto and home.

When you feel ready, start discuss
your inheritance with your spouse or
be involved in your life and finances.
with those close to you about goals an
achieving them can be a tremendous boos
cial success.

Now is also the time to get straight wi
you feel conflicted about the money, or simpl
things out, don't hesitate to seek out a good
therapist. The small amount of time and
spend may be the best investment you will ma

Finally, if you are tempted to go out and b
sive things—the things you've dreamed of havir
good time to remember why so many of the rich s
and even increase what they have. The way they
is to spend only income while holding onto capital (
is the total amount you have to invest).

How Much Is Enough?

Many inheritors fall into the false belief that they
have inherited a "fortune" and their troubles are over.
An amount like $400,000, for example, can look like a
lot of money if you've been earning only a fraction of
that sum each year.

.   If you want to invest safely, however, and make
the amount grow, you should figure on a maximum
income of about $25,000 to $30,000 a year (6% to 7.5%
a year). If you invest all of it for income, you could
safely get $35,000 to $40,000 (9% to 10% a

end of this chapter, you will find listings for a number of remarkable foundations.

Assistance for Inheritors

Over the next 30 years, there's going to be a lot of money changing hands. The combined personal net worth of Americans over 50 is approximately $8 trillion.

This may sound like a lot, but the amounts that most people will inherit are generally not enough to support a lifestyle of the rich and famous. Families in the upper third of the economic scale generally have anywhere from $70,000 to $225,000 to bequeath (though some, of course, will leave much more). This kind of money will buy only a *small* yacht. . . .

Investing wisely, then, so that the principal amount grows over the years can be very important. It is so important, in fact, that it's probably not something you want to jump into as soon as you get the money. First, you need to deal with the emotional issues that may be raised by receiving your inheritance.

The estate lawyers who send out the checks or owner-ship papers to inheritors should have a rubber stamp reading: WARNING! HIGHLY CHARGED MATERIAL! Because talking about issues surrounding money has been taboo, only recently has it become clear that many people have

> **One of the deepest sources of internal conflict can come from receiving money as a result of the death of a loved one. This can be a real mindbender: your good fortune comes because this person has died! Many people find it difficult to deal with the money under these circumstances.**

trouble dealing with their inheritance. We discuss this subject here because too often inheritors resolve their conflicts by losing the money, either by spending it or by investing unwisely. Others put it away in a bank and try to ignore it.

Let's look at some of the emotionally charged issues that come up for inheritors.

One of the deepest sources of internal conflict can come from receiving money as a result of the death of a loved one. This can be a real mindbender: your good fortune comes because this person has died! Many people find it difficult to deal with the money under these circumstances.

Those who handle this particular conflict best tend to look on their inheritance as the last gift from their loved one—a gift that person wanted them to enjoy and benefit from.

Inheritors who resolve *this* conflict, however, often find themselves concerned that their friends or coworkers are not sharing in their good fortune. After years of working and sometimes struggling side by side, suddenly *you* are the one who gets a break.

As if this weren't enough, many inheritors also find themselves in a philosophical bind. If you are proud of always having worked for your money, receiving this "free" money may challenge your image of yourself as a strong, self-reliant person.

Those who inherit large amounts may have to resolve yet another philosophical dilemma: the size of their new

> One of the deepest sources of internal conflict can come from receiving money as a result of the death of a loved one. This can be a real mindbender: your good fortune comes because this person has died!

wealth compared to the poverty of so many millions in this country and the rest of the world. Some feel guilty about this disparity, and this guilt can prevent them from handling the money wisely.

Though each person has to resolve these conflicts and emotions individually, there seem to be a few general concepts that can help. The first is to realize that you are not alone in having these feelings. Knowing that others have successfully worked through similar conflicts can give you a boost.

Another realization that can be helpful is that *money is power*. Resistance to dealing with money can be resistance to accepting new personal power. Whether your inheritance is large or small, it gives you new power to change your life for the better. If you have come into a large amount, you have more power to change aspects of the society we live in. At the end of the chapter you will find a listing for the Funding Exchange. This is the hub of a network of remarkable foundations located in cities around the country. Among other things, they are an invaluable resource for anyone who has inherited.

These foundations provide a range of programs, including seminars on different kinds of investments, assistance in finding a good financial adviser (especially those advisers specializing in socially responsible investments), and conferences and workshops for those with inherited wealth. What this last means is that you can, if you wish, be with other people who have inherited and discuss the personal and practical issues that may concern you.

Isolation is often a common feeling among inheritors. Those who attend these workshops and social gatherings tell of their great relief at finally being able to talk about their concerns with others. Many people who have recently come into an inheritance find that they can learn from those who have already dealt with many of the problems they face.

Among their other resources, many of the foundations publish books and pamphlets for new investors. You will find various investment guides, especially for socially responsible investing; books on philanthropy; and books for women investors, among others.

If you become a donor, you are encouraged to involve yourself in the planning and organization of the foundations' various programs. This includes not only the programs mentioned above, but also community work and educational programs. This kind of hands-on philanthropy is optional—you can become involved to any degree you want—but they do encourage personal participation. They don't just want your money, they want your input and involvement, too.

LOTTERY WINNERS

When Curtis "Mack" Sharp won $5.6 million in the New York lottery in 1982, he arrived at the lottery headquarters with his girlfriend on one arm and his ex-wife on the other. He set up a million-dollar trust fund for his former wife, while his girlfriend received a $10,000 engagement ring and a $13,000 wedding dress. He bought a large house, a large Cadillac, and paid for a $100,000 wedding.

Later, when he settled down a bit, Sharp handed over the management of his assets to a bank. He then proved that his generosity was not limited to himself and his family by helping to establish the largest homeless shelter in New Jersey. He also became a fund-raiser for African relief groups.

Coming into a lot of money via the lottery or other sudden ways can be a wonderful thing. It can give you more freedom to do what you want, set aside money for education or retirement, and be generous, like Mack Sharp. You should be aware, nevertheless, that winning

> Some winners quit their jobs and later regret it. Others wisely stay on the job, at least until they get accustomed to the change in their life.

can have some pitfalls. These do not need to be serious; all you have to do is to watch for them and gain from the experience of past winners.

For starters, people who win large amounts of money sometimes report that they begin to lose their friends. Friends sometimes assume that winners are going to move up in the world and leave them behind. There can be resentment or, occasionally, an assumption that their newly rich friend will lend them money on a long-term basis (such loans put a great strain on friendships, according to winners who have made them).

Some winners quit their jobs and later regret it. Others wisely stay on the job, at least until they get accustomed to the change in their life. This period of getting used to your new situation needs to be taken seriously. Real change in people tends to happen over periods of months and years, not days and weeks. You owe it to yourself to park the main part of the money in a bank and just let it sit, while you begin to get comfortable with the idea of having it.

For the first few months after receiving your winnings, you should hold off on following all the advice you're bound to get. This is the time to sort things out in your mind and talk it over with your spouse or whoever else is involved with the money. It's a good time to think about what's important to you, what you'd like to do, and the directions you want your life to go in.

It's also a good time to start learning about investing. You can do this on your own or with the help of a professional. A personal financial adviser can help you look at all the different aspects of your finances—something that can be extremely helpful for someone dealing with a whole new financial life.

Like people who inherit, some lottery winners feel guilty about having more than others. Some try to deal with this guilt by being overgenerous—or by actually losing the money through bad investments or overspending. If you feel you don't deserve to make more money—or even keep what you have—then there is a very good chance you will handle it unwisely. The message your conscious mind gets from your subconscious is, "Lose it!"

If you experience a great deal of guilt or anxiety, it can be to your advantage to see a counselor or therapist. There are, sadly, big winners out there who have lost it all—and others who feel that the money has ruined their lives. This shouldn't happen to you, and it won't if you're aware of what to watch for.

About 40% of the people in this country play the lotteries. That's a lot of people, a lot of money, and quite a few winners, large and small. Remember that even if you've won only $5,000 or $10,000 or $20,000, investing all or part of it and leaving it alone will turn you into a big winner in 10 to 20 years (see the compound-interest chart in Appendix D).

Those who win millions usually have the built-in safety factor of receiving the money in installments. Even so, however, it's important not to commit too much of it in advance. If you can put away a healthy portion of it each year, you'll still be a winner when your yearly payments end.

For example, if you are a $2 million winner, your money may come to you over 20 years at the rate of $100,000 a year. If you take $17,500 of that each year and invest it at the rate of 10%, by the end of the 20 years you will have over $1 million. This should allow you to continue to get $100,000 a year for the rest of your life ($1,000,000 × 0.10 a year = $100,000).

There is a fantasylike quality to inheriting or winning a lottery. This can make the money seem unreal—and cause people to deal with it in unrealistic ways. All that is required to bring it out of the fantasy realm, however, is to realize the money is the result of somebody's—or a lot of somebodies'—life energy. The money didn't just grow, it was worked for. Understanding this creates a certain respect for what you have, and this respect will help you to use and invest it sensibly.

ENJOYING SUDDEN RICHES WISELY

Money has such stature in our society that it's easy to believe just having a lot of it will make you happy. This can seem especially true to those who have been struggling just to get by. And, indeed, for a while, simply buying and enjoying the things you have never had can be a wonderful experience.

Those who seem to do the best over time among those who come into money, however, are the ones who use it to help themselves do some productive work they enjoy. That and having the chance to be with family and friends seem to be what really makes people happy. Some know this without being told, while others arrive at it the hard way.

If you have been on the low end of the economic scale and have come into some money, you might consider investing in yourself. Perhaps you never had the time or the resources to go to college or even to finish high school. These days, it's pretty easy to take a high school equivalency test and start taking some classes in a community college.

No matter what your age or background, you will not be out of place in a community college. One of my favorite things about the community college I attended for a year was that the students *were* of all different ages and backgrounds.

It's become a cliché, but it really is never too late to go after your dreams. I recently read about an 85-year-old man who graduated from college with the great support and affection of his fellow students. Others—young and old—start new businesses or creative endeavors.

To some, like Mack Sharp, giving away part of what they have is a source of great satisfaction. It's not necessary to be as flamboyant as Mr. Sharp, though, to do a substantial amount of good. Many charitable organizations would welcome not only your money but your volunteer time.

Counseling and Therapy

Once you've learned the basics about personal finance and investing, any further problems in dealing with money can often be traced to emotional sources. If after learning the basics, you find that you are still treating money in an irrational manner—spending beyond your budget, especially with credit cards, investing in very risky ventures, feeling continual anxiety around finances—some internal issues are driving you and need to be resolved.

Many people think that seeing a counselor or therapist indicates a serious emotional condition, requiring years of treatment. In actuality, however, individuals or couples often see a counselor for just a few sessions to work out specific problems.

Here's an example. Sally was mortified because Jeff always paid the household bills late—often so late that they would get calls from the phone company or the department stores. Sally was the type who always paid the bills the moment they arrived.

Being unable to resolve their dispute, they went to see a couples counselor. After only a few sessions, it became clear that Jeff was delaying paying the bills as a way of asserting himself. He was having a difficult time at work with a demanding boss but, in addition, he had always had a tendency to feel put upon and pressured. Now he was resisting this pressure by taking his own sweet time to respond to creditors.

Sally, on the other hand, had used performance as a way of getting love in her family. Paying the bills immediately was her way of being a "good girl." Being "good" had become extremely important because she associated it with getting love.

Once the two of them saw clearly what was driving them, they were better able to understand each other—and modify their behavior.

Money is the single greatest source of disputes among couples. These disputes are not always as easy to resolve as those of Sally and Jeff, but often they are. If a couple has real motivation to work out a problem, it's amazing how quickly they can do so.

Occasionally, however, what starts out as a single problem can lead into deeper issues that need a longer time to resolve. If money to pay for extended therapy is a problem, you can usually find counseling clinics with lower fees or sliding scales. From a purely financial viewpoint, however, I know of no investment that can give you greater return with a lower risk. Working through long-standing emotional blocks can lead to the kind of freer, happier life that transcends any financial considerations.

Just a note to those who have never seen a therapist: You should feel comfortable with and have confidence in this person. Try to choose someone who comes highly recommended, but even then use your intuition. He or she might be an excellent counselor, but not the right one for you. It's an important decision, because you're dealing with very important issues.

> **Although dealing with money seems to be a game you play with forces outside yourself, it is actually more a game you play with yourself. Making this game more conscious can help put the odds in your favor.**

PLAYING THE GAME CONSCIOUSLY

In this chapter, we've talked about the different places you might be coming from as an investor. Your family background, your personal history, and the way you came into your money can all strongly influence your feelings about having it. Becoming aware of how these influences may affect you can be just as important as learning the best ways to invest.

In his book *The Trick to Money Is Having Some!*, Stuart Wilde makes the point that although dealing with money seems to be a game you play with forces outside yourself, it is actually more a game you play with yourself. Making this game more conscious can help put the odds in your favor.

Resources

The Trick to Money Is Having Some! by Stuart Wilde. Hay House, 1995. $12.95 (paperback). This book falls into the general category of "prosperity consciousness"—how to gain wealth by rearranging how you think about money. But whereas many such books and seminars have a rah-rah, missionary zeal to them, Wilde treats the whole subject with refreshing lightness and humor. You may not agree with all he says, but it's a good bet that his ideas will make you take a look at your attitudes toward money and prosperity. An exciting, challenging, and fun book.

Funding Exchange, 666 Broadway, Suite 500, New York, NY 10012. (212) 529-5300. <www.fex.org>. The member foundations of the Funding Exchange are listed below. These organizations are an excellent resource for inheritors, those interested in social investing and social change, or simply new investors looking for a little help (they will recommend honest, competent advisers, among other things).

Appalachian Community Fund
517 Union Avenue, #206
Knoxville, TN 37902
(615) 523-5783
Funding region: West Virginia and the Appalachian counties of
     Virginia, Kentucky, and Tennessee

Bread and Roses Community Fund
924 Cherry Street
Philadelphia, PA 19107
(215) 928-1880
Funding region: Five-county region of greater Philadelphia and
     Camden, NJ

Chinook Fund
212 W. 32nd Avenue
Denver, CO 80211
(303) 455-6905
Funding region: Colorado

Crossroads Fund
3411 W. Diversey, #20
Chicago, IL 60647
(312) 227-7676
Funding region: Chicago metropolitan area

Fund for Southern Communities
552 Hill Street S.E.
Atlanta, GA 30312
(404) 577-3178
Funding region: Georgia, North and South Carolina

Haymarket People's Fund
42 Seaverns Avenue
Boston, MA 02130
(617) 522-7676
Funding region: New England

Headwaters Fund
122 W. Franklin Avenue
Minneapolis, MN 55404
(612) 879-0602
Funding region: Minneapolis/St. Paul

Liberty Hill Foundation
1320 C Santa Monica Mall
Santa Monica, CA 90401
(213) 458-1450
Funding region: Los Angeles County and San Diego

Live Oak Fund
P.O. Box 4601
Austin, TX 78765
(512) 476-5714
Funding region: Texas

McKenzie River Gathering Foundation
3558 S.E. Hawthorne
Portland, OR 97214
(503) 233-0271
Funding region: Oregon

North Star Fund
666 Broadway, Suite 500
New York, NY 10012
(212) 460-5511
Funding region: New York City

The People's Fund
1325 Nuuanu Avenue
Honolulu, HI 96814
(808) 526-2441
Funding region: Hawaii

Vanguard Public Foundation
383 Rhode Island Street, Suite 301
San Francisco, CA 94103
(415) 487-2111
Funding region: San Francisco Bay Area and Northern
  California

Wisconsin Community Fund
122 State Street, #305
Madison, WI 53703
(608) 251-6834
Funding region: Wisconsin

CHAPTER 3

PERSONAL FINANCE

I saw Bill Donaghue on CNBC the other day talking about a surefire, absolutely foolproof way of getting 15% to 20% on your money. Donaghue is a well-known investment adviser and the author of several investment books, so the audience listened attentively. There was a general groan, however, when, (after a dramatic pause), he suggested that they invest in paying off their credit cards.

Groans notwithstanding, Donaghue was illustrating a very important point: You cannot separate your personal financial decisions from your investments. They are inextricably bound together. Suppose you worked hard at picking a particular mutual fund and were rewarded for your efforts by a $1,500 increase for the year. On the $10,000 you invested, this amounts to a 15% return ($10,000 × 0.15 = $1,500). Not bad. . . .

While you're congratulating yourself, however, the year-end tax statements for your credit cards arrive, indicating that over the year you have paid the banks $1,850 in interest payments on your outstanding balances. (If you owe an average of $10,000 at 18.5%, you're paying $1,850 a year in interest.) Suddenly your 15% profit with the fund doesn't look so good. You would have done better—$350 better—by investing $10,000 in paying off your credit cards, thereby "earning" 18.5%.

Similarly, what would be the use of a retired couple's careful management of their investment capital if they neglected to carry enough health insurance? Their entire portfolio could be wiped out by one major operation and hospital stay.

MONEY AND EMOTIONS

Some people seem to be naturally good at managing money: they have a feel for how much they can spend and still stay within a sensible budget. They consider things like insurance, wills, and setting aside enough for Tommy's orthodontia bills. The other 90% of us, though, often have a little trouble. But skills like these can be learned. And they are very similar to the skills you will need to become a successful investor.

The first thing to do is not to steel yourself and vow to stop spending so much—you've tried that and it probably hasn't worked. You need, instead, to sit down and look at your spending and planning habits. Money is very closely tied to emotions: if you begin to change the way you manage money, you can expect to run up against internal resistances. These resistances need to be looked at and considered, not fought and overcome—the fighting is what you've been doing for years.

This process of trying to change and dealing with your emotions can lead you into unforeseen areas. Many people, for example, overspend because they feel discontented with certain aspects of their lives, and the spending lets them do

Some people seem to be naturally good at managing money: they have a feel for how much they can spend and still stay within a sensible budget. They consider things like insurance, wills, and setting aside enough for Tommy's orthodontia bills. The other 90% of us, though, often have a little trouble.

something nice for themselves. If they stop overspending, the feelings of discontent will probably emerge more strongly and demand a real change in their lives. This is just one of many ways our emotions can affect our finances.

I strongly recommend Joe Dominguez's book, which is listed in Resources, as a way of starting to look at your relationship with money. It's enough of a challenge to manage finances and invest successfully without doing battle with yourself at the same time. The exercises in this book will help to get all of you on the same side.

WHAT TO LOOK AT

To be a successful investor, you need to take care of all your finances. Otherwise, you run the risk of having the rug pulled out from under you by some unforeseen event, and watching your hard-won profits go down the drain. Here are the main areas you need to look at:

- Money management: Do you keep your checkbook balanced, or could you take a world tour on the amount of returned-check fees each year? Do you have a budget? Do you stay at least within a few thousand dollars of your budget each month? (Just kidding . . . I hope.)

- Personal financial statement: It's a very good idea to know just what your assets are—and your liabilities. This is the first step toward control of your finances. Financial statement forms are available at most stationery stores. Your bank will also be happy to give you one.

- Insurance: health, automobile, disability, homeowner's or renter's. You need them all, and you need to be sure that the amount you will be paid will be enough. If you have a family or other people who depend on your income, life insurance must be seriously considered.

- Goals: What are your financial goals? And, if you are married, are they similar to your spouse's goals?

- Taxes: Are you paying Uncle Sam only what you need to, or could you benefit from a tax adviser? I recommend getting a good one if you don't have one already. They are not expensive, but could save you a great deal.

- Debt: Are you paying so much in interest on your credit cards or other loans that a missed paycheck or two could cause you major difficulty? Keeping the amount of debt and the interest payments under control can help your financial picture immensely.

- Retirement: You say you're too young to start thinking about it? Think again. The sooner you start, the less you'll need to put away each month and the longer it can grow. (See the compound-interest table in Appendix D.)

You will do yourself a big favor if you get some help in considering these things. At the very least, consult the financial planning book listed in Resources. This is the best I've found on the subject: clear, easy to read, everything that books like this should be (but often are not). You'll be amazed at the things you didn't even *know* you needed to know.

If you feel you could use professional help, you can discuss your finances with a financial planner.

TAXES

Your success as an investor depends partly on how you deal with your tax situation. For example, you need to know the best way to calculate your gains and losses, what deductions you're allowed, how to deal with capital gains and passive losses, the tax benefits of retirement plans . . . need I go on?

The whole subject of taxes requires a more detailed treatment than the format of this book permits. Our job here is simply to impress upon you the importance of either learning as much as you can or hiring a top-notch tax adviser.

If you are going to manage your own investments, the tax book recommended in Resources is very good at presenting clearly an often complex subject. Even if you plan to hire an adviser, you would benefit by reading this book. In dealing with any professional adviser, the more you know, the more you will benefit from the advice.

Your success as an investor depends partly on how you deal with your tax situation.

WILLS

Somewhere in the reams and reams of legal codes in your state there are specific rules about what happens to your money if you don't leave a will. You may think that it will all automatically go to your spouse or next of kin, but this is not necessarily true. Not leaving a will is a great way of enriching lawyers and delighting the kind of bureaucrats who love long, drawn-out, complex proceedings.

Leaving a will that is unclear or legally questionable will also delight the same people. Handwritten, unwitnessed wills are not even accepted in some states; other states require not two witnesses, but three.

See a lawyer and have it done right. It can cost as little as a few hundred dollars, depending on the lawyer and the complexity of the will. The welfare of your loved ones is what is at stake. Parents of young children need to consider who they would want to be the children's guardians in the event of the parents' death. This kind of thing must be laid out properly in the will.

For those who wish to leave money to charity, it is imperative to specify which organizations and how much. Many organizations will help you set up trusts that can benefit not only them, but save taxes for you and your heirs.

Our purpose here is not to make a comprehensive list of all the things to consider, but to emphasize the

> For those who wish to leave money to charity, it is imperative to specify which organizations and how much. Many organizations will help you set up trusts that can benefit not only them, but save taxes for you and your heirs.

importance of doing something soon. The financial planning book recommended in Resources has a good section on wills and estate planning. That book and a good lawyer will tell you what you need to know.

What If Something Happens to You?

You've made a will, you say. Great! But suppose you're the one who handles all the investments. What happens to them if something happens to you?

An older friend of mine recently went to help out upon the death of his brother-in-law. The man's widow had no idea what her financial situation was going to be. All she knew was that while her husband had supported her, there never seemed to be enough money. She was resigned to surviving on Social Security for the rest of her days.

My friend was soon enmeshed in one of the most disordered offices he had ever seen. It took him a couple of weeks to sort through it all, but when he had finished, he was astounded to find that his brother-in-law had accumulated some $300,000 in assets. There were old bank books lying around, shares of various securities stuffed into desk drawers along with worthless papers—my friend likened it to mining for gold in a trash heap.

This story had a happy ending. More often, disorder can lead people to believe that there is *more* there than actually exists. A couple of lessons can be learned from this tale.

First, it's a good idea to get your spouse involved in your investments, at least to the extent that he or she knows what's going on.

Second, putting your papers into some order will make it much easier for whoever has to deal with things. Stationery stores sell books with titles like "Personal Financial Organizer," with pages all set up to record your various investments. That, coupled with written instructions on what to do, will be a tremendous help to whoever has to handle your portfolio.

Lastly, do make sure that whoever needs to knows where your will is. It might be a good idea to write that small, but crucial, bit of information in the same book that lists your portfolio.

Resources

Books

Your Money or Your Life: Transforming Your Relationship with Money and Achieving Financial Independence by Joe Dominguez and Vicki Robin. Penguin Books, 1992. $11.95 (paperback). Once you realize that money = life energy, you may want to look more closely at what kind of job you spend your life energy on. The book grew out of a series of seminars given by Dominguez and Robin which helped people take this closer look. Whether you love your job or want to get out of it, this book will help you find new organizing principles for your finances and practical steps toward reaching your new goals. Dominguez and Robin show you how to: (1) get out of debt and develop savings, (2) reorder your material priorities so that you can live well with less money, and (3) deal with your inner conflicts between values and lifestyles. Highly recommended.

The Wall Street Journal Guide to Understanding Personal Finance, by Kenneth M. Morris and Alan M. Siegel. Lightbulb Press, 1999. $15.95 (paperback).

Credit, mortgages, taxes, college planning—it's all here and more. The Wall Street Journal guides are full of pictures and generally easy to read. This is a good starting book for the basics in financial planning.

The Guide to Tax-Saving Investing, by David L. Scott. The Globe Pequot Press, 1995. $9.95 (paperback). Investing is not just about making money—it's also about keeping as much as you can of what you make. Scott takes you through real estate, retirement plans, life insurance, municipal bonds, and other topics, showing clearly and simply how to save taxes on each.

How to Get Out of Debt, Stay Out of Debt and Live Prosperously, by Jerrold Mundis. Bantam Books, 1990. $6.99 (paperback). Many people think they're ready to invest, when what they really need to do first is pay off excessive debt and rethink their financial lives. This book is for people who have dug themselves into a financial hole and can't see how to climb out. Mundis describes himself as a recovered debtor, and much of the book is based on the techniques of the national Debtors Anonymous program, which helped him to get control of his financial life. Some compulsive spenders may need the support such a group can lend; others may be able to help themselves with this book alone. The program for getting control is all laid out, step by step. All you have to do is follow it.

Quicken Deluxe 99. Intuit, Inc. $59.95. Personal finance software. Here's how to get most of your financial life organized and in one place. Quicken enables you to (1) organize your finances so that the inflow and outgo are visible and clear, (2) write checks or pay bills directly online, (30 fill in tax-related items over the course of a year—making your tax preparation much easier, (4) organize your investment portfolios, and more. Go to <www.quicken.com> for more information on this and other software. If you have further questions, you can probably find a friend or associate who has Quicken—it's become the most common personal finance software.

CHAPTER 4

THE STOCK MARKET

S uppose you decide to form a company. At some point, you'll need to buy equipment and raw materials, and to hire workers. To do this, you're going to need capital. There are several ways of getting this capital: You can invest your own money, you can borrow, or you can sell part of the company to investors.

If your credit is good, you may borrow from a bank, or you may choose to borrow from individuals. The way you borrow from individuals is to issue *bonds*. Bonds are fancy IOUs: your company promises to pay back the lenders in a given number of years. In the meantime, the lenders receive interest payments from the company.

The alternative to borrowing is to sell part of the company to investors. The way you do this is to issue *shares* of the company—shares of your stock, or inventory. ("Shares of stock" has come to be shortened to simply "stocks.") Investors who believe your company's future looks good will buy the stocks and thereby become part owners. Their money is the capital you can use to start or expand your business.

By issuing stock, you have transformed your company from a *privately owned* firm to a *publicly held* corporation. There are still many large privately owned companies, but there are many more firms whose stock is available for investors.

In case you have ever wondered what investment bankers do, this is it. Their job is to arrange financing for new companies or new financing for existing firms. If you wanted to issue stocks or bonds for your company, or arrange for a loan, you would go to an investment banker.

A LITTLE HISTORY

Issuing certificates as proof of a loan or of part ownership goes back to the late Middle Ages, when trade and commerce were beginning to pick up. By the late 17th century, it had become common for individuals to invest in companies. These shareholders were usually wealthy men who took an active interest in the affairs of the company. They would trade shares in the companies directly from each other.

As more people became investors, however, a need developed for intermediaries—*brokers* who could buy and sell shares of different companies for their clients. In cities like London, Paris, and Amsterdam, these brokers began to meet in coffeehouses and parks to trade shares. The New York Stock Exchange had its origins in a regular meeting of 24 merchants and auctioneers under a buttonwood tree in 1792 near what is now Wall Street.

As time went on, these meetings gradually became larger and more formalized until, by the mid-19th century, most exchanges had moved into their own buildings.

Today, despite the exponential growth in the numbers of companies and shareholders, the concept of an exchange is still the same: brokers trading stocks for clients. See the "How Are Your Stocks Traded?" box for a description of how this is accomplished.

Today, there are 142 stock exchanges in major cities around the world, trading hundreds of millions of shares each day. Over 50 million Americans own stocks directly; millions more own stocks through their interest in company or union pension funds, or by owning mutual funds.

How Are Your Stocks Traded?

The traditional method of trading stocks in the parks and coffeehouses was an auction: stocks were sold to the highest bidder, and purchased from the lowest offerer. This method persists today; computerized trading notwithstanding, the price is still determined by what the highest bidder will pay and how low the seller will go.

The trading on the stock exchanges still bears traces of its origins in parks and coffeehouses. The New York Stock Exchange has a trading area in an auditorium-size room called the trading floor. Brokerages from around the country contact their broker "on the floor" of the exchange to place orders for their clients (these days, the orders are placed by computer hookups). The floor broker then contacts a broker—also on the floor—who specializes in the stock being traded (a "specialist"), and arranges the trade.

For years, this was the way all stocks were traded; before the days of computers, brokers would phone or wire the orders. Nowadays, only large orders are handled in this manner. Small orders go directly to the specialist's computer and are executed automatically at the current price.

The pension funds, universities, foundations, churches, and banks that manage trust accounts, called institutional investors, are responsible for about 40% of stock ownership. Foreign investors and foreign governments also own large quantities of U.S. stocks. (During the Cold War years, the communist ideology of the Soviet Union didn't prevent the Soviet government from buying millions of dollars' worth of stocks on the New York Stock Exchange.)

There are presently about 3,100 stocks listed on the New York Stock Exchange, 1,000 on the American Stock Exchange, and 5100 on the Nasdaq Stock Exchange (in 1998, Nasdaq and the American Exchange joined forces and formed NASDAQ-AMEX). Hundreds of companies also list their stock on smaller regional exchanges around the country.

In addition, there are thousands of smaller companies whose stock is not traded on any exchange; they are instead bought and sold in what is termed the over-the-counter market (OTC). As a matter of historical interest, the National Association of Securities Dealers Automated Quotation System (NASDAQ) was originally formed in 1971 to organize the trading of these over-the-counter stocks. This was the first fully automated market for stocks; instead of operating from a central exchange, brokers all over the country communicated stock orders via computer network.

Nowadays, the Nasdaq market is no longer home only to small companies because many Nasdaq firms like Microsoft and Intel have grown into giants. Small companies not on Nasdaq are found on lists of the OTC Bulletin Board (OTCBB) and the Pink Sheets and are traded via computer network. You will not find these stocks in the newspapers, but many are listed on investment web sites on the Internet.

Pre-Owned Stock

When you buy shares of stock in a corporation, you are buying "secondhand" stock—or, as the dealers of expensive cars like to put it, "pre-owned." When you buy and sell these pre-owned shares, you are dealing in the *secondary market* for stocks.

The first time a company "goes public" and offers its stock for sale, it is said to be making an *initial public offering*. Later on, a company may add to the number of outstanding shares by putting out a *new issue* of stock (also called a new offering), adding to the number of its shares already being traded on the markets. *These are the only times the company gets new investment capital*—it makes no profit if the shares already on the market rise in value, because it no longer owns these shares. However, even though it makes no profit from shares traded in the secondary market, the company likes to see the price of its stock go up. Not only does this add to what is called the total *market capitalization* of the firm (the total number of shares multiplied by the share price), but it also means the company will gain more capital when it makes new issues of stock.

Except for the initial public offerings and the new issues, then, the stock you buy through your broker is being sold to you by another investor, not the corporation that originally issued it. The company will give

you a brand-new stock certificate with your name on
it, but this is similar to taking an old dollar bill into a
bank and getting a new one. No new money—or
stock—has been created, just new paper.

All these facts and figures are presented simply to
give you some familiarity with the markets you may be
buying into. There is no difference in the procedure for
buying and selling in the various markets—you just call
up your broker and place the order. There is some difference in the companies whose stock you are buying, however. For example, most of the companies listed on the
New York Exchange are large, well-established corporations, while those on Nasdaq are often smaller, newer
companies. The companies on the over-the-counter markets are smaller still.

These markets for stocks are explained more fully in
Chapter 8. For now, let's turn to the different kinds of
companies whose stocks are traded in these markets.

DIFFERENT STOCKS FOR DIFFERENT FOLKS

The companies with stock available to investors range
from giant, international corporations to tiny electronics
firms with just a few employees. In later chapters, we will
suggest how the new investor might include these different categories in a portfolio.

Blue chip stocks are in the largest and strongest
companies—General Motors, General Electric, IBM,
AT&T, etc. Their stock is considered safer than most,
because of the enormous resources backing it up. "Safe,"
in this case, means that these corporations are very

unlikely to fail, and that they are likely to continue paying dividends to their shareholders even in difficult times. In addition, though their stock prices may go down in bad times, they are likely to rebound in better times.

Secondary issues come from firms a bit smaller and not so well known, but that are, nonetheless, large, well-established corporations. Both blue chip and secondary-issue companies often diversify into many fields, which makes them less vulnerable to a downturn in a single area of the economy.

Income stocks are in companies that have a record of paying good dividends to their shareholders. Utilities— your telephone and gas and electric companies—are at the top of this list.

Growth stocks are generally those from newer firms, for instance, many high-tech companies. Many of these are small, but others are large and still growing fast. Growth companies may be part of a new industry or simply companies making a product with a new twist in an already established industry. If you buy their stock, you are generally hoping for appreciation in the stock price as the company grows. The dividends, if there are any, are usually less than those of the blue chips or the secondary issues, and the risk is greater.

Penny stocks—those that sell for less than a dollar a share—come from very small companies. They are the

Blue chip stocks are in the largest and strongest companies—General Motors, General Electric, IBM, AT&T, etc. Their stock is considered safer than most, because of the enormous resources backing it up.

long shots of the stock market—high risk, but with a chance at great appreciation should the company succeed.

You are also likely to be confronted with terms like "cyclical stocks" and "defensive stocks." *Cyclical stocks* tend to rise and fall with the business cycles of the economy. Stocks of the auto companies and the steel companies that supply them are examples of cyclical stocks. People are less likely to buy cars in depressed times, so corporate profits are more likely to fall—and stock prices will follow suit.

Regardless of the business cycles, however, people always need to eat and have heat and light in their homes. The income of the food companies and the utilities will, therefore, tend to remain more stable in a recession—and so will the value of their stocks. For this reason, they are called *defensive stocks*.

DIVIDENDS

As part owner of a company, you are entitled to part of the yearly profit, should your company make one. The profits are disbursed (usually) quarterly, and the monies are called *dividends*. Your 100 shares of General Electric, for example, will bring you about $50 a quarter, or $200 a year, at the current rate.

Dividends need to be distinguished from *earnings*. The earnings per share of a company are the total amount of after-tax profits divided by the number of shares of common stock ("common" stock is what you normally buy; there is another kind called "preferred" stock, which is discussed in Chapter 18). Out of these earnings have to come various expenses—payments on debts, investment in new equipment, the new yacht for the top brass, and so on. Only after these things have been taken care of are shareholders given their due.

Even in bad times, people usually pay their utility bills, so the dividends of those companies tend to be more secure than those of other industry groups. This stable income means the price of their stock generally fluctuates less than that of other groups.

Dividends are generally offered by older, well-established companies. The new kids on the block are too busy making ends meet and investing in expansion to worry about paying their shareholders. People buy stock in the company because they believe there will be good earnings down the line and this will drive its price up. You can find a company's dividend in the listings in the financial pages (this is explained in Chapter 8).

The large corporations—the so-called blue chip companies—generally give dividends of 2% to 5% of the value of your stock. For example, if you bought 100 shares of GE stock for $7,000, your $200-a-year dividend will mean a return of a little less than 3% on your investment of $7,000 ($200 divided by $7,000 = .0285 = 2.85%). Some companies give substantially higher dividends; these are called *high-yield* stocks.

Investors looking for good income and stability love the telephone, gas, and electric companies. Even in bad times, people usually pay their utility bills, so the dividends of those companies tend to be more secure than those of other industry groups. This stable income means the price of their stock generally fluctuates less than that of other groups.

Occasionally, you will be surprised when you open your quarterly envelope—sometimes pleasantly, sometimes not. You may get an extra payment or your company may raise its dividend. Conversely, in a bad year, you may get less money or, sad to say, none at all. Sometimes, you may get a payment in the form of more stock, instead of cash.

If you like, you can instruct the company to automatically reinvest your dividends in more stock, if the company has such a plan. Over a number of years, this can make for a nice addition to your holdings—and with no brokers' commissions! These are called Dividend Reinvestment Plans, or DRIPS. Do remember, however, that even if the dividends are reinvested, Uncle Sam will want his yearly cut—dividends are always counted as income.

Choosing the Best Stock

So . . . now you know more about stocks. But which stocks are the best ones to buy? How do you choose the companies that are on the way up? Simply on the basis of the increasing number of publications about this subject, companies producing paper would seem like a good investment.

You will soon find, if you invest in the stock market, that the amount of advice available can be overwhelming, not to mention contradictory. One adviser might recommend selling GE stock because of the downturn in defense orders, while another might urge buying it on the basis of its new orders from NASA.

So what to do? Well, there are two ways to go about selecting a stock to buy. One is to do all the research yourself: study the financial strength of a company that interests you, its prospects in its industry group, its sales growth, profit margins, and other pertinent pieces of information. There is more on this kind of analysis in Chapter 18.

This kind of research is the basis of the recommendations you hear for buying and selling (at least it should be!). Some will find this kind of research fascinating, while others will not want to spend the time required to really learn about a company.

The second way to choose is to engage an adviser. Investment managers and stockbrokers are two possibilities. But there is another way to engage advisers: Subscribe to one or more investment newsletters.

NEWSLETTERS

There are professional investment advisers out there who spend their entire day poring over the financial statements of various companies, following the economic life of the nation and world and gazing into crystal balls. (Well, maybe not crystal balls, but there are several who use astrology.) Some of these advisers are top-notch, others are not—and I know what your next question is, even without my crystal ball. The answer is that you look at their record. Past performance may not guarantee future success, but it's still the best way to choose an adviser.

And yes, there is a good way to learn the records of the advisers who publish newsletters. It's called the *Hulbert Financial Digest*, and it is the first newsletter to which you should subscribe if you're serious about picking the best stocks. *Hulbert's* tracks about 140 newsletters, and catalogs the success or failure of their recommendations over the last 10 years. It is easy to choose the top newsletters: their formats are clear and straightforward.

Several excellent newsletters are recommended in this book (including some not covered by *Hulbert's*) that will be especially useful to new investors. Ask for a sample copy of the publication—you can usually get a back issue for free. Some newsletters let you order a trial subscription, usually good for two or three months. (Most

> Especially in the short run, the investing public's *perception* of a company's prospects is extremely important. In addition, the economic climate in both the nation and the world can have a major effect on whole markets or on industry groups.

newsletters are published either monthly or twice monthly.) You can thus see whether its style of investing matches your own before you order a year's subscription.

If you want to look at others, you can subscribe to *Hulbert's* and pick out the ones with the best records in your field of interest. It's a good idea to subscribe to a few and get the benefit of the different perspectives, though more than five can lead to our common enemy: information overload.

Besides giving advice on specific stocks and the condition of the markets, these newsletters often include essays on world politics, historical references, and anecdotes from the publishers' years of investing. While I don't recommend buying individual stocks until you become more knowledgeable, one way of gaining that knowledge is to read the good newsletters. In a few months, you may find that you've absorbed a great deal about investing simply by osmosis.

A word of caution, though: These guys are good, but they're not infallible. Remember that, in the search for certainty, the financial markets are the worst place to look. The best method of picking stocks is usually a combination of listening to the experts and using your own research and intuition.

Sometimes the savviest analysts will pick companies with top-flight balance sheets and excellent prospects, only to see the stock decline because of other factors. Especially in the short run, the investing public's *perception* of a company's prospects is extremely important. In addition, the economic climate in both the nation and the world can have a major effect on whole markets or on industry groups.

Resources

Newsletters for the New Investor

Hulbert Financial Digest, (888) HULBERT. Monthly. $135/year (but specials often bring the price down substantially); $37.50-five-issue trial subscription. Useful as it is, Hulbert's should be taken as just another tool, not gospel. Be aware that various people have taken issue with Mark Hulbert's method of rating newsletters' performance.

Also remember that the '90s—where most of the statistics come from—were go-go years when most stocks rose dramatically. You will see some very impressive statistics, especially from the growth-oriented newsletters. It's hard to predict, but the next decade may be a time when more conservatively oriented newsletters will be the most successful.

You need to beware of ads that refer to Hulbert's ratings. You will often see the phrase "top rated by Hulbert's." The key question here is, "For how long?" Try to choose the letters that have performed well over a number of years, not the one that had a couple of lucky picks during the last quarter and showed a 70% increase.

Profitable Investing, Philips Publishing Inc. (800) 777-5005. Monthly. $99/year. Richard Band is your basic conservative investor, an expert on utility stocks, bonds, and high-yield money market funds. He is also generous with general investment advice.

Books

The Money Masters by John Train. Harperbusiness, 1994. $15.00 (paperback). This book tells the stories of nine famous investors. Though they each emphasized different things, certain qualities were common to all nine: a firm discipline that nevertheless allows for flexibility, creativity, and patience. An excellent and entertaining book from which the new investor can get a good deal of background information about the world of investing. Train has a follow-up to this book called *The New Money Masters* (Harperbusiness, 1994. $16.00 [paperback]). This one covers famous investors and traders from the 1980s and is also an excellent read.

CHAPTER 5

BUYING AND SELLING
STOCKS

The basics of buying and selling stocks are not difficult to understand. The more complex aspects, like
how to pick the best stocks or when to buy and sell,
will be dealt with in later chapters.

Stock certificates represent ownership in a company.
Perhaps some of the excitement of stocks comes from the
fact that, especially in America, people dream of owning a
business or at least part of a business. If you were to buy
100 shares of International Business Machines stock, you
would be an owner of one of the great corporations of the
world (along with a few million other investors, who
together own 922,852,000 shares).

As an owner, your fortunes will be tied to those of the
company. If its sales of home computers increase, your
quarterly dividend payment and the value of your stock
may go up. If the smaller computer companies cut
sharply into IBM's sales, the stock may go down.

As in any market, an increase in the number of people wanting to buy a stock will drive the price up, an increase in the number of sellers will drive it down. This is the law of supply and demand.

Of course, the reasons that people buy or sell are not always related to the actual value of the company. If rumors abound about an amazing new kind of computer chip, the stock analysts will start worrying about the companies that produce computers with the old chips. The public listens to their worries and begins to sell its computer company stock, including IBM.

Meanwhile, however, IBM is working on a new chip of its own, which they feel is equally as amazing as the other chip. But its stock goes down because the investing public is not aware of the significance of IBM's new chip. They *believe* that losses are coming, so they sell their IBM stock. (This, of course, creates a buying opportunity for those who know the whole story.)

So . . . suppose you're one of the few who realize that IBM is a good buy at this new lower price. How do you go about actually buying some shares of IBM stock? What you do is find a stockbroker.

BROKERS

"Broker" is just another word for dealer or agent. Their business is to act as go-betweens in the buying and selling of stocks and bonds, and their income is in the form of fees—called *commissions*—for these services.

Most stockbrokers are members of brokerage companies. These companies deal directly with individuals on the various stock exchanges and computer networks who actually do the buying and selling of securities. (The term *securities* includes stock certificates and bonds; *equities* refers specifically to stocks.)

First you need to know that there are two kinds of brokerage houses: full-commission brokers—also called full-service brokers—and discount brokers.

Until the 1970s, there were only full-commission brokers. They recommended stocks to their clients, answered questions, and were always there for advice and consultation. They all charged pretty much the same commissions, which followed the "minimum fixed commission rates" set by the New York Stock Exchange.

In 1975, however, the Securities and Exchange Commission (the federal government body charged with regulating the securities industry) decided that these "minimum rates" amounted to price-fixing. The New York Exchange was ordered to abolish them, and the field was cleared for price competition between the brokerages.

The so-called discount brokerages were started on the hunch that many people didn't really want all the advice given by brokers, and would be willing to forgo it in return for lower commissions. They were right: Substantially lower commissions drew a great many customers. There are now numerous discount brokerages, some of which have grown very large very quickly.

Commissions

How much commission can you expect to pay when you buy 100 shares of IBM? Suppose IBM is selling for $90 a share; you give the broker the $9,000 for the 100 shares,

Want to pay commissions of just $10.00 per trade? Get online and trade at your broker's web site.

plus about a $120 commission at a full-commission broker. When you sell the stock, you pay another $120 commission. At a discount broker, you might pay a $50 commission, which is more than a 50% savings. These prices vary greatly, even among the discounters.

Brokers have complicated systems for calculating commissions; some are based on the number of shares traded, some on the dollar amount of the transaction. All brokers have a commission minimum, however. A minimum of $50 would translate to a commission of 5% on a trade of $1,000 of stock ($1,000 × .05 = $50). On larger transactions, the commission will be a much smaller percentage of the dollar amount. For example, at a discount brokerage, you might only pay a $125 commission on a trade that involves $20,000 worth of stock.

Want to pay commissions of just $10.00 per trade? Get online and trade at your broker's web site. Prices vary for online trading, but they are always substantially less than phone trading.

About Brokers

So . . . what are the best ways to choose a broker?

After you have finished this book, you will have a good idea of the various ways to get investment advice. Then, as you read more, talk with friends, and generally learn more about the markets, what kind of investing you want to do will become clearer. At that point, what kind of broker would be best for you should also become clear. Today, thanks to the free market, you have quite a few choices.

The larger full-service brokers, such as PaineWebber or Merrill Lynch, offer a whole range of services to their customers. In addition to the advice you get from your personal broker, you have access to financial planning, tax consulting, free seminars, research material, and free reports on promising companies. Your higher commissions pay for these.

Incidentally, the various brokerages call their brokers by different names: "financial consultants," "account executives," "institutional salesmen." Regardless of what they are called, their main job is to advise you and trade securities for you.

If you like the idea of a smaller, local firm, you will find quite a few in any city. They may not provide as many services, but will do just as good a job at trading securities. Whether their advice is as good as the larger firms' depends more on the firm and individual broker. The most important thing is to find a broker you feel is competent and has your best interests at heart.

Large discount brokers such as Charles Schwab, Fidelity, and Quick & Reilly will not give you advice, but they will provide various services. You can have a checking account, a Visa card, set up a trust or an individual retirement account, and place buy and sell orders 24 hours a day. The brokers you talk to are usually accustomed to new investors and happy to answer any questions about the mechanics of buying and selling. Commissions are roughly one-half to two-thirds those of the full-commission brokers.

A growing number of brokerages "discount the discounters." If you eventually begin to trade securities fairly often and/or in large quantities, the fees can be quite small: sometimes as much as half the cost of the larger discounters and a quarter to a third the cost of the full-commission brokers! These companies don't usually provide as many services as their big brothers, though as they become better established, more services are beginning to appear.

The super discounters are not hard to find—just open any financial newspaper and zero in on the largest ads. You can send for their brochures and compare their commission schedules and services. If you're online, you can check out the broker's web sites—Chapter 22 describes how to do this. Remember that trading online is always the cheapest.

Many banks also buy and sell securities for you, and many financial advisers and managers are licensed to trade securities. If you decide to hire an adviser, this may be the simplest way for you to buy and sell.

What you are paying for with a full-commission broker is a personal investment adviser, specializing in stocks and bonds. It's important to remember, however, that you are also getting a salesperson whose income depends on commissions.

Many new investors assume that because they are inexperienced, they should engage a broker as an adviser. This is not necessarily true. Many brokers are less well trained in the art of analyzing securities than they are in the art of selling. To earn greater commissions, some engage in questionable practices, such as urging clients to buy or sell stock simply to earn commissions for themselves. These practices are discussed more fully in Chapter 9.

Before you choose a full-service broker, I hope you will study this chapter—and the rest of the book. There are good brokers out there, just as there are other good financial advisers. To separate them from the turkeys, however, you need to know what to look for.

How to Buy and Sell

Later chapters will discuss in more detail the different types of brokerage accounts, the various ways of buying and selling stock, and how to read the stock tables in the newspaper. For now, here is a brief explanation just to dispel some of the aura of mystery that many new investors perceive around the trading of stocks.

Once you have decided on a broker, you will open an account—in this case, a "regular account," or "cash account." You will deposit money to purchase stocks in your brokerage account, money that will earn interest just as it would in a money market account at your bank.

Now, suppose you have decided to buy stock in IBM. All you do is call the broker and say, "I'd like to buy a hundred shares of IBM." The broker will say, "IBM is currently trading at ninety and three-quarters" (meaning $90.75 a share). "Shall I execute the order?" You say, "Yes, go ahead," and that's it! (Selling is exactly the same procedure; all you do is substitute the word "sell" for "buy.")

Your account is debited $9,075 (100 shares × $90.75 = $9,075) plus commission, and you have bought into the world of high technology. If you don't have enough in your brokerage account to cover the cost of the purchase, the broker will send you a bill, which you must pay in three business days.

You will receive a fancy certificate saying that you own 100 shares of International Business Machines

> **Holding stocks and bonds in street name is generally the preferred method, since it relieves you of the responsibility of safeguarding the documents.**

Corporation. You can hold on to this certificate yourself if you want, preferably in a bank safe-deposit box, or you can ask your broker to safeguard it for you. This is called holding the securities "in street name" (meaning the name of the brokerage company).

Holding stocks and bonds in street name is generally the preferred method, since it relieves you of the responsibility of safeguarding the documents. It also means you don't need to deliver the certificates to the broker each time you sell some stock. The broker will send you monthly statements that list the shares you own in each company and their current value.

CHANGES IN OUTLOOK

Once you have invested in a company, you may discover some changes in your outlook. Your fortunes now depend not only on the company's performance in the marketplace, but on the national and world economy as well. If the economy takes a nosedive, so will the stock market, and probably your stock too. The reverse is also true: good times will be good for the market.

Why is this? Because in times of recession, most companies don't make as much money. Earnings tend to be smaller, which means that payments to shareholders (dividends) are also smaller. Investors know this—and they also know that a great many other people are going to be selling, which will drive prices down. So they often get rid of many of their stocks and put the money in whatever seems safe, like bank savings accounts or government bonds.

The reverse is true when the economy starts to pick up. Investors take their money out of banks and start buying stocks in anticipation of higher corporate earnings—and because they know that stock prices will go up as other investors start buying. Since there are so many people who want to buy, those who hold the stocks can demand higher prices for them. As a result, the overall value of the stock market starts to rise.

Of course, you don't have to sell your stocks just because the market is down. Later, we'll discuss the pros and cons of holding investments through good times and bad. You need to be prepared for the ups and downs of the business cycles, though, and for the probability that your stock's value will go down in bad times, even if the corporation that issued it is doing well.

You may have done your best to invest in a company you believe will do well over the long term. But, as with any investment, your fortunes now depend partly on events beyond your control. You may find yourself reading with new interest not just the financial pages, but the national and world news. Welcome to the World of Investment!

Resources

Here's an excellent resource for choosing an online broker: At <www.sonic.net/donaldj/>, you are presented with a number of online brokers and their commission schedules. In addition, you will find commentary about the quality of each broker's web site—some are much easier to use than others. There is more on choosing online brokers in Chapter 22.

CHAPTER 6

MUTUAL FUNDS

When some new investors see the complexities and risks involved in choosing a portfolio of individual stocks, they often throw up their hands and start looking for a good investment adviser. They would like to manage their own accounts, but it all seems like too much to add to their already busy lives.

There is, however, a third way. It's possible to buy a portfolio of hundreds of stocks and hire a whole group of professional managers to look after them for you. This is what you do when you buy mutual funds.

Most companies produce goods or services. You invest because you believe a company will show a profit selling these goods or services. Mutual funds are also companies—investment companies—but *their* way of making profits is to invest in the stocks and bonds of the firms that produce goods and services. You invest in a mutual fund because you believe the managers of that fund are skilled at choosing which companies will be the most

> **The number of funds has more than doubled in the last eight years, to over 8,000. These funds handle hundreds of billions of investor dollars.**

profitable. If they make the right choices and the stocks of these firms go up, the shares of the mutual fund also rise in value.

When you buy shares in a mutual fund, you are combining your money with that of thousands of other investors. The managers of the fund use this pool to invest in the securities of many different companies. They diversify so that should one or two companies do poorly, their poor performance will be balanced by the good performance of the others.

Quite a few individuals have decided that mutual funds are the right place for them. The number of funds has more than doubled in the last eight years, to over 8,000. These funds handle hundreds of billions of investor dollars.

Mutual funds come in all sizes. Some have total assets of less than $1 million, whereas others manage investments in the billions. The largest, the Fidelity Magellan Fund, has assets of over $74 *billion*. The number of different companies in which a fund may own stocks and bonds also varies greatly—from 20 to 200 is common, though some of the larger funds own stock in 300 or 400 companies.

Almost anywhere you look in the Investment World, you will find a mutual fund. There are funds that specialize in growth stocks, bonds, international securities, even real estate. For the speculator, there are funds that own gold mines, silver mines, or stock options. If you are a socially conscious investor, you can buy funds that own only the securities of socially responsible companies.

Mutual funds are an easy way to invest in a specific area. For example, suppose you think the price of oil is on the way up. Instead of making a risky speculation on an oil futures contract, you can put your money in a mutual fund that specializes in energy companies. If you want to invest in gold, you don't have to go to the trouble of buying gold coins or bullion—or even shares in Cousin Jack's Australian gold mine: You can invest in a fund specializing in gold-mining companies. As you might guess, the stock prices of these companies follow the price of gold very closely.

You're going to hear a lot about mutual funds in this book, because they're perfect for the new investor. Why?

- Professional managers have records that can be checked in much less time than it takes to research an individual company.

- There is safety in diversity: each fund's portfolio represents a number of companies.

- A good balance in your own portfolio is easy to achieve by buying several different kinds of mutual funds. You'll see how to do this in the chapters on portfolios.

A further advantage is that you can start investing in a mutual fund for as little as $2,500, sometimes less (Pax World Fund has a minimum of just $250). This makes them perfect for small investors. Once you have started with your initial investment, you can then continue to add money as you wish. Many people invest a set amount each month—there is usually a minimum of $25 to $50 for these additions.

HOW TO BUY

Shares in mutual funds are bought and sold somewhat differently from stocks. Instead of ordering a certain number of shares, you place fund orders using round dollar figures. You will say to your broker, "I want to buy five thousand dollars' worth of the Vanguard Equity Income Fund." The broker will then make the purchase and may charge you a commission for the service.

To Broker or Not to Broker
(That Is the Question)

In setting up your portfolio, the question inevitably arises: Do you want to buy through a broker or directly from the individual funds? The answer is that dealing through a brokerage account is almost always easier, but sometimes more costly.

Discount brokers commonly charge a minimum commission of about $30 each time you buy or sell a mutual fund. Fees generally run at the rate of 0.6% on the first $15,000; 0.2% on the remaining $15,000 to $100,000 (this may vary among the different discounters). Note that the figure is 0.6%, not 6%; 0.6% = .006.

A $10,000 purchase would cost $60 in commissions ($10,000 × .006 = $60). A $50,000 purchase would be 0.6% on the first $15,000 = $90, plus 0.2% on the remaining $35,000 = $70, for a total of $160.

As you can see, discount brokerage commissions are not very high for middle-range and large buyers of mutual funds, particularly when looked at as a percentage of the purchase. A purchase of $5,000, for example, would cost the minimum $30 fee—which is only 0.6% of the total. And the buyer or seller of $50,000 worth of a fund would pay only a 0.32% commission on the purchase ($160 = 0.32% of $50,000).

These days, most brokerages have a large

number of funds that you can buy for free—no fees, no commissions. Charles Schwab, for example, has its "OneSource" funds, which are free of commissions. Ask your broker to send you a list of all the mutual funds they carry; this brochure will specify which funds carry no fees.

What all this means is that it is usually preferable to buy mutuals through a broker. Dealing with a broker offers the convenience of buying and selling with one phone number and having all your funds in one place. The brokerage will send out a monthly statement listing all your funds and showing their present values. This can make things much easier, particularly for those who are setting up a portfolio of investments for the first time.

There are exceptions to this rule: your broker may not carry a smaller mutual fund, in which case, you will have to buy it directly from the fund office. And for those who can't afford the broker's minimum initial purchase (commonly around $2,500), it may be necessary to buy a fund directly (often, the funds require smaller initial investments than brokerages).

Unlike most investments, you can also buy mutual funds without the aid of a broker. You can call up the fund office directly; for example, you could call the Vanguard office, ask them to send you an application, and return it with the $5,000 for their Equity Income Fund. (The toll-free numbers of the various fund offices can be found in the books listed at the end of this chapter.) In this particular case, you would not be charged any commission by the fund.

Some mutual funds charge a kind of initiation fee, which they call a *sales load*, or simply a *load*. The

Vanguard funds are all *no-load* funds, so there is no fee to buy into the Equity Income Fund. Other funds, however, may charge 2% or 3% of the amount of your purchase—or more. To buy into the United Science and Technology Fund, you will pay a 5.75% load. If you were to buy $10,000 worth of this fund, this would mean a payment of $575 in fees (5.75% = .0575 × $10,000 = $575). A 10% rise in the fund during the first year would amount to a $1,000 profit on paper—but your actual return would be only $425 after you subtract the $575 load.

Some funds charge a fee when you *sell* your shares in the fund. This fee is called a *back-end load*, as opposed to the more common *front-end load* when you buy in. It is also called a *redemption fee* or a *deferred sales charge*.

Logically, you might assume that the funds that charge high loads do better than the no-load funds—that the managers must be doing *something* to earn the extra money. This, however, has been statistically proved not to be the case. Overall, there is virtually no difference in the performance of load and no-load mutual funds. Some individual funds may do better than others, but this is true of the no-loads as well as the load funds. So why pay these fees, when you can buy a fund that is just as good with no fees? Why, indeed?

There are many excellent funds with no loads and minimal or nonexistent 12b-1 fees. Except in rare cases, there is no reason you should pay more than the yearly management fees when you own a mutual fund.

You need to be aware that some of the larger brokerages and investment management companies have their own mutual funds—and these funds usually have loads attached to them. You may be directed to these funds by your broker, but you can ask to be directed away from them—to high-performing no-load funds.

All the funds charge management fees of 0.5% to 1% a year. These you should expect—after all, the managers have to get paid somehow. You won't see these fees on the statement of your account; they are deducted from the fund's assets before the total value is calculated—"off the top," as it were.

Some funds, both load and no-load, have what are called *12b-1 plans*. These plans allow the fund managers to use the assets of the fund to pay for such expenses as advertising, brokers' commissions, and sending out informational material. The 12b-1 charges can range from 0.10% to 1.25% per year and, like the management fees, are deducted directly from the fund's assets.

These fees are essentially "hidden loads." For example, if you have owned a fund for five years, a 12b-1 fee of 1% a year would be the approximate equivalent of a 5% front-end load.

Be sure to watch for the various loads and fees when you check out the particulars of a fund (the recommended books will list all the fees). There are many excellent funds with no loads and minimal or nonexistent 12b-1 fees. Except in rare cases, there is no reason you should pay more than the yearly management fees when you own a mutual fund.

OPEN-END FUNDS AND CLOSED-END FUNDS

The mutual funds we are discussing in this chapter are called *open-end funds*. All this means is that, unlike most companies, the fund has no limit to the number of shares it issues. When you buy into a fund, they will simply print up new shares for you. (You can ask that the share certificates be sent to you, though most people opt to have them kept at the fund office.)

Open-end mutual funds are not traded on the stock exchanges (you will find them listed in a separate section of the financial pages). This is because you buy and sell shares only from the fund itself, not from other investors on the open market.

Closed-end funds are similar to the open-end ones in that they own securities of many different companies. Closed-end funds, however, like most publicly owned companies, issue a *limited* number of shares, and these shares are traded on the stock exchanges. As with other stocks, you buy shares from other investors through a stockbroker, not from the fund office. Closed-end funds are discussed in detail in Chapter 13.

READING THE MUTUAL FUND TABLES

Each day, the total value of all the securities and cash in an open-end fund is added up. This total is divided by the number of shares the fund has issued, and the resulting figure is called the *net asset value* (NAV). This is the price of one share of the fund, and it is the figure you will see in the mutual funds section of the financial pages.

If the NAV figure is followed by "NL," this means the fund is a no-load fund. If, on the other hand, another, larger number follows the net asset value, the fund has a front-end load attached. The second number is the offer price—the amount it will cost you to buy a share of the fund.

FIDELITY INVESTMENT

Fund	NAV	Offer Price	NAV Change
Balanced	11.93	NL	+0.06
Blue Chip Growth	17.60	18.14	+0.09

The Fidelity Balanced Fund is a no-load (NL) fund. You can buy one share at the net asset value price of $11.93. The change in the NAV from the day before is +0.06; that is, yesterday the price was $11.87.

The Fidelity Blue Chip Growth Fund is a load fund. The $18.14 is the cost per share—$0.54 higher than the net asset value. This reflects a load charge of 3%. If you buy into the fund, you will pay $18.14 per share, but should you turn around and try to sell the same shares back to the fund, you would get only $17.60 for each. For you to show any profit, the net asset value will have to increase past $18.14.

As we mentioned above, mutual funds are usually purchased in round dollar figures. If you order $1,000 of the Fidelity Balanced Fund at $11.93 per share, they will send you a notice saying that you bought 83.8222 shares ($1,000 ÷ $11.93 per share = 83.8222 shares). You should be prepared for such decimalized figures when you buy mutual funds.

If, over the next few weeks or months, the companies owned by the Balanced Fund do well and the net asset value goes up to, say, $13.25, you would multiply this new figure by the number of your shares to arrive at the value of the shares ($13.25 × 83.8222 = $1,110.64). You will be ahead by $110.64.

How Prices Are Set

Because open-end mutual funds issue new shares to new buyers, the law of supply and demand does not affect the price of these shares. Stock prices rise and fall according to the demand by investors for the *limited* supply of shares issued by a company. Sellers can demand a higher price if the stock is popular. In the case of mutual funds, however, the only seller is the fund office. Instead of demanding a higher price from new investors, the fund simply issues them new shares at the going price.

The price, or net asset value, of shares in an open-end mutual fund is determined solely by the total value of the assets held by the fund. This is one of the few instances in the investment world where supply and demand are not at work in setting a price.

FUND FAMILIES

A mutual fund is usually part of a "family" of funds—a group of funds owned by one management company. In order to encourage people to invest all their money with them, management companies create funds with different investment purposes. The Fidelity Group of Funds, for example, offered 115 different funds at last count, each of which had a different focus for its investments. This is unusually large—most fund families consist of anywhere from 5 to 30 funds. Some of the other large companies are Scudder, Dreyfus, T. Rowe Price, and Vanguard.

Do certain families of funds perform better than others? Yes, but the individual investor should concentrate more on individual funds—their performance over time, the loads and fees, and the prospects for the type of investments owned by the fund. Occasionally, it's useful to know about the parent companies: for example, all Scudder funds are no-load, and the Vanguard funds generally have low management fees.

DIVIDENDS AND DISTRIBUTIONS

Because the stocks and/or bonds owned by a mutual fund produce interest and dividends, the fund will accumulate income over the course of a year. In addition, the securities may increase in value; if the fund managers sell these at a profit, this sale will also produce income in the form of capital gains.

This income is passed on to shareholders in the form of *distributions* during the year. You can receive checks monthly or quarterly if you need the income. If, on the other hand, you are investing only for the growth of your capital, you can ask the fund to automatically reinvest all your income in additional shares of the fund.

These reinvested amounts may not seem very large at first, but when compounded over the years, they can make for a substantial increase in your holdings. *The new investor should know that the performance figures for mutual funds almost always assume all income is reinvested.* (You should also know that the performance figures do not subtract taxes from the income generated by the fund.)

The amount of dividends and distributions from a mutual fund will depend on the kind of investments it owns. Funds investing in high-rated corporate bonds may give returns of 6% to 8% based on the income from the bonds. A fund investing in small-growth companies, on the other hand, might have little or no income from dividends. Any profit you make from this fund will be the result of appreciation in the market value of the stocks owned by the fund.

Whether you receive the distributions in cash or have them reinvested, Uncle Sam will want his cut. At the end of the year, the mutual fund office will send you a form listing the dividends, interest, and capital gains for the year—all the information you need for your taxes.

Investors are sometimes confused by the tax rules surrounding mutual funds. Believe it or not, the Internal Revenue Service has a very helpful booklet explaining these rules, complete with examples of how the rules work in different situations. Ask for Publication 564 at an IRS office.

A Fund for Every Purpose

No matter what part of the World of Investment you're interested in, you can almost always find a mutual fund that covers it. There are five general categories of funds and then a very large number of specific categories.

In addition, you can find all different levels of the risk-reward thermometer among the many funds. In spite of the safety inherent in owning many different companies, some funds are quite risky because they invest in things like junk bonds or stock options. Other funds are extremely conservative, investing only in top-rated bonds and blue chip stocks.

General Categories

Aggressive Growth Funds. You would invest in an aggressive growth fund to maximize the chances of increasing your investment capital in a short period

No matter what part of the World of
Investment you're interested in, you can
almost always find a mutual fund that covers
it. There are five general categories of funds
and then a very large number of specific
categories.

of time (i.e., get rich quick). Because the companies held
by the fund are often in the process of growing, their stock
dividends are commonly small or nonexistent.
Distributions will, therefore, tend to be minimal.
Aggressive growth funds, as a group, are the most
volatile—they tend to lose the most value in bear markets
and gain the most in bull markets.

Growth Funds. Growth funds—also called conservative growth funds—are interested in a long-term appreciation of capital. They are likely to invest in blue chip
companies that pay dividends, but are still oriented
toward growth. Income will be higher and risk lower than
with the aggressive funds, but these funds can also lose a
good deal of value in a bear market. Because of the high
quality of the stocks, however, recovery is usually excellent when the market improves.

Growth and Income Funds. Growth and income
funds (also known as income or equity-income funds)
attempt to provide a substantial income, while still
encouraging growth of capital. They tend to invest in
convertible bonds (see Chapter 7) and utility stocks.
These securities usually fluctuate less than those of the
growth-oriented companies, so these funds tend to be
more stable.

Balanced Funds. Moving on down the risk-reward scale, the first purpose of the balanced funds is preservation of capital. The portfolios of these funds are "balanced" between stocks and bonds; traditionally they will hold 60% of assets in stocks, 40% in bonds. Like the growth and income funds, the balanced funds provide high income, but will be even less volatile in response to market fluctuations.

Bond Funds. Investors put their money in bonds and bond funds because they yield a high cash income and provide balance in a portfolio of stock funds. The interest payments from top-rated bonds will continue even in a depressed stock market. Although there are funds that hold high-risk bonds called "junk bonds," most bond funds are purchased for their stability and high income yield.

Specialized Funds

Here are a few of the more popular types of specialized mutual funds.

International Funds. International funds have provided good diversification for their investors over the last 20 years. These funds invest in the stocks and bonds of foreign companies, thereby providing welcome diversity to an all-American portfolio. Some international funds invest all over the world, while others cover a specific area, like the Pacific Basin or Europe. You can find international funds in all of the five general categories listed above: aggressive growth, growth, growth and income, balanced, and bond.

Socially Responsible Funds. Relatively new on the scene, the socially responsible funds invest only in companies that exhibit a social conscience. Companies that take care of the environment and are aware of the rights and needs of their workers are "in"; firms that produce pollution, weapons of war, cigarettes, or alcohol are "out." Most socially responsible funds have performed very well over the last five years. See Chapter 12 for more about these funds.

Precious Metals Funds. For risk-tolerant investors only! Precious metals funds invest in gold and silver mines, bullion, other rare metals like platinum, and, occasionally, metals futures contracts. These funds are not for the weak-hearted; the funds nevertheless provide an easier way of investing in metals than actually buying coins or bullion.

Index Funds. In recent years, funds that track stock indexes have become extremely popular. In Chapter 8 we will discuss the various stock indexes used to measure the performance of the stock market, such as the Dow Jones averages and the Standard & Poor's 500 (S&P 500). Right now, all you need to know is that the S&P 500 Index tracks the ups and downs of the stocks of 500 large corporations on the New York and American Exchanges and the Nasdaq Stock Market. It is an excellent indicator of the direction of the stock market as a whole.

Index funds buy stock in all the companies of an index. For example, the Vanguard Index 500 Fund invests in the stock of all 500 companies in the S&P 500. Investing in an index fund like this one is as close as you can come to investing in the entire stock market. What's the advantage? One advantage is that the managers of such funds don't have much to do in the way of buying and selling, so management fees are small.

Index funds that tracked large corporation indexes like the S&P 500 did extremely well during the 1990s because these large companies increased sharply in value. In 1998, for example, the S&P 500 Index Funds outperformed all but 14% of the actively managed funds. But whether the next decade will see a repeat of this performance is an open question.

Some of the other specialized funds invest in the securities of companies in these categories: real estate (companies that hold income property and real estate sales companies); small companies; utilities; technology; health care; energy; and biotechnology. There are also specialized bond funds, such as those holding only tax-free municipal bonds or government bonds.

CHOOSING THE BEST FUNDS

Information on mutual funds is not difficult to find. The American Association of Individual Investors (AAII) issues an excellent yearly guide to no-load funds. This is listed at the end of this chapter, along with a few other guides. Your broker will have a booklet listing the funds traded by the brokerage. Barron's (the weekly financial newspaper) puts out a comprehensive guide to the funds each quarter; you receive this as part of your subscription, or you can buy that particular issue at the newspaper shop.

These guides will list the investment category of the fund, the loads and fees, and the dividend yield during the last year. They will also show the "performance" of the fund during the last few months and over several years—that is, how much you would have gained (or lost) had you invested a given amount in the fund. Some of the recommended books will give more detailed information, such as the investment objective of a given fund and its performance compared to other funds in the same category. All the guides will list the address and 800 number of the fund office.

Pax World Fund

Let's look at an example of a mutual fund. Pax World Fund was started in 1970. It is a no-load, "balanced" fund: roughly 60% of its portfolio is in stocks and 40% in bonds. Shareholders number about 70,000; assets are $920,000.

Pax is a socially responsible fund; it excludes companies that manufacture weapons or are engaged in the liquor, tobacco, or gaming industries. It presently owns 38 different stocks. Here are its largest stock holdings:

Stock	Shares	Value	% of Net Assets
AirTouch	700,000	$50,488,000	6.03%
Gap	750,000	$42,188,000	5.04%
SBC Comms	703,000	$37,683,000	4.50%
Amgen	300,000	$31,369,000	3.74%
Merck	200,000	$29,538,000	3.53%

All bonds owned by Pax are top-rated government bonds.

Following are the rates of return, in percentages, for the last four years:

1995	1996	1997	1998
29.19	10.36	25.12	24.63

To figure the increase for an investment in any year, multiply by the percentage shown. For example, in 1997, there was an increase of 25.12% (an excellent year). If you had invested $1,000 at the first of the year, you would have had $1,251 at the end. Notice how the rates of return vary widely from year to year. You should expect this from any mutual fund that invests in stocks.

Because stocks have done so well in the last few years, returns from PAX are not quite as high as those from many stock funds. However, the balanced format, which includes bonds, will often do better than stock funds in years when stocks are down.

If you are thinking of buying a fund, you can call the fund's 800 number and ask them to send you a prospectus. This short booklet will tell you the investment policy of the fund, its performance since its inception, and the companies in its portfolio.

A word of caution: The past-performance figures for mutual funds can be misleading, particularly for the funds specializing in a narrow market group. For example, a fund specializing in energy stocks may have had a fantastic record for the past year, but its performance this year may be terrible if the economic climate is difficult for the energy companies. Try to find the funds with a good record over several years *and* good prospects for the future.

A few of the newsletter editors I mention in this book, like Richard Band and Richard Young, recommend mutual funds in addition to individual securities. These newsletters are an excellent source for top-performing funds.

Until you gain experience and a feel for the markets, I recommend that you avoid buying individual stocks and bonds. Mutual funds are an excellent place for the new investor to start.

If you are thinking of buying a fund, you can call the fund's 800 number and ask them to send you a prospectus. This short booklet will tell you the investment policy of the fund, its performance since its inception, and the companies in its portfolio.

In Chapter 14, we'll discuss not only which categories of funds have performed the best in the past, but which ones show the most promise for the future. And in Chapters 15 and 16, we'll look at how to choose the funds most appropriate to your situation. Finally, in Appendix A, you will find a short list of the current best-performing funds to choose from.

Resources

The Individual Investor's Guide to No-Load Mutual Funds. The Resources section of Chapter 1 explains how to join the American Association of Individual Investors (AAII). The yearly edition of this manual comes free with membership. If you don't want to join the AAII, the guide is available in bookstores, but the price is $24.95! (It's more cost-effective to join AAII.)

Either way, this book can be extremely helpful to new investors. The performance of about 500 no-load funds is reviewed over the past five years. The first few chapters present useful information about funds in general, and interpretations of the performance figures. An excellent place to start.

Morningstar Mutual Funds (800) 735-0700. Binder: $495/year; $55/three-month trial. Principia Software: $895/year (updated CD every month). This is the service to sign up for if you plan to buy a number of mutual funds. Your subscription gets you a large three-ring binder with the particulars on 1600 different funds. Every two weeks, you receive an update on 150 funds, which you add to the binder. The information on each fund is updated every 20 weeks. Instead of the binder, you can get the Principia software, which contains the same information in a less bulky form.

Morningstar provides you with much more detailed information than most fund guides—and more of it. Despite the amount of information, however, the presentation is clear and straightforward. There is a guide that explains in plain English the reasons for all the different facts and figures. This is for the investor who wants to be really thorough in managing his or her portfolio.

Morningstar also has online reports about the funds they cover, though these are not as extensive as the reports in their binder or software. Check out Chapter 22 for the best ways of finding online information about mutual funds.

Each family of mutual funds has its own web site. To find them, first go to *Ask Jeeves* at <www.ask.com>. Jeeves is one of the best search engines and will enable you to find all kinds of information, much of which is pertinent to investment. In the question box, type in "Vanguard Mutual Funds" or "Fidelity Mutual Funds" and you will be given the link to their web site. At the Vanguard site, you are presented with much more information than you really want to know about the Vanguard "Family" and how to become a part of it. Stay focused and click on "Our Funds," then find the particular fund you want to know about. Take a look at the general information offered about the fund on the first page, then, under "Fund Facts," click "Performance." This will show you how well the fund performed during the last year, three years, five years, and ten years, and allow you to compare this performance with an index of similar funds. The information offered at these sites can be very useful, but be sure to get an additional assessment of the fund from an independent source, such as Morningstar, before you buy.

CHAPTER 7

FIXED-INCOME INVESTMENTS

S tock dividends, even those of giant corporations, rise and fall every year. If you own part of a company through your stock purchase, then your yearly return will depend on how well that company performs. In addition, of course, the value of your stock will rise and fall according to the fortunes of the firm. Fixed-income investments are an alternative to this kind of uncertainty; in this case, you are a *lender* instead of an owner. Lenders have a good deal of clout because everybody wants their money; banks, corporations, even the federal government will pay you a relatively high rate of interest for the use of your money—and they will guarantee this rate for a certain length of time. This is why these loans are called "fixed-income investments."

In this chapter, we're going to take a look at the various ways of getting a fixed income, and the advantages and disadvantages of each.

CDs

When you open a savings account at your local bank or credit union, you are essentially lending your money to the bank. They are willing to pay you interest for the use of your money because they can lend it to others at a higher rate.

With a regular savings account, you can withdraw all your money at any time. The banks, however, would like you to leave your money with them for a longer period of time, so they will know how much they have to lend out. For this reason, they created *certificates of deposit*, or *CDs*. If you commit a certain amount of money for a certain length of time, they will pay you a higher interest rate than that of regular savings accounts.

You can buy certificates of deposit for periods ranging from three months to five years. The most common CDs have terms of six months to two years, and the minimum deposits range from around $250 to $1,000, depending on the bank and how long the term is.

The interest you receive from CDs will be several percentage points higher than that of regular bank savings accounts. For example, if regular savings were paying at a rate of 2% to 3%, six-month CDs might yield 5%, twelve-month CDs 5.5%, and two-year CDs 6%. Different banks and credit unions will have different interest rates for their CDs—it pays to shop around.

> **The most common CDs have terms of six months to two years, and the minimum deposits range from around $250 to $1,000, depending on the bank and how long the term is.**

The rates *offered* by the bank will change with the prevailing interest rates, but once you have purchased a CD, your interest rate will be locked in until the expiration date (this is why CDs are fixed-income investments). These days, there are a few exceptions to this rule, and a few CDs have interest rates that fluctuate—so be sure to check.

When prevailing interest rates are low, it's not a good idea to lock yourself in to a long-term (two- to five-year) CD with a low return. The prevailing rates are likely to go up before the CD expires. You won't be able to take advantage of these new, higher rates, though, because you will be charged a fee if you withdraw your money before your CD matures (this fee may be as high as 90 days' interest on CDs with a term of a year).

CDs are a better place to park your extra money, or part of your emergency fund, than regular savings accounts. Not only will you receive a higher interest rate, but because of the CDs' early withdrawal fee, you will probably think twice before making any "impulse" withdrawals from your savings.

Like regular savings at almost all banks, CDs are covered up to $100,000 by the Federal Deposit Insurance Corporation (FDIC). You should be absolutely sure that your bank is covered by the FDIC. This means that if the bank should fail, you will receive all the money you have on deposit, up to $100,000.

MONEY MARKET ACCOUNTS

Another way of lending your money for interest is to open a money market account. These days, almost every financial institution has some form of money market account.

Just what is the "money market"? The federal government, banks, and large corporations all have a need to borrow money for the short term—less than a year. The government issues Treasury bills (T-bills) and Treasury notes, banks borrow by way of very large CDs ($100,000 and up), and large corporations put out IOUs called "commercial paper." It's not possible for the average investor to invest in most of these "money market securities," but banks and other institutions buy them by pooling depositors' money.

What does all this mean to the individual investor? By having a bank invest your money in the money market, you can earn substantially more than with a regular savings account. You may earn a bit more with a CD, but CDs have less liquidity. You can always withdraw funds from a money market account. You can even write several checks a month on the account.

Banks usually set a minimum of $1,000 to $2,000 on money market deposit accounts (MMDAs). If your bank is insured by the FDIC, you are covered in the MMDAs up to $100,000.

Money market interest rates can fluctuate dramatically. Once you've invested your money, you may earn more interest one month and less the next. In the spring of 1990, the return was about 7.5%; but during the rest of the decade, you could expect only 4% to 5% on your money. Because of this fluctuation, MMDAs cannot strictly be called fixed-income investments; they do, however, offer safety and interest rates substantially higher than those of regular savings accounts.

As a matter of interest, the going interest rates on most money market accounts are pegged half a percentage point below the rate of U.S. Treasury bills.

So which is better, CDs or MMDAs? This depends on a couple of considerations. Longer-term CDs may give a slightly higher return, but money market accounts have more liquidity. CDs lock in a rate of interest for a given period, but if interest rates go up during that period, you'd be better off in an MMDA.

This is one of those decisions that can give people headaches—but really don't matter all that much. Over the long term, one or two percentage points can make a large difference, but over the short term, you can always transfer your money if one or the other kind of account looks better. They're both insured and they're both better than regular passbook savings accounts, if you can meet the bank's minimum deposit requirements.

These days, many banks have minimum deposit requirements for passbook savings and even some money market accounts. You may find that you are being charged a monthly fee if your account is less than $500—and that this fee often amounts to more than the interest you are being paid! What this means, if you are a small depositor, is that you are better off squirreling your money away in a piggy bank until it reaches the level where you will not be charged a fee. Open a savings account then, but as soon as you can meet the minimum, take your money out of regular savings and open a money market account or buy a CD.

CREDIT UNIONS

Unlike banks, credit unions usually welcome small savings accounts—and without any monthly fees. Credit unions are an excellent alternative to banks. Because they are cooperatives, owned by their members, they are usually smaller, friendlier, and more sympathetic to the small borrower. In addition, you have the satisfaction of knowing that your savings allow the credit union to lend money to your neighbors or coworkers.

If you have access to a credit union where you work or in your community, I would strongly recommend you give it a try. The interest rates are usually comparable to those of the banks, and your money is insured by the federal government (at most credit unions—be sure to check). These days, many credit unions offer the same services as banks: CDs, auto loans, credit cards, and checking accounts.

There are now 14,650 credit unions across the country, with $200 billion in assets and 62 million members. For help in finding one near you, or in starting your own credit union, you can contact the Credit Union League in your state. Look in the phone book in your city or the nearest city. If you can't find the league office in your state, you can call the Credit Union National Association at (800) 358-5710. They will put you in touch with the closest league office.

For those interested in putting their savings to work where they are most needed, there are a growing number of community development credit unions which lend to such groups as small, inner-city, and minority-owned businesses. To find one near you, you can contact the National Federation of Community Development Credit Unions, 120 Wall Street, 10th Floor, New York, NY 10005, (212) 809-1850. This is an excellent way to put your savings to work in a socially active manner.

BONDS: HOW TO LEND MONEY TO GENERAL MOTORS

You become part owner of a corporation by owning its stock. But suppose you *lend* money to this same corporation—or to the federal government. This is also a type of investment, because you will receive payments for the use of your money.

The way you lend money is to purchase *bonds* issued by corporations and governments. Bonds are essentially IOUs that give you interest payments in return for the rental of your money. Corporations figure they can make more than the 6% to 8% they pay you by investing your loan in their own operations. About 80% of their borrowed money comes from issuing bonds.

> **Bonds are the Volvos of the investment world: not terribly exciting or stylish, but extremely safe and dependable.**

Unlike stocks, whose dividends may fluctuate according to the fortunes of the company, bonds are fixed-income investments. This means the interest payments you receive will stay the same during the life of the bond. You don't gain more profit when the firm issuing the bonds does well, but neither do you receive less if the company falls on lean times.

Bonds, like other fixed-income investments, offer the advantage of a stable return. You don't have the chance to make a large profit, as you do with riskier investments, but neither do you leave yourself open to a major loss. Bonds are the Volvos of the investment world: not terribly exciting or stylish, but extremely safe and dependable.

For local, state, and national governments, bonds are an alternative to taxes as a way of raising money. Unlike the corporations, however, governments usually do not invest their bond income in money-making endeavors. Bonds are a way for governments to borrow at less interest than a bank would charge them for a loan.

You can buy and sell bonds through stockbrokers, very much the way you buy and sell stock. Just as with a stock, you will receive a certificate, which you can keep in a safe-deposit box or at your broker's.

Bonds are issued with a specific interest rate and a specific date at which they will "expire" or "mature." At this "maturity date," the borrower must pay back the entire amount of the bond—the so-called *face value.*

Most bonds are similar to "interest-only" loans, in that the principal is not paid off until the loan comes due. This is different from the kind of loans most individuals are used to; each payment on an auto loan, for example, includes interest and principal, so that the loan is paid off in several years.

Instead, the issuer of the bond will pay you interest, usually every six months, then repay the amount of your original loan on the maturity date. (There are exceptions to this, as you will see in Chapter 21, on individual bonds.) The face value, interest rate, and maturity date are all printed on the bond certificate.

Bonds are generally regarded as extremely safe investments, especially those issued by the federal government and large corporations. There are, however, corporate bonds with a low safety rating. Buyers of these so-called "junk bonds" receive higher interest than they would for top-rated bonds, but run the risk of default by the issuing company (a default in payments means your bond could end up worth nothing).

The bonds with high safety ratings, however, can provide a good balance to stocks in a portfolio. Bonds yield a steady return—substantially higher than the dividends from most stocks—which you can either use as income or reinvest.

One reason bonds are safe and stable is that interest on a company's bonds must be paid before any dividends to stockholders. And, though bond prices do fluctuate, they do so much less than stocks. Bonds as a category, then, come out a notch or two lower than stocks on the risk-reward thermometers.

The Rule of 70

There is a simple way of determining how long it will take your money to double at any compound rate of interest. Take the interest rate and divide it into 70:

the result will be the number of years for the amount to double.

For example, suppose you invest $10,000 at 7%: 7% into 70 = 10. It will take approximately 10 years for your $10,000 to double at a rate of 7%, compounded each year. If your rate of return was 12%, however, your money would double in $5\frac{5}{6}$ years, or 5 years and 10 months (70 divided by 12 = 5.833, or $5\frac{5}{6}$). This will not be an exact number, but it's useful for quick figuring.

There are many different types of bonds, each with different characteristics. And the factors that make individual bonds and the bond market go up and down are generally different from those that affect the stock market. You will find descriptions of the different types of bonds and how to buy them in Chapter 21.

Most of these details, however, are useful only to more experienced investors. Individual bonds, like individual stocks, are generally not appropriate investments for the new investor. Mutual funds that hold their assets in bonds are a much better place to put your money.

Compound Interest and Mutual Funds

Compound interest is one of the reasons most mutual funds don't perform quite as well as the overall stock market, as measured by stock indexes such as the Standard and Poor's 500. Even no-load mutual funds have management fees, which subtract about 1% a year from the total value of the fund you own.

Suppose the stock market as a whole goes up 10% in a given year. If your mutual fund performs as well as the stock market, your gain will be only 9% after the 1% management fee is subtracted. If the fund has other expenses, like the 12b-1 fees mentioned in Chapter 6, your gain will be even less—maybe only 8%. We have just seen the difference between growth at 8% and growth at 10%.

What this illustrates is the importance of buying mutual funds that charge low management fees and have very low or nonexistent additional expenses, such as 12b-1 fees. It also illustrates the importance of choosing the very best mutual funds—the ones that will equal or outperform the overall market. We'll learn how to do this in Chapters 14 and 15.

How Compound Interest Works

Just as a CD or a money market account will earn you 2% to 3% more than a regular passbook savings account, a bond mutual fund will usually earn 1% to 3% more than a money market account.

But are a few percentage points of interest worth the trouble of taking the money out of your local bank and investing it in some mutual fund? If a certificate of deposit is giving 6%, why try for 8% with a corporate bond fund? The extra 2% would mean only $200 more a year, if you were investing $10,000. After all, your money is fully insured at the bank, and—at least in a money market account—you have immediate access to it.

The answer to this question is contained in the compound-interest chart in Appendix D. Referring to this chart, notice that at 6% your $10,000 will become $20,000 in twelve years, assuming that all the interest is reinvested at the end of each year—"compounded annually," in bank terminology. But notice that at 8% compounded annually, the $10,000 has doubled itself in only a little over *nine* years!

This example illustrates how important two, or even one, percentage points can be over the long term. In 30 years, your $10,000 will have grown to $100,000 at 8%. At 6%, however, it would be only $57,400. Not a bad chart to remember when you're investing for long-term objectives like college educations or retirement. (Remember that in this scenario, growth is the only objective; you don't receive any spendable income from your investment—all of the interest is reinvested.)

Why do these one or two percentage points make such a difference? Because when you "compound" interest, you add it on to the principal. The next time you figure the interest, you figure it from this new, larger number.

For example, you invest $10,000 in a bond fund from which you receive an annual return of 10%. Interest is usually paid either quarterly or every six months, but for the sake of simplicity in our figuring, we're going to add it on at the end of the year.

On December 31, then, 10% × $10,000, or $1,000, will be credited to your account. You now have $11,000. Next year, the 10% interest will be paid not on the original $10,000, but on this $11,000. 10% × $11,000 = $1,100, which gets added to the total, making $12,100.

The third year, the 10% is figured on the $12,100, giving you $1,210. Adding it on, you now have $13,310.

Notice how the interest payments keep getting bigger as the principal amount gets bigger. When you get up to 10 years, the principal amount has grown to about $25,900. This means the interest payment will be $2,590. The larger interest payments mean the principal will grow at a faster clip each year.

If, however, you're getting 8% instead of 10%, the amount will grow more slowly. At the end of 3 years, $10,000 invested at 8%, compounded annually, will have grown to about $12,600. At 10 years, it will be $21,600, substantially less than the $25,900 at the 10% interest.

At 20 years, the difference has become dramatic: $46,600 for the 8% fund, $67,200 for the 10%. Such are the wonders of compound interest. This is why people get excited over a few little percentage points.

Stocks Versus Bonds

While we're on the subject of compound interest, this is a good time to talk about why so many people invest in stocks instead of choosing the relative safety of bonds. Bonds—especially U.S. government bonds and top-rated bonds from the giant corporations—are about as rock-solid safe as investments get. Furthermore, though they may fluctuate in value, bonds are not likely to take the kind of dive as stocks did in 1987. So why risk your money in the stock market?

The answer is that while stocks are indeed riskier over the short term, in the long term they have outperformed bonds hands down.

From 1970 to 1990, inflation charged ahead at an average yearly rate of 3.36%. Regular savings accounts didn't stay very far ahead of inflation: $10,000 invested in 1970 and compounded over the years would have grown to $45,000 in 1990. If you subtracted the value of

Stocks are among the few investments that have beaten the tax and inflation bites with plenty to spare.

the dollar lost to inflation during that period, you would be left with only $11,400—a total profit of just $1,400.

In the same 20 years, $10,000 invested in corporate bonds would have topped out at $56,000. Stocks, however, as measured by the Standard and Poor's 500 Index, would have made $10,000 grow to $82,500.

If you turn to Appendix C, "Total Returns: 1925 to 1994," you'll see an excellent example of how compound interest works. You will also notice that the figures shown are impressively in favor of stocks.

The table shows that $1.00 invested in corporate bonds in 1925 would have grown to $38.01 in 1994; $1.00 invested in stocks, though, would have amounted to almost $3,000 dollars! (All of these figures assume that all earnings are reinvested.)

It's important to remember the twin demons of inflation and taxes in figuring total returns. If inflation is growing at an average rate of 4% and taxes take a bite of another 2.8% out of your total portfolio, then a 6.8% growth in your investments will amount to no growth at all.

Let's look at how the tax bite works. Suppose you receive 10%, or $1,000 on a $10,000 investment, and are taxed at the rate of 28% on this income. Your tax is $280 a year ($1,000 × 0.28 = $280). So your after-tax return is only $720.

Another way of looking at this, however, is that your capital amount—the $10,000—has been decreased by $280, or 2.8%. So while inflation is busy lowering the value of your capital by decreasing the amount it can buy, taxes attack your capital head on. Added together, their total damage comes to 6.8%. Your tax rate may be higher or lower and the inflation rate may vary from year to year, but these figures are close to average rates over the last 20 years.

This is just one more reason the stock market needs to be a part of an individual portfolio: Stocks are among the few investments that have beaten the tax and inflation bites with plenty to spare.

Bond Mutual Funds

So now we have to ask another question: Why invest in bonds at all, if stocks have done so much better? The answer is that in the World of Investment, it's good to have as many bases covered as possible. We just don't know how stocks will perform in this new century. In Chapter 15, we'll go into more of the reasons for diversifying a portfolio of investments. Right now, let's consider mutual funds that invest in bonds.

As you will see in Chapter 21, the various factors to consider when buying individual bonds can get quite complex. Bond mutual funds, also known as "fixed-income funds," make it much easier for the new investor. The managers of the funds decide which bonds to buy and sell—and the best times to do so. All you have to do is choose the best fund. The great majority of investors have chosen this route: individual investors in bond mutual funds outnumber holders of bonds by about 25 to 1.

Like stock mutual funds, there are many different kinds of bond funds, with different investment purposes. There are super-safe funds that own only U.S. government securities, speculative funds that invest in junk bonds, and a whole spectrum in between. Here, we are interested in bond funds primarily for the safety and steady income they provide; for this reason, we're going to avoid the more speculative funds and deal only with the conservative ones.

These conservative funds buy government securities and high-rated corporate bonds. In the mutual funds section of Appendix A, we list a few fixed-income funds that are not only the safest, but have also given good returns over the years. These are the kinds of funds we include in our model portfolio in Chapter 14.

CHAPTER 8

FINDING AND INTERPRETING FINANCIAL INFORMATION

The individual investor needs two kinds of information: descriptive and analytical. You need to know what's happening and, especially if you're a new investor, you have to know what it means—how you should respond to the information. And, of course, you have to get acquainted with the terminology: what is this Dow you're always hearing about? What do all those numbers and letters mean in the stock tables?

In this chapter we will talk first about the best places to learn what's happening in the financial markets and where to find the best interpretations of these events. Then we'll get into the terminology and discuss such things as the various stock markets and stock indexes.

One of the greatest challenges to the new investor is tackling the vast amount of information and opinions pertaining to investing, and not just in the media. Everyone from your Uncle Fred to your next door neighbor seems to have some stock to recommend or some little nugget of

absolutely essential advice. New investors can often be swayed by what they read or hear, particularly if it is presented in an authoritative manner.

In fact, the inexperienced investor reading a financial paper can sometimes seem like a drunk in a department store. "Consolidated has a new chairman who has saved six other companies from bankruptcy" (check out Consolidated); "Analyst says gold has made a bottom and is ready to take off" (I've always wanted to buy gold—I guess now is the time); "Oil prices rise sharply" (Hmm, don't stocks usually go down when oil rises? Maybe I should think about selling some stocks), and so on, lurching from one possibility to the next.

How do you deal with this mountain of material? After all, we do need at least some of this information to make intelligent decisions.

First, remember where you are. You're not in Kansas anymore—you're in the Wonderful World of Investment, where all things seem possible. Each helping of information must be taken with several grains of salt. Remember, if that gold analyst were right even 60% of the time, she wouldn't need to be writing for *Barron's*. Remember, oil prices often go up and down like a bungee jumper and the stock market may or may not be affected.

What will help the most, however, is focusing yourself on the areas that appeal to you. As you set up an investment plan, you will then gravitate naturally to the information that pertains to your interests.

But where is the best current information and analysis? For general current information, you have your pick of the financial papers: the venerable *Wall Street Journal*, or the upstart *Investor's Business Daily*. If you tend to be overwhelmed by the quantity of information in the dailies, you can subscribe to the weekly journal, *Barron's*.

Your best bet is to go to your local library and read the different papers. You should be able to sense pretty quickly which one suits you best. The stock tables are definitely easier to read in Investor's Daily, but the manner in which the rest of the news is reported is really a matter of personal taste. They all give the necessary information.

What about the magazines for individual investors? *Money, Financial World, Personal Investor*—all the slick monthlies with their color illustrations, charts, and easy-to-read articles? Or how about the heavyweights for businesspeople—*Forbes, Fortune,* or *Business Week?*

Again, you might consider a trip to your public library to sample the various publications; if you find one you like, cut-rate subscriptions are usually available for new readers.

Unlike the financial newspapers, which focus almost exclusively on stocks and bonds, magazines are more likely to run articles about all areas of investment and finance, from real estate to personal money management to business cycles. There are certainly some useful articles in the financial journals, but it's usually necessary to sift through a good deal of other information that may not interest you. These are, after all, written for as broad a base of readership as possible.

In our information-oriented society, it is now possible to tune in the radio or TV almost any time of day and hear discussions of the discount rate or the possibility of a rise in the silver market. During the day, CNBC carries up-to-the-minute news of the markets, as well as interviews and analysis. Many public broadcasting channels carry the *Nightly Business Report* in the evening. On Friday evening, Louis Rukeyser brings you his financial experts on Wall Street Week, and various segments of the economy are discussed on *Adam Smith's Money World*, both on PBS.

Whether these programs are useful has to be your own decision. I have heard insightful discussions and gotten interesting information from all these sources. A good thing to remember, though, when you're listening to the "experts," is that there is almost certainly another "expert" whose view is diametrically opposed to the one you're hearing. You won't have to look very far to find her, either—just listen to a discussion on the same subject on another program the next day.

During the last few years, the Internet has become a rich source of information for individual investors. In fact, many of the financial publications mentioned above now have online versions. The sheer amount of raw information and analysis available online, however, can quickly overwhelm you. In Chapter 22, we will sort this all out and discuss how to find the best web sites for your needs.

Perhaps the best way to refine and limit the information you receive is to subscribe to a few good financial newsletters. When you decide on a specific advisory service, you have already begun to specialize in the kind of investments that interest you. The information you then receive is pertinent to your situation and your portfolio.

As for analysis of the economy and the specific markets, in my experience it is the advisers who write the newsletters who do the best job—at least this is true of the advisers recommended in this book. It can be useful to read a weekly paper like *Barron's* for up-to-date reporting of financial events, but you may find that most of the analytical investment information you need is contained in your monthly or bimonthly advisory newsletter.

Investors who buy and sell individual securities with some frequency may choose to subscribe to one of the daily financial papers. For the long-term investor, however, the time span of a few weeks between newsletters is just about right.

READING THE TABLES

Even though we recommend that the new investor stick to mutual funds, it's a good idea to know a few more things about the stock market—like how to read the stock tables. (The majority of funds are made up of stocks, after all.)

To begin with, what do all those funny-looking numbers and letters mean? The various financial papers may have the numbers arranged differently, but if you look at any stock table you will find these figures:

(1) 52 wk HiLo	(2) Div	(3) Shares	(4) Yld	(5) P/E	(6) Hi	(7) Lo	(8) Last	(9) Change
$40\frac{3}{8}$ 29 AT&T	1.32	6982	3.3	15	40	$39\frac{5}{8}$	$39\frac{7}{8}$	$+\frac{1}{8}$

(1) The high and low prices per share over the last 52 weeks. These are interesting figures. Overall, 75% of listed stocks fluctuate by more than 50% over a period of a year.

The prices of all stocks will fluctuate as the overall market goes up and down. Some, however, will rise and fall much more sharply than the market, and some less. This comparison of a stock's volatility compared to the market's volatility is called its *beta coefficient*. A stock with a beta of 1.00 tends to vary in price exactly as much as the overall market.

Eastman Kodak, for example, has usually had a beta of about 1.00. AT&T, like most utilities, has had a much smaller beta—around 0.65. Risky new technology stocks, on the other hand, may have betas as high as 2.00. A general rule is the higher the beta, the higher the risk. Some stock tables list betas, though you will usually see them only in more comprehensive descriptions of stocks.

(2) The total amount of dividends per share over the last year, in this case $1.32 per share. This does not necessarily mean the same dividend will be given during the next year. The larger companies tend to have more stable dividends than the smaller ones. The dividend is not the same as a company's total earnings. (See Chapter 4 for more about dividends and earnings.)

(3) The total number of shares traded that day, in 100s. This means you add two zeros to the number shown. On this particular day, 698,200 shares of AT&T were traded. Stock analysts watch these figures very closely. A sharp increase in the number of shares traded combined with a price increase means that a number of individuals and-or institutions are bullish on the stock. The reverse is true, of course, for a high volume of shares coupled with a price decrease.

(4) The yield is the dividend divided by the stock price, expressed as a percent. In this case, $1.32 divided by $39\frac{7}{8}$ = 3.3%. This means if you invest in AT&T at the current price, you will get a cash return of 3.3% of your investment. This figure does not include the stock's increase or decrease in price over the past year—only the dividends.

(5) A company's earnings for the year divided into the current stock price results in a very popular figure called the *price-earnings ratio*, or P/E ratio. This number is watched very closely by many analysts. The idea is that if

Each firm has a code name called a ticker symbol in addition to its full name.

a firm's stock price falls but the earnings remain high (causing a low P/E ratio), the stock is likely to rebound. In analyzing any stock, however, remember that the P/E ratio is only one of a number of things to consider. ("Earnings," you'll recall, refers to *total* yearly earnings, not dividends.)

(6), (7), (8) The high, low, and closing prices the stock traded at during the day. After these numbers, you will see the net change from the previous day (in *Barron's,* the numbers are weekly figures instead of daily).

The stock markets have not quite made it into the decimalized modern world: most prices are still quoted in fractions (there are plans to start decimalizing early in the next century). To do any figuring on calculators, you must convert prices into decimals. A price of $20\frac{1}{2}$ means $20.50 per share—or $2,050 for 100 shares; $20\frac{1}{8}$ translates into $20.125; 100 shares at this price would be $2,012.50 (100 × $20.125). Prices of the costlier stocks will go up and down by quarters and eighths. The lower-priced issues often move in sixteenths, thirty-seconds, and, occasionally, sixty-fourths. See Appendix B for the decimal equivalents of the fractions.

(9) The net change in price from the previous day. In this case, one share of AT&T rose just an eighth of a point (12.5 cents) from yesterday's closing price. Notice, however, that during the day the price ranged from a low of $39\frac{5}{8}$ to a high of 40.

Abbreviations

The papers have begun to improve on this score, but it can still be difficult to find a given company in the stock tables. Each firm has a code name called a *ticker symbol* in addition to its full name. General Electric is GE, for example, Apple Computer is AAPL, and so on. You need to use these symbols when ordering stock from your broker.

Unfortunately, the newspapers use neither the full names of the companies *nor* the ticker symbols, preferring instead to employ their own, often unintelligible combinations of the two. For example, *Barron's* lists Northeast Utilities (symbol: NU) as NoestUt, Atlanta/Sosnoff (ATL) as AtalSos, and First Bank System (FBS) as FtBkSy. To make things more confusing, in searching for First Bank System in alphabetical order, you don't look for "FtBkSy," you look for "First": the listings are in the alphabetical order they would be in if the full name were used.

To their credit, the editors of *Investor's Business Daily* have made a real effort to list the company names intelligibly. Now, if the other papers would only follow suit, life would be made much easier for all of us, especially for the new investor trying to find GTE Corporation (GTE) in its proper alphabetical order. What they don't tell you is that companies whose names consist only of capital letters are listed at the *beginning* of their alphabetical letter. You will find GTE near the beginning of the G listings. You will not find IBM at the beginning of the I listings, however, because that company's name is still officially International Business Machines—you'll have to look under "International."

Scattered among the company names and assorted numbers in the stock listings are various letters: pf, n, s, wt, x, and many more. There are boxes at the beginning of the tables listing the various letter symbols and their meanings. These symbols are important. "Pf," for example, means preferred stock, which is quite different from common stock; "b" (in *Investor's Daily*) means the company is bankrupt, a rather significant thing to know if you're thinking of investing in it. Unfortunately, some of these letters mean different things in different papers—another good reason for finding one paper you like and sticking with it.

You will need to know the ticker symbols for each company when you watch the price quotes on the electronic display at your broker's or on the financial channels on TV. These displays are still called tickers after the old machines in the brokerages that would tick as they printed out the latest stock prices. (The paper tape from these machines was the same ticker tape that used to be thrown from windows of skyscrapers for parades. The tape made wonderful streamers.)

The ticker has a few more abbreviations. Here's an example of a ticker describing transactions on the New York Stock Exchange.

This display would be read as follows:

T	IBM	GE	T	CTV
$40\frac{1}{4}$	5s 98	2,000s $75\frac{1}{2}$	$40\frac{3}{8}$	2s $21\frac{3}{4}$ $\frac{5}{8}$

One hundred shares of AT&T (symbol: T) were traded at the price of $40\frac{1}{4}$ ($40.25 per share). When no quantity of shares is listed, you assume that it is 100 shares. In the next quote, IBM is trading at 98; "5s" means 500 shares were traded. Moving on, 2,000 shares of General Electric went for $75\frac{1}{2}$. A hundred more shares of AT&T were traded, now at the price of $40\frac{3}{8}$. Finally, 200 shares of Commscope (CTV) were traded at $21\frac{3}{4}$, followed by 100 more at $21\frac{5}{8}$. In this case, the ticker has omitted the 21 because it's clear from the previous quote that the amount is $21\frac{5}{8}$. The quantity of shares has been omitted, so you assume that it's 100 shares.

Occasionally, the ticker will fall behind; at these times, only the fractions will be displayed. You are expected to know that "T $\frac{1}{4}$" actually means "T $40\frac{1}{4}$."

STOCK MARKETS

The New York Stock Exchange (NYSE), the American Stock Exchange (AMEX), and The Nasdaq Stock Market are the markets listed in the papers (even though the

> **The companies listed on Nasdaq, together with other small company stocks, account for a higher trading volume of securities than the New York Exchange.**

Nasdaq and the American Exchange have joined forces, their stocks are still listed separately. You may also see a regional exchange if there is one located nearby; for example, newspapers in the San Francisco Bay region list stocks of the Pacific Stock Exchange located in San Francisco.

The New York Exchange (sometimes called the "Big Board") accounts for about 80% of the volume of shares traded on the organized exchanges (excluding Nasdaq). These days, however, the companies listed on Nasdaq, together with other small company stocks, account for a higher trading volume of securities than the New York Exchange.

There are about 11,000 other stocks that you will not find listed in the newspapers. These make up the so-called over-the-counter market. Most of these are so-called "penny stocks"—low-priced stocks of small companies—and are carried by listing services such as the OTC Bulletin Board and the Pink Sheets.

Many fine small companies are among those listed in the over-the-counter market, but there are also quite a few marginal ones. Unless you have personal knowledge of a specialized field or of the prospects of a specific small company, it would generally be wise to steer clear of the over-the-counter stocks until you gain experience.

There are a couple of good reasons for this. First, it can be very difficult to measure risk in many cases, because of limited information about the small companies. In addition, a number of stock manipulations and other funny dealings have been associated with these lightly traded issues. Yes, the next Xerox or Apple Computer may be hiding among these issues, but your chance of finding it is poor until you learn more about the factors that bring about successful growth.

If an OTC company starts to grow, it can apply for a listing on Nasdaq. This requires a certain amount of earnings, net worth, and a minimum share price now set at $3 a share (after listing, the price may drop below $3 for a while without losing its listing).

If our former OTC company grows quite large, it can apply for admission to the American Stock Exchange or the New York Stock Exchange. Each has more stringent requirements for admission, with the New York Exchange being the most exclusive. The NYSE is where the big boys— General Motors, IBM, General Electric—hang out, though there are some very large, newer companies, like Microsoft and Intel, that have elected to remain with Nasdaq.

BID AND ASK

When you buy almost any of the Nasdaq stocks, and quite a few of the thinly traded stocks on the exchanges, you will come across what is called the *spread*: the difference between the current price at which you can buy a stock and the price you can sell it for. These are the *bid and ask prices*. In the stock tables, you will see only one price— the "bid" price.

International Remote Imaging Systems (IRIS, NAS-DAQ) may be listed in the paper at $^{11}/_{16}$ (that's 11/16 of a dollar, or 68.75 cents per share; this means you will pay $68.75 for 100 shares). Eleven-sixteenths is the bid price—the price "bid" by the broker who specializes in trading IRIS stock. This is the price you can sell it for if you already own it.

But if you want to buy IRIS, you will be quoted another price when you call up your broker, in this case

$^{13}\!/_{16}$ (81.25 cents per share, or $81.25 for 100 shares). This is the "ask" price—the price demanded by the specialist. This is the lowest price at which you can buy the stock.

The spread, in this case, is the difference between $^{13}\!/_{16}$ and $^{11}\!/_{16}$, or $^{2}\!/_{16} = ^{1}\!/_{8}$. This amounts to 12.5 cents per share, or $12.50 for 100 shares ($12.50 is the difference between the ask price of $81.25 and the bid price of $68.75). This $12.50 goes to the specialist; it does not go to your broker—the brokerage office gets its own commission from you. If someone wants to sell 100 shares of IRIS, this specialist will buy them for $68.75 and sell them to you for $81.25, pocketing the difference (not a bad business, eh?).

This spread is important to know about because it can add up to a substantial amount. If you bought 10,000 shares of IRIS, for example, your broker's commission might be about $ $100 (with a discount broker), but the spread would come to $1,250 ($8,125 minus $6,875). This means your IRIS stock will have to go up by more than 1/8 for you to recoup your $100 commission and the $1,250 spread. When buying a bid-and-ask stock, you need to think of yourself as already in the hole for whatever the spread is, plus your commission.

When buying the heavily traded stocks on the exchanges you will buy and sell at the one quoted price—no need to worry about bid and ask.

INDEXES

"The Dow Jones Industrial Average rose ten and one-half points today in heavy trading, the S&P fell half a point, while the Major Market Index. . . ."

Dow Jones averages? S&P? Major Market Index? Are these truly useful things, or simply more gobbledygook to confound the new investor?

Yes, the market indexes are important, because they show in which direction the markets are heading. And, unless the stocks or mutual funds you own are very unusual, they will be sensitive to the ups and downs of the market. Each index covers a different sector of the market.

The Dow Jones Averages

First of all, the granddaddy: the Dow Jones averages, started by Mr. Charles Dow in 1884. You will notice in the papers that there are actually four Dow Jones averages: the Industrial Average, the Transportation Average, the Utility Average, and the Dow Jones Composite Average, comprising the 65 companies included in the first three.

The Dow Jones Industrial Average (also known as DJIA, the DJs, or simply the Dow) is the one most often quoted. The Dow is made up of 30 of the largest industrial companies from different sectors of the economy (such as IBM, AT&T, Sears, and Exxon). Each day, the closing prices of these 30 stocks are added up and the numbers manipulated by a special formula. If the prices of the majority of these stocks rise during the day, then the Dow will also rise, and the market will be said to have "posted a gain."

For years, the Dow has been the most-quoted index, but recently many analysts have become critical of the Dow as being too narrow a measure of the stock market. Most of the other indexes include many more companies and, therefore, are better indicators of the direction of the greater market. On any given day, some of these indexes may be up while others are down. What this means is that it's necessary to look at all the major indexes to get a feel for the overall stock market.

Other Indexes

The Standard and Poors 500 (S&P 500) is a composite of four indexes monitoring 400 industrial, 20 transportation,

40 utility, and 40 financial companies. These 500 corporations account for approximately 75% of the total amount of
equities in the U.S. market.

"The Market"

Analysts speak of "The Market" as if it were an entity
unto itself. Everyone always seems to be trying to figure out what "The Market" is going to do. What the
stock market actually *is*, of course, is no more than a
vast conglomeration of individual investors, traders,
and institutions driven by hopes, fears, and rumors.

It can be useful, though, to think of this monster
as a separate entity, because not only is it affected by
its investors, they, in turn, are affected by the market's ups and downs.

As an example, suppose IBM comes out with a
very poor quarterly earnings report. Many investors
decide to sell their IBM stock, and this causes the
stock price to drop sharply. Because IBM is the
largest corporation selling computers, other investors
decide that IBM's poor earnings may be indicative of a
slump in the entire industry and start selling stocks
of other computer companies.

The Dow Jones Industrial Average starts to go
down, because IBM is a major component of that
index, and this makes investors wary of the entire
market. Buying drops off and selling increases, driving the Dow down even further.

What has happened here is that some individuals
and institutions reacted to the drop in IBM, and this
reaction drove the market down. *Other investors then
reacted to the fall in the market itself.* "The Market"—
not IBM—was affecting these investors. This is why
it's helpful to view the market as an individual entity.

The S&P 500 is made up of large companies on the American Exchange and Nasdaq, as well as the New York Exchange, so it gives a much broader indication of the market than the Dow does. It is the index that analysts always seem to use when making comparisons—for example, "This mutual fund outperformed the S&P 500 for the last five years."

- The AMEX Market Value Index measures the performance of more than 800 companies on the American Stock Exchange.

- The Nasdaq Composite Index keeps track of the over-the-counter stocks listed on Nasdaq (not the over-the-counter stocks). This is the index that most often goes in a different direction from the Dow Jones Industrials. Investors often feel differently about the prospects for the smaller, more speculative companies listed on Nasdaq than they do about the giants monitored by the Dow.

- The Value Line Index and the Wilshire 5000 are the most inclusive indexes, including companies from the major exchanges and Nasdaq.

- In the financial papers, you will also find indexes for the major international stock markets. Among the most quoted are the German DAX Index, the Japanese Nikkei Index, and the British Financial Times Industrial Index (the FTSE, whimsically called the "Footsie").

The newspapers publish all kinds of statistics relating to the indexes: the percentage change from the previous day, the change over 12 months, graphs and charts showing the rise and fall of various averages over 30-year periods, charts of the volume of stocks traded and how this relates to the averages, etc., etc., *and* etc.

Just a few years ago, a movement of 50 points in the Dow Jones Industrial Averages would generate a lot of excitement. Nowadays, such a move, whether up or down, is greeted with a yawn and a statement that the market is essentially "flat." This is because the Dow tripled in value during the last half of the 1990s; what this means is that 50 points is now a much smaller move in terms of percentage. With the Dow at 3,500, a 50 point drop meant that the index had lost 1.5% of its value—a significant amount. With the Dow at 11,000, 50 points is no more than .45% of the total index—nothing to get excited about.

Because each index has a different numerical basis, the percentage gain or drop is the most important figure to watch for. A 50 point gain in the S&P 500 Index, for example, would be very significant. If the Index were at its present value of 1,350, a 50 point gain would mean a change of 3.7%—a signal that a major rally was taking place. Most information providers will now give the percentage gain or loss in the indexes.

Serious investors will want to study these statistics to discover which ones are useful to them, and to get a better overall sense of the markets. The sheer volume of numbers, however, should persuade you to do this gradually. Don't get overwhelmed—it's not cost-effective.

What the new investor wants to achieve is a feel for the averages, and what makes them go up and down. In Chapter 20, we'll go into more detail about the reasons the stock market rises and falls. Right now, though, you can begin to get a feel for the market by watching the averages and noting the reasons the analysts give for the ups and downs.

Though it's useful to stay aware of the fluctuations in the stock market, it's also important for the long-term investor to take these fluctuations in stride. No matter how good the company or mutual fund, it will almost always be sensitive to a drop in the overall market. It is also true, however, that a good mutual fund is likely to recover quickly when the market turns around. Don't get discouraged and sell at a loss simply because your stock fund has been dragged down by a bear market. Like the South, y'all gonna rise again!

OTHER KINDS OF INFORMATION

It will soon become obvious to the new investor that general economic and political information can be just as important as specific information about a company. Say this hot software company is expanding its markets in China and the prospects look terrific. But what if there are signs that the political climate is changing in China and the American companies may be excluded? Similarly, what good will it do to research the best energy mutual fund if there is a growing oil glut that will depress oil prices and oil stocks?

Before long, by paying attention to national and international news, you will find yourself understanding and even occasionally anticipating market reactions. You will know, for example, that those strikes in the South African gold mines will probably drive gold prices up.

One thing that can discourage new investors, however, is how quickly the markets react. Before you can buy gold, or gold-mining stocks, you may find that the prices have already risen. Sometimes they rise weeks in advance in anticipation of an event. If many investors believe that the miners are going to go on strike, they will quickly bid up the price of gold.

> **You'll be surprised at the number of areas where you have a natural advantage over other investors simply because of your specific knowledge.**

One of the best things you can do is to keep your eye out for information that other people are not likely to see. For example, what area of the economy does your job or your interests make you an expert on? If the company you work for is involved in the wholesale food business, you might notice a growing number of orders for low-sodium, "healthy"-type foods. You can then begin to research which companies are producing these kinds of foods. You'll be surprised at the number of areas where you have a natural advantage over other investors simply because of your specific knowledge.

Just a further clarification about buying with the help of specific knowledge about a market, in this case the wholesale food market: This is not the kind of illegal "insider trading" you may have heard about. The illegal kind relates to buying or selling stock with inside knowledge of specific actions a company will take. For example, an officer of a corporation might know that his or her company is about to make an offer to buy another firm. If this person buys the second company's stock in anticipation that it will rise when the offer becomes public, that's illegal insider trading.

CHAPTER 9

FINANCIAL ADVISERS

So . . . after reading this book and other materials, consulting with your friends and family, and considering the whole subject for a few months, you decide you would like to hire a financial adviser. What do you do now? The next step is to decide whether you want someone who will deal with your complete financial picture, or just your investments.

A *financial planner* will go over your entire financial life with you: your goals, your income, outgo, and possible budgets, insurance needs, tax planning, as well as investment strategies to reach your goals. Such a process can be extremely useful. If your finances have seemed like a mess, you'll be amazed at how good the ordering process can make you feel. A friend of mine once likened it to financial therapy.

Money is one of the two areas of life that people think and worry about the most. If this area is out of control, it can profoundly affect the rest of your life. There's no guarantee that putting it in order will help the other most common concern, i.e., love and sex, but it *is* a fact that money is the major source of disputes among couples.

In addition to helping you look at your overall financial picture, a planner may also manage your investments, if you choose. Or you can simply ask the planner to assist you in getting your financial house in order, and then invest for yourself.

Suppose, on the other hand, you feel capable of handling your personal finances, but would like someone to manage only your investments for you. In this case, the person you would go to is an *investment manager*. After discussing at length your goals, investment preferences, and risk tolerance, the manager will invest your money for you and charge a fee for the service (the different kinds of fees are discussed below).

Your third alternative is to invest for yourself, but hire an *investment adviser*. With an adviser, you will do all the buying and selling; the adviser's role is just to provide information and advice.

The only fee charged by investment advisers comes from providing advice on various types of investments. As such, they need to be differentiated from the multitude of other people who may fill the role of adviser, such as stockbrokers or insurance agents. The difference—and it can be an important one—is that these latter two will get commissions if you buy on their advice.

Financial planners and advisers go by many different names and are licensed differently in different states. Whether they are called certified financial analysts,

> **If someone you know well has dealt with an adviser for a few years (at least) and found this person to be honest and skillful, you're off to a good start.**

chartered financial consultants, registered investment advisers, or something else, however, they will generally fall into one of the above three categories.

HOW TO CHOOSE

Obviously, choosing a good financial adviser is not something to be undertaken lightly. There are two main things to consider when making this choice, in addition to a few technical considerations.

To begin with, of course, you want to be absolutely sure that the adviser you choose is competent and honest. There are some real turkeys in the profession, ranging from inept to out-and-out crooked. The first and best step is to get referrals from friends, family, or business associates. If someone you know well has dealt with an adviser for a few years (at least) and found this person to be honest and skillful, you're off to a good start.

But even though an adviser may come highly recommended by friends, *you* have to decide for yourself what you think about this person. Do you feel comfortable talking about your finances with him or her? Does it seem that the adviser is really listening? Do you *like* this person? It's important that you listen to your feelings, and not decide simply because you have heard how much money your friends have made. If you're comfortable with your adviser, the relationship is more likely to last and be fruitful.

If you are searching on your own, a good place to start is with the Funding Exchange, listed in the Chapter 2 Resources; they will direct you to a member organization in your area that will help you find an adviser. These organizations subject their recommended advisers to an ongoing screening process. If a number of clients were to complain about any adviser, he or she would be dropped from their list.

It's a good idea to interview a few different advisers (we are using the term "adviser" here for convenience— substitute "planner" or "manager" if that's who you are interviewing). Here are the questions you will want answers to:

1. Who are the adviser's clients? Are they roughly similar to you? Some advisers deal mostly with large institutional accounts; smaller accounts might be neglected because the profit to the manager would be less. If you know nothing about the adviser, you could ask for a few client names and phone numbers.

2. What professional registrations does the adviser have? Many states require that advisers demonstrate competence by taking various tests. In addition, the Securities and Exchange Commission (SEC) requires advisers to tell you in writing of their experience and education, the kind of work they do, and the manner in which they are paid. These things, together with information on any violations of the law, or bankruptcies, are contained in a document called the *ADV Form*.

   You can ask to see the adviser's ADV Form or you can send for a copy of it from the SEC, Public Reference Branch, Stop 1-2, 450 Fifth Street NW, Washington, DC 20549. Phone: (202) 272-7450.

3. How is the adviser compensated? By the hour? A fixed fee? Or is the fee based on a percentage of your assets to be managed? Fees can vary greatly and may depend partly on the size of your portfolio. Annual fees of 0.5% to 3% of total assets are common. Hourly rates may range from $50 to $300. However the fees are calculated, advisers who are paid by fees are called *fee-based advisers*.

Many people prefer to deal with advisers whose only income is based on fees. The reasoning is that such advisers will be more likely to concentrate on the best investments for the client, not on what will gain them the greatest commission.

Advisers may also be compensated by commissions: they're called *commission-based advisers*. If the adviser charges only a small fee, or none at all, for a financial plan or for advice, it is probable the adviser will be receiving commissions from the companies he or she recommends.

For example, many of the large financial-planning firms and stock brokerages have their own in-house mutual funds and insurance programs. These mutual funds usually have fees, or loads, to buy in to them—which you will pay. Your adviser may get part of this load money as a commission. This is how you pay for his or her services, instead of paying an hourly fee.

There is nothing wrong or illegal about this, though the possibility for a conflict of interest exists here, as you may be directed toward the investments that pay the highest commission to the adviser.

For this reason, many people prefer to deal with advisers whose only income is based on fees. The reasoning is that such advisers will be more likely to concentrate on the best investments for the client, not on what will gain them the greatest commission.

My belief is that you should not rule out the commission-based adviser if you feel comfortable with him or her, think the planning program is a good one, and believe your interests will come first. Do take care to check out the recommended investments, though. That's why you're reading this book—so you can do this knowledgeably!

Smaller advisory firms or individual advisers are more likely to be fee-based, the ones in the larger firms commission-based. You will need to decide whether you want to deal with a large firm or a small office. This is essentially a matter of personal taste. Some feel more secure dealing with a large company, while others believe they will get more personal attention from a small firm or an individual.

4. If you opt for an investment *manager*—someone who will handle all your investing for you—you have to decide just how much control this person will have over your money. A *discretionary account* gives the manager the right to invest your assets without first obtaining your approval. With a *nondiscretionary account*, either you or the manager may decide on an investment, but you have to approve that it be carried out.

The new investor should know that the most flagrant abuses in the field come from managers who have been entrusted with their clients' money in discretionary accounts. In many states, financial planners and managers operate with a minimum of government supervision or certification.

Extraordinary care must be taken in investigating and choosing someone to whom you will entrust your money.

This is changing, but slowly; many people who call themselves "planners" or "managers" have actually had very little training or experience. Others are nothing but con artists. The North American Securities Administrators Association estimates that investors are cheated out of $500 million a year by dishonest financial managers.

This means that extraordinary care must be taken in investigating and choosing someone to whom you will entrust your money. Alarm bells should start sounding in your head if a planner:

    a. insists that you open a discretionary account

    b. promises high returns from risky investments

    c. is not registered with the state regulators

    d. is evasive about educational background or experience

5. Finally, when interviewing advisers you will want to discuss your investment preferences. You must be sure, for example, that your adviser understands your personal tolerance for risk. In the process, you can ask about the adviser's performance record with the kind of investments you choose.

If you are discussing investing in a portfolio of mutual funds, for example, ask to see the past performance of the funds the adviser has chosen for other clients' portfolios. The performance of the adviser's past recommendations should be compared to that of other funds in the same investment categories.

If you are interviewing several managers or advisers, you can compare their performance figures.

Insurance "Advisers"

Recently, certain financial "advisers" have appeared on the scene whose main job is to sell insurance. These people are given a minimum of training by insurance companies and then sent out to masquerade as financial planners or advisers. You will recognize them by their great emphasis on all kinds of insurance.

Other planners will deal with insurance, too, but it will be only part of a balanced financial plan.

One of the best ways of choosing a financial adviser is by noting whether this person speaks *intelligibly*. Some advisers will purposely make things sound difficult, so that the client will feel confused and in need of advice. Others are simply not good at making themselves clear.

Either kind of adviser is someone to avoid. Whether or not you are managing your own portfolio, you absolutely need to understand what's going on.

I think you will agree that finding a good adviser or manager is one of the more important steps you can take in becoming an investor. If you choose this route, the information here should assist you in making a good choice.

Resources

Check out Resources in Chapter 12. Co-op America's *National Green Pages* directory is an excellent place to find ethical investment advisers and money managers.

CHAPTER 10

REAL ESTATE: OWNING A HOME

They ain't makin' any more of it.
—WILL ROGERS ON WHY LAND IS A GOOD INVESTMENT

What do you think of when you hear the words real estate? A safe place to invest? Or a good way to get rich? For years, real estate has been extremely popular with the average investor. Millions of people are investors simply through owning their homes.

There is a great deal to learn if you are interested in real estate, either as a home owner or an investor. The place to begin, though, is determining *whether* real estate is the right investment for you. We're going to start you off on that track in this chapter. If you decide you want to go ahead, the Resources at the end of this chapter and the next chapter list several recommended books and an excellent newsletter.

More people have invested in their own homes than in any other type of investment. Is owning a home for you?

Owning a home has generally been an excellent investment. Will Rogers might have added that in contrast to the breakdown in the land-producing industry, the people-creating industry is doing just fine. Once more, this is a question of supply and demand, so property has generally appreciated—and faster than the rate of inflation.

There are, of course, other factors to be considered— factors that the financial gurus like to call "intangibles"— such as the satisfaction of owning your own place. For every intangible on one side of the ledger, however, there is another one on the other. Many people, for example, consider being able to call up the landlord when the water pipes are spraying all over the kitchen to be a very important intangible. With the homeowner, the buck stops here—and there can be lots of bucks involved.

So should you invest in a home? There is much to be said for the financial advantages, but this is one of those decisions that depend a great deal on the intangibles. The important thing is not to rush into buying a home because everyone, especially your father-in-law, says you have to. "Look at all the money you're pouring down the drain in rent" is usually the argument.

Certain people are very happy owning their home and other people would rather rent. And even though they require more discipline than making monthly house payments, there are other excellent ways to invest your money.

Try making a list of all the things you would like about owning a home—and another one of the things you know you wouldn't like. Have you always dreamed of owning a home? Do you like to putter around trimming hedges and fixing odds and ends? (I believe that enjoying puttering is a prerequisite to happy home ownership, unless you can afford to hire people to maintain everything for you.)

You need to make a list of the finances involved, too. At today's high real estate prices, many individuals or couples find themselves with very large monthly payments—much more than rent for a comparable property.

On the other hand, there are some excellent tax advantages to owning a home. In the next few pages, we'll discuss some of these pros and cons.

FIX-UP

Many people dream of buying an older home, fixing it up while living in it, then selling it and buying a more expensive one. I have done this and seen other people do it. It can work if you're willing to do much of the work yourself. If you have to hire contractors, the increase in value will generally not match the expense.

There are exceptions to this rule: In a rapidly appreciating real estate market, improvements can bring good returns. And a run-down building purchased at a very low price can also show a profit, even with professionals doing much of the work. The finances of such a project, however, need to be carefully worked out.

If you are reasonably skilled, enjoy this kind of work, and have enough spare time, you will probably do well— given a stable or appreciating real estate market. If you are inexperienced at fix-up work, have a full-time job, children, or other commitments, beware! Living in a construction zone and working on weekends is a good definition of a high-stress situation.

MORE PROS AND CONS

An argument can be made that buying a house is a kind of enforced savings account: you can't take your down payment out, and even though the monthly mortgage payments may be high, you are gaining *equity* by gradually paying off your loan. (Equity is the amount of the

> An argument can also be made for getting into a rising real estate market, even if you plan to move. If you buy a house and the prices in your area go up, you are able to buy another house more easily, because you can sell yours for more.

property you actually own. If you made a 20% down payment, you have a 20% equity in the property. The bank owns the other 80%.)

As the amortization schedules show, however, this equity buildup is significant only if you hold on to the house for a number of years. If you tend to move every few years, you won't gain very much equity, especially with a 30-year loan, because most of your payment goes toward the interest on the loan. This is important, because the average holding time for residential property these days is less than five years.

An argument can also be made for getting into a rising real estate market, even if you plan to move. If you buy a house and the prices in your area go up, you are able to buy another house more easily, because you can sell yours for more.

But buying in a high-priced housing market can be riskier than is generally believed. Suppose you pay $250,000 for your house, putting 20%, or $50,000, down. This will mean a loan of $200,000. A 30-year loan at 9.5% will leave you with payments of $1,680 a month plus about $250 in taxes (depending on your area) and $50 insurance, for a total of $1,980 a month.

Depending on your credit history, amount of debt, etc., etc., the bank will want your income to be at least $6,000 a month, or $72,000 a year. The general rule of thumb is that no more than one-third of your income should go to house payments ($1,980 is about one-third of $6,000).

On the plus side, there are important tax advantages to owning a home. The greater part of your mortgage payments in the early years of the loan go to pay interest on the loan. This interest is a deductible item on your federal income tax, which can mean substantial savings on your tax payment.

If you have a secure, high-paying job, or income from other sources, you may not worry about your ability to meet your mortgage payments. In the recession of 1990–91, however, a fair number of people lost their jobs and couldn't make their payments, and thus lost their homes and their equity when the banks were forced to foreclose on the loans and repossess the houses.

How an Amortized Home Loan Works

It's pretty simple. Each month you make the same payment; part of it goes to pay interest on the loan to the bank, and part of it goes to pay off the principal (the total amount you owe). At first, most of your payment will go toward the interest, but each month more and more will go to pay down the principal.

For example, if you borrow $100,000 at 10%, to be paid back over 30 years, your first monthly payment will be $877. Of that, $830 will go to pay the interest and $47 will go to pay down the principal.

Next month, however, the total amount you owe will be only $99,953, because you have paid off $47 of the loan. So, since you are charged 10% interest only on the amount you owe, the interest part of your payment will be slightly less. This time, you will still pay $877, but of that, $829.60, instead of $830, will be interest. This means $47.40 will go toward paying down the principal. The principal has now been reduced to $99,905.60.

This doesn't sound like much of a change, but it builds up over time. By the end of the second year, the principal has been paid down to $98,700. This means of your $877, $819.21 will go toward interest and $57.79 will be subtracted from the principal. The principal gets reduced very slowly on a 30-year loan.

Here's how the loans progress over a period of years. The dollar figures are the amount of the principal left to pay at the end of each year (the original principal being $100,000).

Year	2	5	10	15	18	20	25
20-yr	$96,300	89,300	72,000	44,400	20,300	0	
30-yr	$98,700	96,200	90,200	80,500	72,100	65,000	40,000

Notice how slowly the principal decreases during the first few years. And notice how much faster the 20-year loan gets paid off. At the end of 25 years, there is still $40,000 owing on the 30-year loan.

Monthly payments on a 20-year, $100,000 loan are $965, about $100 more than the $877 for the 30-year loan. But because the 20-year loan gets paid off 10 years earlier, you end up paying many thousands less in interest. At the end of 20 years, you would own the house free and clear, while a 30-year person would still be making payments.

This should make it clear that if you plan to hold on to a house for a number of years, a shorter-term loan is in your best interest. In fact, you will do better with the 20-year loan if you hold the house longer than five years. The amount of the loan you will pay off will more than offset the larger monthly payments.

Most lenders will allow you to pay more than your regular monthly payment. Thus, if your income should rise, enabling you to make larger loan payments, you could pay off your 30-year mortgage in 25 or even 20 years and save a bundle on interest. Be sure to check when you obtain the loan whether increased payments are acceptable.

At your local bookstore, in the section on real estate, you can probably find a small booklet that will tell you the monthly payments for an amortized loan of any amount at the prevailing interest rates. Ask for a payment table for monthly amortized mortgage loans. If you can't find a booklet there, you can contact Contemporary Books, 180 N. Michigan Avenue, Chicago, IL 60601, (312) 782-9181. Ask for their Monthly Interest and Amortization Tables ($5.95).

There were also those who wanted to move, but were caught in the falling real estate market. A common sight in those days was "For Sale" signs in front of houses with several asking prices crossed out and new, lower prices added.

This should make it clear that if you plan to hold on to a house for a number of years, a shorter-term loan is in your best interest. In fact, you will do better with the 20-year loan if you hold the house longer than five years. The amount of the loan you will pay off will more than offset the larger monthly payments.

Is Buying a Home for You?

Cons	Pros
Can be very expensive: payments, repairs, etc.	Traditionally a good investment
Time consuming	Enforced savings
Greater responsibility	Helps credit standing
Ties up capital; in a down market, a house can be difficult to sell	Can borrow against equity
Equity buildup is negligible if you move often	Mortgage interest deductible on income tax (large item!)
More difficult to move quickly	Personal satisfaction and other intangibles
Risk of losing equity if you can't make payments	Equity buildup
	More freedom: remodeling, pets, gardens, etc.
	Greater security: can't be evicted at owner's whim

So when I say that owning a home has generally been an excellent investment, I mean that *over time* residential property has tended to appreciate. Like the stock market, the real estate market experiences a good many ups and downs. If you're planning on buying and holding, these fluctuations won't bother you much. If you need to move often, they may interfere with your plans.

There is, as you can see, much to be considered in buying a house of your own. There is even more to consider if you are thinking of building. If you are leaning in either of those directions, I hope you will read some of the excellent literature listed below. These books will tell you how to go about buying or building—all the practical things to consider, once you've made your decision.

But I would like to emphasize again that, regardless of what your father-in-law says, it is *not* necessary to own a house to be financially stable or smart. There are arguments to be made on each side, and much comes down to the so-called intangibles—which really translate into personal preference.

When Good Credit Is a Secret

Say that you bought that house five years ago and you think it might be time to refinance your mortgage. Interest rates are now substantially lower than when you bought and, if you qualify, you could save a couple of hundred a month on your payment. And why shouldn't you qualify? You've taken great care to make all your payments on time, not just for the mortgage, but for other bills too, including credit cards.

However, after applying to another lender who offers lower rates than your present mortgage holder, you are refused the loan. The reason given is "insufficient credit data." A call to the credit bureau reveals that no record of your mortgage payments has been registered. In addition, very few of your credit card payments have been recorded. How can this be?

Until recently, virtually all creditors reported payment data to the three major credit bureaus: Equifax, TransUnion and Experian (formerly TRW). In the last few years, however, an increasing number of lenders are keeping the records of their best customers secret. The reason is that they don't want other lenders to offer lower rates to these customers. For example, if you've been paying off your mortgage at 9%, your bank is very happy to have you continue, especially if interest rates have gone down to 7%. The same is true of credit card companies: they don't want any competition either.

Unfortunately, there's not a great deal you can do about this situation, except switch banks (you may be able to convince a new lender that you have been making payments on time). Lenders are not required to report payment information, although there have been laws proposed that would make it mandatory. You could insist that your bank reveal your payment history—or offer you a refinance at the same low rates as the other lender. Your leverage is the bank's desire to hold onto you as a customer. You can also support legislation making this kind of withholding of data illegal.

Resources

The Complete Home Buyer's Bible, by William T. Molloy. John Wiley & Sons, 1996. $19.95 (paperback). If the dream house you want to buy is located on a hillside, shouldn't you know what to look for in proper soil drainage? There are many things in this book that you may not know about, like improper soil drainage filling your basement with water or undermining the foundation. All the steps that go into buying a home are dealt with here in a readable, entertaining fashion, from real estate agents to mortgages to closing fees. There are even a few illustrations, including one showing how soil drainage is supposed to work. If you are on your way to becoming a homeowner, you need this book.

How to Plan, Contract and Build Your Own Home, by Richard M. Scutella and Dave Heberle. Tab Books, 1991 (paperback).
    This is a thorough treatment of the title subjects, enhanced by numerous illustrations. The book has a roomy quality to it: plenty of white space, with no clutter or confusion, kind of like a well-designed house. A very useful book for the prospective home builder.

<www.mortgage.com>. Here is a great web site for finding out how much you could borrow for a home loan. You fill in your

income and expenses and how large a down payment you could make—and the approximate amount you can borrow is instantly displayed. This site will also help you to find the best rates for different kinds of mortgages. And, if you're ready to start looking for a house, you can even find a lender and do much of the paper work online. This will give you a chance to prequalify for a loan before you begin your search.

<www.realtor.com>. If you're looking for a home, here's a good place to start. Pick the area of the country you want to buy in, then choose your criteria for a home (price range, how many bedrooms, bathrooms, etc.). I filled in my criteria and was presented with six homes, several of which looked promising. This, of course, should only be looked on as a preliminary tool, before you start the actual search, but it can be especially useful if you're moving to an unfamiliar area. You can also get some basic information about the town or city, such as what schools are available, what the crime rate is, a rough profile of the population (professionals, retired people, etc.).

This service is nationwide, but many local realtors also have their own web sites. At a number of these sites, you can take virtual tours of houses, meaning that you will see pictures of various rooms, landscaping, views, etc. Again, this has to be seen as just a preliminary step in your search, but it can give you a good idea of what's available.

CHAPTER 11

REAL ESTATE
AS AN INVESTMENT

RENTAL PROPERTY

"HOW I MADE 10 MILLION DOLLARS IN REAL ESTATE WITH NO MONEY DOWN WHILE HOLDING TWO JOBS AND RAISING SIX CHILDREN—YOU CAN DO IT TOO!" It used to be that the hucksters in real estate were out selling swampland in Florida. Now they're selling get-rich-quick schemes. Their books, seminars, and home study courses make great profits seem ridiculously easy to obtain. And because there is usually at least some truth to their claims, they have an air of plausibility.

You can indeed make money in real estate. It takes quite a bit of time, energy, and, perhaps, a certain knack, but there are people who do it. The advantages of buying rental properties as investments are readily apparent. You can borrow up to 80% of the cost, sometimes more, and this gives you very high leverage. (*Leverage* is a favorite word in the investment world. A "highly leveraged investment" is simply one in which you put down a small percentage of the purchase price and borrow the rest. Remember your high school physics? Using a lever, you can lift large weights with a minimum amount of energy.)

What this high leverage means is that you can buy a property worth $100,000 using only about $20,000 of your own money and borrowing the rest from a bank. This means that if the property should appreciate 20%, to $120,000, you would realize on paper a 100% appreciation on your investment of $20,000.

During the 1980s, when the baby-boom generation was buying homes, it was not unusual for property owners to realize this kind of profit in just a few years or less. By 1990, however, the demand for new homes fell off with the recession, and the value of real estate in most areas stopped or reversed. During the rest of the decade, real estate recovered its growth, but nowhere near that of the "go-go" 1980s.

There are certain substantial tax advantages to owning rental property. For example, on the assumption that your building decreases in value as it gets older, you are allowed to deduct this "loss"—or *depreciation*—from your income each year. In addition, if you make improvements, thereby increasing the value of the property, you can deduct the expense of the improvements from your income. Real estate can, therefore, be a good *tax shelter*, especially if you have a high income.

So why isn't everybody investing in rental property? Why aren't people beating down the doors of the real estate offices? One answer is that the great appreciation in real estate values has left rental income in the dust. In other words, in many areas, the yearly income from rents is no longer enough to cover the mortgage loan payments and other expenses.

Except in the areas where property values have not kept pace with the rest of the country, it is becoming difficult to buy a house, apartment building, or commercial property where the rents will cover expenses. This means out-of-pocket payments each month for the owner—something few people are prepared to do.

Being a Landlord

It takes a good deal of time, energy, and skill not only to acquire a good property but to manage it successfully. It also helps to have some knowledge of building repairs, or at least to know some good repairmen.

But most important, unlike stocks, bonds, or most other kinds of investments, rental property gets you directly involved with people. As a landlord, you suddenly find yourself mixed up in people's lives—and this can include their finances, their bad habits, or their occasional dishonesty.

I once owned several rental properties, and it was never easy. There was always something: So-and-so couldn't pay the rent because he lost his job; the sewer pipe had to be replaced, which meant the toilets and other fixtures couldn't be used for a week. I had to get a court order to force out one tenant who hadn't paid rent for six months. (In response to abuses by some landlords, the courts have made it difficult to evict tenants quickly, even for nonpayment of rent.)

Yes, you can check tenants' backgrounds, and yes, you can even get a management company to do it all for

> I had to get a court order to force out one tenant who hadn't paid rent for six months. (In response to abuses by some landlords, the courts have made it difficult to evict tenants quickly, even for nonpayment of rent.)

you (for a handsome fee). But you cannot control all the variables when you are dealing with people. Often you find yourself struggling with moral questions: Should you evict the family whose breadwinner just lost a job and can't make the rent payment? Or should you wait a month? Two months? Since you are probably depending on the rent to cover the mortgage payments, you can imagine the possible dilemmas.

I never enjoyed all the various difficulties that came with owning rental properties, and I'm happy to be out of the business. To my friend Bob, however, being a landlord was an entirely different experience. With a minimum of capital and a maximum of wheeling and dealing, Bob managed to acquire half a dozen different houses, some of which he divided into two or more units. He had skills as a designer, carpenter, and general handyman, so he was able to do much of the remodeling and repairs himself.

What made him even more suited to the rental business, though, was that he *enjoyed* it. He was your basic hands-on landlord; I remember driving around with him in one of his beat-up cars to visit a few properties. He would fix a water heater at one place, dicker about rent with a tenant at another (in the process, getting into a long, totally unrelated conversation), then meet with a prospective tenant at yet another. He had his own unorthodox style that worked well for him.

It's not necessary to be a character like Bob to succeed in the property rental business, but you should enjoy dealing with people. It also helps to have some understanding and patience with such things as stoves, furnaces, and leaky roofs.

RAW LAND

Sounds kind of unappetizing, doesn't it? But I prefer this term to "undeveloped land," because the latter makes it sound as if development is inevitable. Whether raw land is an appealing addition to your holdings depends on your needs.

Buying land is like making any other investment in that plenty of research is necessary. It's not enough to buy and hold, hoping that population growth will eventually drive the price up. You could wait a long, long time in the states that are losing population.

The best places to buy, of course, are in the areas that appear due for development. The price of land can appreciate dramatically when developers get interested.

While good returns are possible with this strategy, the new investor needs to know that it is not always easy to pick which areas are going to grow. There are experienced speculators who lose their shirt trying to do this. A city's expansion may turn in another direction, or the economy may go sour, putting developments on hold. In the meantime, the landholder is stuck with payments on a loan, taxes, and no income from the investment. A risky business, this.

As with other real estate investments, then, buying land should be something you do after you have learned a good deal about it, done the necessary research, and feel comfortable with the risks.

IF IT STILL LOOKS GOOD TO YOU . . .

If the prospect of owning real estate—income property or land—still looks good to you, take note of the Resources section at the end of the chapter. If you're online, your next step is to go to John T. Reed's web site and read his advice to beginners. Click on "Suggested sequences for starting a real estate investment program" and "List of different real estate investment strategies" for starters. If you're not online, call or write for information about Reed's books and his monthly newsletter. If you do go ahead with real estate, the practical information contained in these publications will make them a great place for your first down payment.

The next step is to find a friend or acquaintance who owns property and make a nuisance of yourself by asking every conceivable question. There is no better way to get a first-hand view of what it's like to own property than to have a friend walk you through everything that's involved in managing it. Then, if you take the next step, and decide to start looking at property, you will need to consult with a tax expert on your specific tax situation.

It's a good idea to decide what kind of building you want, what areas you like, and how much you want to pay before you start talking to real estate agents. Most agents I have known have been straight, honest people, ready to help you find the right piece of property for your needs. As salespeople, though, they have their own agendas: they have properties they are interested in selling, and may steer you toward them.

If you are sure of what you want, however, you are much more likely to be shown only those properties that fit your needs and your budget.

Those who inherit a piece of real estate are often unacquainted with the market in the area where it is located. Under these circumstances, it's a good idea to have the building appraised by an independent real estate appraiser. This should be done before approaching a real estate agent about selling the property.

OTHER WAYS OF INVESTING IN REAL ESTATE

REITs

There are real estate investments that involve less responsibility and fewer hassles than rental property or

> REITs may be *equity trusts*, which buy, sell, and rent out properties, *construction and development trusts*, which give short-term loans to developers, or *mortgage trusts*, which give long-term loans to real estate investors.

raw land. These methods are good for people with less money to invest. For example, *real estate investment trusts*, or *REITs*, are essentially closed-end mutual funds that invest in specific areas of the real estate market. They are listed on the exchanges and on Nasdaq and can be purchased through a stockbroker.

REITs may be *equity trusts*, which buy, sell, and rent out properties, *construction and development trusts*, which give short-term loans to developers, or *mortgage trusts*, which give long-term loans to real estate investors.

Remember that even though you may be relieved of the responsibilities of direct management, your success as an investor in an REIT still depends on the overall market for real estate—and on the skill of the managers. Despite a lot of ups and downs, REITs, as a group, have generally performed well during the last twenty years, but many individual REITs have done poorly. As in the case of stocks, you need to choose individual companies with care.

There are some sound ones out there, but you need to check certain things verycarefully. All the following questions should be answered to your satisfaction before investing money in a trust or partnership:

Have the distributions or dividends been paid on time—and have they been up to the original projections?

Has the cash flow increased?

Are the economic conditions good in the areas where the properties are located?

Are the properties themselves of a high quality?

In a partnership, does the management have an active repurchase plan so that you can sell your shares if you want to? (very important!)

Are the managers reputable, skillful businesspeople?

I think a well-run REIT is an appropriate place for a small amount of a portfolio. It makes for a healthy diversification into real estate, without the kind of day-to-day management details of owning property on your own. The answers to the above questions must look good, however. Too many people have lost money because they didn't ask them.

Partnerships

It is also possible to invest in a *real estate general partnership*. This is organized by a *general partner* who buys and manages the properties. You, as an investor, are a *limited partner*. As such, your liability is usually limited to your original investment, though you will share in the profits and losses. There are some tax advantages similar to those for owning your own property, but these are complex enough that you should consult with a tax expert.

Public partnerships are registered with the Securities and Exchange Commission; you can buy them through

If you feel bullish about the real estate market, a real estate mutual fund is a good place for a new investor to start. As you learn more about the market, you could expand into the more specialized REITs your broker. Watch out—there will be a "load" to get in. There are also private partnerships, which you can learn about from brokers, from newspaper advertisements, or by word of mouth.

Real estate partnerships have fallen into disrepute in recent years because of abuses by some general partners. The regulatory agencies are trying to make it more difficult for investors to be cheated, but until that happens you would do well to avoid investing in a limited partnership.

Mutual Funds

As you might imagine, there are real estate mutual funds—though only a few. These differ from the REITs in that they are open-end mutual funds that invest in many different kinds of firms associated with real estate. A real estate fund portfolio might include real estate brokerage companies, building companies, and different kinds of REITs.

You would buy in to a real estate fund if you expected the construction and sales of homes and commercial buildings to do well all over the country. If you feel bullish about the real estate market, a real estate mutual fund is a good place for a new investor to start. As you learn more about the market, you could expand into the more specialized REITs.

Second Mortgages

Another way of getting at least halfway involved in real estate is to lend money to those needing to finance properties. Banks or other institutions are usually the holders of the main loan on a house, the "first" mortgage. Home buyers sometimes need additional financing, however, and take out a second loan, using their house as collateral. This loan is called a second mortgage. Second mortgages are often held by individual investors who are attracted by their relatively high rate of return.

In larger cities, it's possible to invest in second mortgages through finance companies, which guarantee the loans. This is a relatively safe way of getting 10% to 13% on your money—if you are satisfied that the finance company is sound and well managed.

The only problem could arise in a severe recession that caused many people to default on their mortgage payments. This could put a strain on the company that guarantees the loans.

It's also possible to get 15% or more on your money by buying second mortgages directly from other lenders. Often a holder of a second mortgage will want to cash out and will sell the contract at a discount. If you buy the contract, you will then be the one to receive monthly payments from the homeowners who are paying off the loan. Needless to say, this requires thorough research into the value of the property and the creditworthiness of the homeowners. Anyone lending money for second mortgages should have a good knowledge of real estate and be wealthy enough to absorb possible losses.

Resources

John T. Reed's *Real Estate Investor's Monthly*, 342 Bryan Drive, Alamo, CA 94507. (925) 820-7262. Monthly. $125/year. Website: <www.johntreed.com/realestate.html>. If you are thinking of buying property as an investment, then you need John T. Reed's newsletter, which has received good reviews from such well-known financial writers as Jane Bryant Quinn, who calls him smart and witty. It's a good bet that any aspect you can think of concerning the buying, managing, and selling of income property has been or will be covered in the newsletter.

A subscription to Reed's newsletter gets you a list of the topics covered in back issues. You will also receive a description of the various books and cassette tapes written or recorded by

Reed, such as *How to Manage Residential Property, Real Estate Investment Strategy, Aggressive Tax Avoidance for Real Estate Investors*, and *High-Leverage Real Estate Financing*. There are others—all of them very useful to the would-be investor.

Reed can be quite outspoken in support of issues he feels strongly about. You may not agree with everything you read in the newsletter, but you don't have to agree with his opinions to follow his excellent advice on practical matters.

On Reed's web site, you will find not only a list of his many books and tapes and advice for beginners, but also a "View of various gurus." If you are moved to take an expensive seminar on how to make millions with no money down, better see what Reed has to say about the real estate guru who is teaching it. You may be impressed, as I was, at the number of well-known authors and seminar leaders who have declared bankruptcy. . . .

The subjects covered in Reed's newsletter, the books, and the tapes are the nuts and bolts of real estate investing. They stand in sharp contrast to the dozens of dubious books and seminars that claim making a fortune in real estate is easy. It's not.

PART 2

INTERMEDIATE INVESTING

CHAPTER 12

SOCIALLY RESPONSIBLE INVESTING

When socially responsible investing first began to achieve national recognition in the 1970s, the Wall Street establishment reacted with disdain. *Fortune* magazine dismissed it as "insignificant, do-good nonsense." But twenty years later, we see the giant mutual fund companies starting up their own social funds. And the newest and best book on the subject, *Investing with Your Values* (see Resources), is published by Bloomberg Press, an old, established financial publisher.

To what do we owe this dramatic change of opinion regarding socially responsible investing? In one word: *success*. Funds invested in a socially responsible manner now account for ten percent of all money invested in the U.S., or $1.2 trillion. A number of social and environmental mutual funds have shown returns near the top of their class; for example, both the Citizen's Index Fund and the Domini Social Equity Fund have outperformed the S&P

500 Index Funds during the last three years. In 1998, the Citizens Index Fund returned 42.8%.

This success has not gone unnoticed by the Wall Street Establishment. In 1995, *Fortune's* annual survey of "America's Most Admired Corporations" led off with this statement: "There is a growing appreciation that corporations cannot live by numbers alone. Reputation is increasingly seen as something more than the record of earnings growth rates." This same report listed "responsibility to the community and the environment" as one of the eight criteria used in the study.

So is this growing movement something you might be interested in? In this chapter, we're going to make the case for investing according to your values and you can decide if it fits your world view.

PROFITS AND VALUES

In an ideal world, the economic system would help to nurture human society and preserve the ecology of the natural world. In the nineteenth century, corporations were chartered for socially useful purposes and were strictly regulated by state legislatures. In the latter half of the nineteenth century, however, corporations used their economic power to rewrite the laws, thereby doing away with many of these governmental limitations. The purpose of a corporation became simply to make as much money as possible for its shareholders—an ethos that continues into the present day. If employees work in unsafe conditions for low pay, if the environment is damaged and the natural capital of the Earth depleted—this is not the concern of corporate management. They must focus on the bottom line—or face the wrath of the shareholders.

Corporate shareholders, then, share responsibility with management for this concern with immediate profits, and the lack of long-range planning. And this is where the individual investor comes in. Investors don't have to buy stock in firms whose products and services harm the environment or degrade human society. If they believe that corporations should do more than simply focus on profits, they can invest in companies that exhibit more social conscience.

Socially responsible investing, also known as socially conscious, ethical, or simply social investing, means placing your money with companies whose products or services either do no harm to the environment and society—or actively promote the welfare of both. There are two reasons for investing in this manner: first, because you hope to make the world a better place and believe that corporations can help to do this and, secondly, because you want to put your capital to work in harmony with your values.

For example, many investors exclude cigarette companies from their portfolios simply because they don't wish to make a profit from a product harmful to people's health. Mutual funds that invest in a responsible manner usually avoid firms involved in tobacco, liquor, weaponry, or nuclear power. They also tend to exclude companies with poor environmental and labor practices.

Profiting from Tobacco

Imagine how it would be to own stock in a tobacco company. The more cigarettes people buy, the greater the profit for the company, the more dividends the stockholders get and the more the value of the stock goes up. At the same time, the more cigarettes smoked, the larger the number of people who contract lung cancer and heart disease. Therefore, the more people get sick and die, the more money investors make.

Carrying this further, in 1995, an Oxford-based study in *Lancet* forecast that over the next fifty years, *one-fifth* of the population in the developed countries of the world may die prematurely from smoking-related diseases. This figure comes to 250 million people, but it approaches a billion people when you include the developing countries, where the tobacco merchants are busy pushing their product.

This is why many investors choose not to place their money with tobacco firms.

Socially responsible investing—often abbreviated to "SRI"—has roots that go back to the early part of the twentieth century when religious groups avoided placing capital with any company engaged in practices they regarded as "sinful." At that time, this meant no liquor, gambling, tobacco, or pornography. The modern SRI movement started in the 1960s when student activists demanded that universities divest themselves of companies that produced weapons of war.

In the early 1970s, several mutual funds were started that avoided defense firms, and concentrated instead on companies that were friendly to social change

ANNUALIZED RETURNS: DOMINI SOCIAL EQUITY FUND VS. S&P 500 INDEX

1995	35.17%	37.50%
1996	21.84%	23.07%
1997	36.02%	33.40%
1998	32.99%	28.58%

and the environment. The movement grew steadily through the '70s and '80s as more investors became aware of the power of their capital.

One of the focuses of the SRI movement during this time also became one of its greatest successes. During the 1970s and '80s, a growing number of investors refused to support firms that did business with the oppressive regime in South Africa. Businesses that continued to operate in that country were exposed to public scrutiny and disinvestment in their stock, and the result was that many pulled out. Nelson Mandela speaks of this disinvestment, and the resulting damage to the South African economy, as one of the key factors that eventually brought down the apartheid regime.

If you should ever have doubts about the power of socially conscious investing, this is a good example to remember. Repressive regimes depend on the income they get from the international corporations that do business in their country—not just from taxes, but also from bribes and kickbacks given to the rulers. If the corporations can be influenced to withdraw from the country, this is often the deciding factor that brings down the oppressors.

At present, many SRI professionals recommend avoiding companies that do business with Burma, because of the repressive policies of the military junta in that country. In Resources, you will find publications that will keep you up to date not only on the best places to invest, but also the key places to avoid.

PROACTIVE INVESTING

Professionals in the SRI movement have their list of companies to avoid. As we mentioned above, these generally include manufacturers of weapons, alcoholic beverages, tobacco, nuclear materials, and companies involved in gaming. The process of choosing what to include and exclude in your portfolio, however, is, by necessity, a very personal one. For some, any firm that performs research on animals is automatically out. Others may not want to exclude the defense industry because they believe that weapons are necessary for national defense. Socially responsible investing asks each individual to search his or her personal values and invest accordingly.

But, happily, SRI is not just a matter of choosing companies that "do no harm" and excluding those that do. Many firms have progressive labor practices, support local community programs, and engage in active environmental programs. When you place your investment capital with these companies, along with millions of other investors, the message you are sending to the business community is clear and unequivocal: we support corporations that act in a socially responsible manner—and we will not support those that don't.

There is a third category of SRI firms, after the ones that do no harm and those that have progressive labor and environmental practices. These are businesses whose products and services are designed to *solve* pressing environmental problems. An increasing number of companies are engaged in recycling, sustainable energy, pollution control, and natural foods. While most of these firms are still small, their stock can be an important part of a social investor's portfolio.

Of these three categories, the largest is still composed of "do-no-harm" firms—those companies whose

The process of choosing what to include and exclude in your portfolio, however, is, by necessity, a very personal one.

products and services generally have a neutral social impact. Luckily, this neutral category includes most of the hi-tech firms that have done so well in the last decade. Further enlarging this category, a number of large corporations have endorsed SRI principles and are working to improve their "social status" in the investment world.

But suppose that investing in a socially responsible manner sounds good to you. How do you go about finding the best companies in all three of the above categories? These days, there are a number of excellent resources for the social investor that you will find at the end of this chapter. Some will tell you where to look for promising SRI companies, others will suggest what to avoid, and a few newsletters will make recommendations of specific stocks.

AES Corporation
A Model for 21st Century Business

"The AES Corporation announced that net income increased for the thirteenth consecutive year. Net income for 1998 is up 67% from 1997 to $307 million."

"Majority of brokers rate AES as a 'strong buy.'"

"AES is high on the list of the Washington Post's Top 100 Public Companies."

The superlatives just keep coming for AES Corp. Founded in 1981, it has rapidly grown into one of the world's largest independent power suppliers. AES owns or has interest in ninety-three power plants in fourteen countries, with many more under construction, and employs 40,000 people. The stock has been a darling of Wall Street for the last few years, increasing from $10 a share in 1996 to $50 in 1999.

The growth in yearly earnings explains Wall Street's interest:

AES NET INCOME (MILLIONS):

1998	$307
1997	188
1996	125
1995	107
1994	88

But this phenomenal financial success tells only half the story. Behind the scenes, AES is run differently from most corporations. The managers have turned the company into what could be a model for businesses in the twenty-first century, a place where workers are part owners and managers, and where concern for the environment is an integral part of company planning.

The owners of AES started with the novel belief that workers should enjoy themselves on the job. Consequently, morale is extremely high at AES and turnover extremely low. Workers take turns at jobs traditionally reserved for management; for example, a team of workers might take responsibility for negotiating financing for a new project. The company books are open for all to see and employees are encouraged to learn about such things as profit-and-loss statements. They are also encouraged to make suggestions, not just about their departments, but about anything to do with the company. In addition, AES has developed an advanced employee stock option plan (ESOP): by purchasing the company stock, the workers at AES have also become owners.

The company's philosophy can be summarized as follows:

- Workers are also owners
- Workers are also managers
- The workplace is a community
- The corporation is a good neighbor in the immediate community
- The corporation is part of a global community

In line with this philosophy, AES involves itself in social projects in the towns surrounding its power plants. Another part of being a good neighbor is to produce as little pollution as possible: emissions from AES power plants average 55% lower than mandated.

But AES sees itself not just as a contributing member of the surrounding community, but also as a global citizen. For example, the company has planted 55 million trees in Central America to absorb the carbon dioxide produced by their new coal-burning plants. And in South America, a project with Oxfam America will assist indigenous peoples to gain title to and manage 3.7 million acres of their homeland.

As we saw in the statistics above, these extra expenses don't seem to have hurt the company's bottom line. Rather, AES is living proof that it's possible for corporations to take an active interest in social and environmental concerns while still making excellent profits. I would even argue that by involving employees in the running of the company and making AES a company they can be proud to work for, that the owners have probably elevated profits. In addition, they have almost certainly attracted many socially concerned investors.

> Is this the way corporations will look in the twenty-first century? SRI investors can help make it so.

Choosing Consciously

Investing in a socially conscious manner can sometimes be difficult. If you want to avoid companies that invest in countries like Burma, employ unfair labor practices, produce weapons, or damage the environment, you will have to research them very carefully. For example, that utility company building a solar electric plant may also own several nuclear power plants. The corporation that deals so fairly with its employees may also be a large military supplier.

How about smaller companies? Many of these may be suppliers of parts for military hardware built by the large corporations. Certain small companies in the biotech sector have done very well for their investors during the past few years. Biotechnology, however, usually means testing new products on animals—a process that can involve cruel, often torturous techniques.

Each new investor needs to decide what is acceptable to him or her. These days, there is a lot of help available—the books and newsletters listed at the end of the chapter will inform you about the social and environmental stances of the companies they consider to be socially responsible.

One thing the new investor needs to know is that the various socially responsible mutual funds use quite different "screens" to determine which companies to invest in. You will have to decide by reading a fund's prospectus whether you agree with the managers' philosophy.

You also need to be aware that some funds calling themselves "environmental" actually invest in some of the largest polluters. In the *Greenmoney Journal* (see Resources) you will find listed the mutual funds that invest in companies with a true social conscience.

The Power of the Ballot

Some investors feel their investment choices become too limited when they leave out all the companies that are not entirely socially conscious. Many of the larger corporations, for example, have areas where their social concerns are lagging.

There is, however, yet another way of exercising your social concerns. When you buy equities, you become part owner of the firm. As such, you have a vote in the affairs of the company. (Only holders of common stock can vote; preferred stock or bonds carry no right to vote.)

If you have owned at least $1,000 worth of stock for twelve months, you are eligible to vote. Within a year of buying stock in a company, you will get a notice of the next shareholders' meeting and the issues being put to a vote. Often, some of these issues have to do with social or environmental concerns.

You can usually vote by mail—you don't need to attend the meeting in person. The issues up for voting are usually placed on the agenda by individual shareholders

Voting for the Environment

who have formed groups, or blocs, large enough to have some influence. Your number of votes is almost always equal to the number of shares you hold. So your 100 shares in General Electric may not seem like much, but by joining a bloc of a few thousand other shareholders, you can have a major impact.

Do you think GE is placing too much emphasis on marketing its nuclear technology? Do you believe nuclear power is not only a danger to the environment but a bad investment for the corporation? Well, so do quite a few other shareholders. So far, in this particular case, there haven't been enough who feel this way to change company policy, but who's to say what might happen in a few years?

As you can see, then, there is an alternative to completely avoiding companies involved in activities you disagree with. More and more people are coming to believe that the private sector must take greater responsibility for the social and environmental problems it helps create. As this number grows and includes more shareholders, even the great multinational corporations will be strongly affected.

The Securities and Exchange Commission regulates the procedure by which shareholders can place an issue on the ballot for the annual shareholders meeting. To learn more about this process, you can contact Co-op America, listed in Resources below.

SOCIALLY CONSCIOUS SOUL-SEARCHING

Socially responsible investing may prompt you to do more than a little soul-searching. There are many ways in which we, as investors, can express our concerns. Just how socially conscious do you want to be with your money? Are there areas you feel more strongly about than others? How would you feel about investing in a company that was involved in a practice you disagreed with?

What about investments that might be termed socially neutral, such as rare coins? Do you want any neutral investments, or do you want all your money to be at work in socially conscious ways?

Do you want to lend money to the federal government by buying government bonds, thereby encouraging further deficit spending? Do you want to put your savings in a large bank, where it might be lent to socially irresponsible corporations? Or would you rather it be in a community-based credit union? There's a lot to consider when contemplating socially responsible investing, but the knowledge that your money is at work in a manner helpful to the world can be a powerful source of satisfaction.

A recent prize-winning study by Michael Russo at the University of Oregon (*Academy of Management Journal*, 1997) demonstrated that firms with superior environmental records had higher returns on investment than their competitors. A number of other studies have also indicated that environmental performance means better financial performance. Among utilities, eco-efficiency has found to be strongly correlated with higher stock prices and lower debt financing (*Energy* magazine, Winter, 1999). This is further proof that socially aware investing is smart investing.

SRI is at the cutting edge of investing. At its best, it incorporates the spirit of social change from the 1960s, coupled with a hard-headed view of investment realities. There are many actions we can take to encourage the kind of sustainable policies that will preserve and restore the environment; likewise, we can act in ways that will bring peace and prosperity to the world. Placing our investment capital wisely is one of the most important actions we can take to ensure that our values are reflected in the world around us. This is truly twenty-first century investing.

Resources

Co-op America. 1612 K Street NW, Suite 600, Washington DC, 20006. (800) 58-GREEN. <www.coopamerica.com>. Membership for one year: $20.00. Do you need help in finding a socially responsible investment adviser? Want to know about green businesses, or which companies to avoid because they run sweatshops? Join Co-op America, an organization for everyone concerned about the environment and responsible investing. Co-op America puts out several very useful publications, including the *National Green Pages,* which lists green businesses of all kinds. This is one of the premier sources and advocates of SRI.

Environmental Services News on Yahoo will keep you up to date on the latest environmental news, including updates on companies that work in the environmental field. <http://biz.yahoo.com/news/environmental.html>.

The Greenmoney Journal, West 608 Glass Avenue, Spokane, WA 99205. (509) 328-1741. Quarterly. $35/year, $50/two years. If you are serious about socially responsible investing, then you need to get this journal. Publisher and coeditor Cliff Feigenbaum has made *Greenmoney* into a real forum for concerned investors. There is a "Green News" section, a list of publications, a "Green Events Calendar," and a performance update on SRI mutual funds, as well as excellent lead articles.

Since 1995, *Greenmoney* has had a web site: <www.greenmoney.com>. This site has similar information to the journal, but is updated continuously.

New Energy Report: Investing in the Environment, 84 Canyon Road, Fairfax, CA 94930. (415) 485-5825. Six issues. $60/year. The *New Energy Report,* edited by Sam Case (the author of this book), reports on small companies whose products or services are aimed at solving the great environmental problems of the day. Companies focusing on renewable energy, recycling wastes, nonpolluting transportation, and organically produced food are the growth companies of tomorrow. While these small companies are appropriate for only a small portion of your portfolio, they have the possibility of growing very large.

Investing with Your Values, by Hal Brill, Jack Brill, and Cliff Feigenbaum. Bloomberg Press. 1999. $23.95 (paperback). This is the definitive book on socially responsible investing. It is the one you want if you decide to invest according to your values because it covers all aspects of social investing. It is also the book that is going to place SRI even more firmly in the mainstream of the investment world and lead it into the twenty-first century.

"Definitive" books in their field are not always entertaining and easy to read, but this one is. Highly recommended.

The Socially Responsible Guide to Smart Investing: Improve Your Portfolio As You Improve the Environment, by Samuel Case. Prima Publishing, 1996. $19.95 (hardcover). As we saw in the chapter above, there is a proactive kind of social investing that involves placing your capital into firms that are actively working on environmental problems. *The Socially Responsible Guide* describes the growing field of environmental business and shows investors how to find the most promising companies involved in recycling, renewable energy, clean transportation, responsible waste disposal, and environmental merchandising.

CHAPTER 13

INTERNATIONAL INVESTING

F or years, only the very rich invested in foreign countries. But recently, with what the economists like to call the "globalization" of world markets, it has become much easier to put money into foreign assets. This gives the individual investor a much greater choice; investing only in the United States has the same disadvantages as investing in only one stock; that is, you don't have enough diversification in your portfolio.

During the 1970s, for example, after correcting for inflation, the U.S. stock market as a whole was actually worth less at the end of the decade than at the beginning. A balanced portfolio that included investments in the major foreign economies, however, would have ended up comfortably on the plus side.

To be an international investor these days, it's not necessary to open an account in London or Zurich (although you can, if you like the idea). There are several ways to put money into foreign corporations and other investments without going any further than your own stockbroker. The first, and easiest, way is by means of our good friends, the mutual funds.

MUTUAL FUNDS

International funds and global funds—that's what you're looking for. The international funds are more truly international; the global funds may have as little as 25% of their assets in foreign securities—be sure to check the prospectus. There are a growing number of these funds and they invest in all sorts of different markets. There are funds that invest in the Pacific Basin, some that specialize in Japan, others in Europe, and quite a few that invest in companies all over the world. Some invest only in stocks, some in bonds, others in both.

You can find the best-performing international funds the same way you find the best domestic funds (see Chapter 6). You will also find a few suggestions in the realm of international funds in Appendix A. Again, however, be aware that the best-performing funds over the last year or 10 years may not be the ones to buy now.

Good examples of the wisdom of this warning are the funds that invest heavily in Japanese stocks. During the 1980s, buyers of these funds made out like bandits because the Japanese economy was on its way into orbit.

> **There is a closed-end fund for almost every country with a major economy and some for smaller economies, like the Irish Investment Fund.**

In 1990 and 1991, however, the stock market came back down to earth—hard. At one point, the Nikkei stock index had lost almost half its value from a year earlier. Needless to say, the owners of the Japanese-based mutual funds were extremely unhappy. So do your best to look to the future and not just the past.

CLOSED-END COUNTRY FUNDS

Most mutual funds are known as open-end funds because there is theoretically no limit to the amount of shares they can sell. Closed-end funds are similar to the open-end mutual funds in that they are investment companies that own a portfolio of stocks in different companies. The closed-end funds, however, sell only a limited number of shares, like most corporations, and the shares are traded on the stock exchanges. For this reason, they are called "publicly traded funds."

Some closed-end funds invest in a portfolio of American stocks. Others—the "country funds"—invest in stocks of a certain country. There is a closed-end fund for almost every country with a major economy and some for smaller economies, like the Irish Investment Fund. The share prices of these funds may be found among the stock listings; the financial papers also list them in a special section, usually after the open-end mutual funds.

The country funds provide a way of investing in individual world economies, but they are ornery investments, kind of like untrained horses. A case in point: You see that the Irish economy is doing well, so you buy 100 shares of the Irish Investment Fund for $14 a share. In only a few months, the Fund shoots up to $25 a share and you are accepting congratulations all around. But then, another month passes and you open up the paper one day to discover that the share price has dropped to $18. "Impossible!"

you exclaim, but, over the next couple of weeks, the price continues to fall, bottoming out at $15.

"What happened?" you demand of your broker, or whoever is handy. "Did I blow it in researching the Irish economy?" No, Ireland still looks like a winner. What happened was this: suddenly, a large investor (a) decided he had made a good profit and it was time to sell his shares in the fund; (b) read an account—along with other investors—of how certain small economies were not doing well; or (c) decided that violations of the peace accord in Northern Ireland would affect the Irish economy.

When this investor sells his 50,000 shares and the stock begins to fall, other investors decide somebody must know something they don't, and begin to sell their stock. Pretty soon, everyone's jumping ship and nobody wants to buy except at a very low price—so the stock goes down to $15 a share. In such ways are financial decisions often made in the World of Investment.

This kind of thing can happen with any volatile stock, but it seems to happen with regularity among the country funds, particulary those of the smaller countries. Occasionally there is good reason for a decline; for example, after years of increases, holders of the Korea Fund saw all their gains wiped out in 1997 as the Korean economy took a sharp dive. Often, however, volatility is due more to the fears and perceptions of the investing public.

HOW TO BUY SOMETHING
FOR LESS THAN IT'S WORTH

As we explained in Chapter 6, the net asset value of an open-end mutual fund is the total value of its assets divided by the number of shares outstanding. A greater demand for shares does not increase the net asset value because new shares are issued as more people buy into the fund. Because there is an unlimited supply of shares, the law of supply and demand is not a factor, so when you buy into an open-end fund, the net asset value is the price you will pay per share.The story is different, however, in the case of closed-end funds.

Closed-end funds figure their net asset values in the same way as the open-end funds. But in the financial tables, you will notice two prices listed after these funds—the net asset value and the share price—and these prices are usually different. This means that often you can buy shares of a fund for *less* than their net asset value.

How can this be? It can be because we're back to supply and demand again. These funds are called "closed-end," remember, because they issue a limited number of shares. If investors decide that the Korea Fund is a hot property, there will be more buyers for this limited number of shares—and their price will be bid up, regardless of the net asset value.

In the closed-end listings, you will notice yet a third figure, after the NAV and the price. This is the percent of difference between the net asset value and the price per share. If the price is 10% more than the NAV, it is said that the fund is trading at "10% over net asset value," or is trading "at a premium of 10%; if the price is 10% less, it is trading at a "10% discount to net asset value."

At times, this difference can be extreme. In early 1999, the perception of many investors was that Indonesian stocks were underpriced because of the economic crash in that country during the previous year. There were days when shares in the Indonesia fund traded 90% over the net asset value of the fund! Conversely, during the same period, shares in the Latin America Investment Fund were trading 27% *under* net asset value.

There are two things to consider, then, when buying a closed-end fund: whether the companies it owns will do well and what investors feel about the chances for the

> **If you are willing to wait and take a little risk, watch for the funds of countries with strong economies that are currently in disfavor with investors.**

fund. This is an excellent example of what the new investor (or any investor) needs to consider in making any purchase. An individual company, for example, may have a fine balance sheet and terrific prospects, but the price of its stock won't go up until the investment community decides it's a good buy.

In the case of the closed-end country funds, their prices will go up according to how well their country's economy is performing *and* whether investors believe that economy will perform well in the future.

Some advisers will tell you to jump at the chance to buy funds trading at discounts to their net asset values, but I have reservations. I see the situation as no different from that of any good company whose share price has been driven down by fears and misperceptions. Such companies can be sound investments, especially if you're willing to wait a while, but their stock will start to rise only when investor sentiment changes.

If you are willing to wait and take a little risk, watch for the funds of countries with strong economies that are currently in disfavor with investors. When the shares start trading at a 10% discount to net asset value or more, that's the time to do some research on the country in question.

If the prospects for the economy look good, then take a look at the share prices and the net asset values of the fund over the last few months. Is the present price higher than the lowest price during this period—or is the fund still on its way down? If it's turned the corner, now is the time to buy if you're interested. All you need is a little luck and a change in investor sentiment.

The luck is often easier to come by than a change in sentiment. The investing public as a whole is not always known for its rationality. The meteoric rise and fall of the country funds provides one of the best illustrations of how perceived value can often be more important than real value in determining what people will pay for a given stock in marketplace.

For the new investor, open-end mutual funds are the best places to start your international investing career. As you begin to get a feel for the international markets, a few well-researched country funds would be appropriate for a small amount of your portfolio.

Eventually, however, if you find that you enjoy sending your money on world tours, you will want to invest in individual companies. One simple way of doing this is to buy ADRs.

ADRs

In order to make it easy for Americans to invest in them, many foreign corporations—large and small—trade shares on American stock exchanges. These shares are called *American depository receipts*, or ADRs.

Despite a rather complex arrangement between international banks that makes this possible, buying ADRs is very much like buying any other stock. The advantage to buying into a foreign corporation in this way is that you avoid such difficulties as transferring your money abroad, and foreign taxes on dividends and on capital gains.

There are over 600 ADRs traded in this country. The financial papers list those of the larger corporations. Your broker should have a more complete list, if you are interested.

It's important to remember that whether you buy an ADR or stock in the same corporation on an exchange in its own country, you are buying in to that country's economy. In unstable political climates, economies can change overnight. If you buy shares of Benguet Corporation, for example, you are speculating not only on gold-mining and engineering projects in the Philippines, but also on the often violent politics in that country. A revolution would almost certainly bring about economic turmoil, resulting in a sharp fall in the Philippine peso as well as a sharp devaluation of stock prices.

Such factors also have to be considered when buying open-end mutual funds that specialize in only one or two countries, and in buying the closed-end country funds. As you might imagine, the First Philippine Fund is one of the most volatile of the country funds.

TRADING IN INTERNATIONAL MARKETS

It is possible to open a trading account almost anywhere in the world. Through brokerage houses and banks, you can buy securities, foreign mutual funds, precious metals, and real estate—in short, just about anything you can buy in this country. Some international investors open savings accounts in countries where interest rates are higher than in the United States and-or the currency seems likely to appreciate against the dollar.

Opportunities are excellent for those who know what they're doing. There is a fair amount to learn, because international investing involves certain complexities that are necessary to know about: Tax rates, rules about taking money out of a country, different investment procedures, and, of course, different languages are just a few of the things confronting the international investor.

This is not to discourage you, however. I think foreign markets are eminently worth knowing about. The material listed at the end of this chapter will give you a good start, if you're interested. It's not all that difficult to learn—it's just a good idea to know as much as you can before putting down any real money.

As you become more knowledgeable about and comfortable with international markets, you can start looking for a good international broker. As a rule, only the large brokerages such as Merrill Lynch and Dean Witter have international divisions. Once you have found a broker, he or she can trade securities for you on exchanges in almost any country. And because these are full-service brokers, you can discuss your proposed purchases with them, or consider their recommendations.

CURRENCY

The new international investor needs to know that each country's currency is constantly going up or down in value compared to other currencies, because of the performance of a country's economy relative to the economies of other countries.

The new international investor needs to be aware that the currency of every country is constantly rising and falling in value in comparison to the currency of other countries. There are two reaons for this volatility: first, Country A's economy may be performing better or worse than Country B, or investors may *believe* that Country A's

Whether you buy an ADR or stock in the same corporation on an exchange in its own country, you are buying in to that country's economy. In unstable political climates, economies can change overnight.

economy is—or will be—performing better or worse than Country B.

Currencies are traded like other commodities, so demand for a country's money will send it up against other currencies. During much of the 1990s, for example, investors bought dollars, because the American economy looked safe and was growing faster than many other economies; this caused the dollar to appreciate against most other currencies. On the other hand, when investors—and particularly speculators—perceive that a country's economy is on the skids, they will sell great quantities of that currency, often causing massive devaluations in that country. This was what happened in several of the Asian countries in 1997 and 1998.

If you make an investment in a foreign country, you have to buy units of that country's currency with dollars. Should the value of that country's currency go down relative to the dollar, the value of your investment will also go down. When you come to sell your investment and change the foreign currency back into dollars, you will get fewer dollars than you put in.

The reverse is also true. If you had bought German marks in 1988, used this money to invest in German stocks, and then sold them two years later, you would have realized a 20% profit on the currency exchange alone because during that time the German mark appreciated 20% against the dollar. The stock of the companies you bought was priced in marks, and in 1990, changing these marks back into dollars gave you 20% more dollars.

This means that when you invest abroad, you need to consider more than just the type of investment. You need to have a feeling for how well that particular foreign currency is likely to do against the dollar.

Starting out in mutual funds that invest internationally avoids this whole problem. You don't have to worry about the currency exchanges, the managers of the funds do. That's what you're paying them for.

INTERNATIONAL SOCIAL INVESTING

The number of environmentally aware corporations and investors is growing all over the world. The movement is particularly strong in Europe.

There are now a few international mutual funds that invest in a socially responsible manner. Investors who wish to buy stocks in individual companies with advanced social and environmental policies should contact a socially aware investment professional.

Don't let the seeming complexities of foreign markets keep you from opportunities. Investing abroad can be not only profitable but fascinating. Suddenly, you may find yourself listening to the BBC, or reading some obscure journal on the economies of the Far East. International investing is a constant reminder of how interdependent the world has become, as well as how fast it is changing.

Resources

Dessauer's Journal, Philips Publishing. (800) 777-5005. Monthly $149.00/year. John Dessauer is one of the better known advisers on international investing. His journal includes general articles on the world economy and short updates on stock markets in various countries. Dessauer also has a portfolio of recommended stocks from around the world (including the United States) that have done very well. This journal is an excellent place for the new investor to enlarge his or her knowledge of world markets.

CHAPTER 14

THE MODEL PORTFOLIO

U p to this point, I've been giving you an overview of the most important areas in the World of Investment. In this and the following two chapters, I'm going to ask you to start thinking about how *you* might fit into this world. This does not mean it's time to start buying. It's simply time to consider what kinds of investments might meet your needs.

To make this easier, we're going to look at a model portfolio—a group of investments created with a specific purpose in mind, in this case *long-term growth*. This chapter outlines the investments that make up the model. In Chapter 15, using the model as an example, we'll talk about what goes into the building of a successful portfolio. And then, in Chapter 16, you'll be able to look at the portfolios of a few individuals, and, perhaps, compare your needs and goals with theirs.

As I have emphasized throughout this book, it is usually wise for the new investor to start out investing in mutual funds. The diversification already present in their portfolios adds to the safety we are looking for. In addition, the performance of the fund managers against the overall market can be easily checked.

Over time, some investors will stay with the funds; others, as they gain experience, will want to begin buying individual securities. The model portfolio is presented as a place to start for both kinds of investors.

Let's take a look at the categories included in the model portfolio.

Balanced/Equity Income/Utilities.   We begin with this category for the sake of the good income and stability these funds provide. There is also good growth potential in stocks that yield a high dividend. (*Yield*, remember, refers only to yearly income, not appreciation in value. A "high-yielding" stock is one with a large, yearly dividend.) Remember that in figuring the overall growth of a stock or mutual fund, we are including the reinvestment of dividends. If a dividend amounts to 5% to 8%, the reinvestment of it will cause an investment to grow much faster than a dividend of only 1% to 3%.

Most of the companies that give large dividends are utilities, so this is what you find in most equity income funds. Utilities are an excellent way of adding safety to any portfolio, because their stock prices don't fall as far as others in bad times, and usually rebound more quickly. This is because the utility companies usually continue to pay good dividends, even in bad times.

Balanced funds emphasize preservation of capital as well as growth and income. They will often have much of

It is usually wise for the new investor to start out investing in mutual funds.

their stock portfolio in utilities—and the bonds in their portfolios will also provide good income.

High-income stocks are a specialty of two conservative newsletter advisers recommended in this book. Richard Band's newsletter *Profitable Investing* is listed in the Resources section for Chapter 4, and Richard Young's at the end of this chapter. Young shows that investing in the highest-yielding stocks in the Dow Jones Industrial Average would have provided a much greater return over 30 years than investing in the lower-yielding Dow stocks.

The first 20% of our capital will, therefore, be invested as follows: 10% in the best equity income fund we can find, 10% in the best balanced fund.

Growth Funds. Certain funds have been star performers over the last 10 years—and show every sign of continuing their success. These are in the fund categories of "growth" or "aggressive growth." We have listed a few in Appendix A. Take a look at these, but do some research on your own, too. We're going to put 15% of our model portfolio into two growth funds with the best records and the best prospects, 7.5% in each.

Index Funds (Stock). These have been the star performers during the latter part of the 1990s, particularly those funds that track the S&P 500 Index. These funds buy stock in all of the companies in the S&P 500 Index, and simply hold onto them. Because there is very little active management involved (almost no buying and selling), management fees are lower than those of other mutual funds, so return to the investor is higher. Fifteen percent of the model portfolio will go into two index funds, 7.5% in each. Although the index of stocks is different for each fund, both are large company indexes.

International Funds. The U.S. stock markets outperformed most of the other major stock markets in the world during the 1990s. Some of the smaller markets did well in the first part of the decade, but crashed and burned in the second half. Investors in stocks and mutual funds of Russia, Brazil, Korea, Thailand, and Indonesia watched as their holdings were halved in value, or worse. Many sold out and vowed never to return.

What this demonstrates is the importance of buying mutual funds that invest in a number of different countries all over the world. And right now, it encourages us to invest in areas where the economies are more stable, such as Europe. The continuing economic unification of Western Europe should bring great benefits to the economies involved.

Considering these facts, we're going to invest 5% of our capital in a European growth fund and 10% in another growth fund that invests all over the world. We'll put our money in the two no-load funds with the best records *and* the best prospects.

Small-Cap Stocks.   These are stocks of smaller companies. "Cap" is short for "capitalization": the total capitalization of a company is equal to the number of outstanding shares of stock multiplied by the value of each share. These stocks are generally low-priced issues. "Low-priced" in this case means $10 a share on down, with special emphasis on those under $5 a share.

During much of this century, small-company stocks, as a whole, have handily outperformed those of the larger corporations, including the blue chips (see Appendix D, "Fifty Years of Returns"). During the 1990s, however, the big companies have been stronger.

The stocks of individual small companies tend to fluctuate more than those of the large corporations. They are vulnerable to downturns in their sectors and in the greater economy. Owning a group of them in a diversified mutual fund, however, spreads out the risk. We'll put 15% of our portfolio into two mutual funds whose holdings include a number of top-performing small companies in various fields, 7.5% in each.

> **Individual bonds will not usually fluctuate very much in value, but their yield in yearly interest is greater than that of most stocks.**

Small-cap stocks are discussed in greater detail in Chapter 19.

Bonds (Fixed Income). Because of their low risk and steady return, bonds provide a good balance for a portfolio composed mostly of stocks. Unlike stocks, individual bonds will not usually fluctuate very much in value, but their yield in yearly interest is greater than that of most stocks. As this money is reinvested and compounded, the bond fund will grow in value. We're going to invest 7.5% in a bond fund with a portfolio of government bonds and AAA-rated corporate bonds. An additional 7.5% will go to a fund specializing in international bonds for a total of 15% in bonds.

Cash. We're going to keep the final 5% of our money in a money market account, either at our broker's or at the same office as one of our mutual funds. This money market cash will give us interest, too—not as much as the bond funds, but normally anywhere from 3% to 6%, depending on the credit markets.

In actuality, we will have substantially more than 5% of our capital in cash, because the managers of stock and bond mutual funds commonly hold 5% to 20% of *their* assets in cash. The percentage of fund assets invested in the stock and bond markets depends on the fund managers' perception of the condition of these markets. If the managers see a rocky road ahead, they will sell some of the fund's securities and keep the proceeds in cash for a while.

Buyers of individual stocks will want to keep anywhere from 10% to 20% of their capital in cash. This not only provides added safety but allows an investor to take immediate advantage of any buying opportunity. Our portfolio now looks like this:

20% Equity income/Balanced
15% Growth
15% Stock Index
15% International
15% Small companies
15% Bonds
5% Cash
_____
100%

We own twelve separate funds, plus the money market fund. This is not a difficult number to keep tabs on, particularly because this is to be treated as a buy-and-hold portfolio.

Beating the Averages

In the stock market sector of the investment world, a great premium is placed on "beating the averages." What this has come to mean is making better profits with your stocks, or stock funds, than the overall stock market does. If the market, as measured by the S&P 500 Index, increased in value by 10% in a given year, then an 11% increase in your portfolio would constitute beating the averages.

The kind of enthusiastic advertisements for investment advice you see in the newspapers suggest that it's easy to do better than the S&P 500. This is not the case: In any given year, the S&P 500 outperforms the majority of professional financial managers and advisers. This is one reason why S&P 500 Index funds have been so popular recently.

It's possible to place too much emphasis on beating the averages while ignoring other important factors. The stock funds in the model portfolio were chosen partly because their investment categories have often done better than the overall stock averages. They were also chosen, however, because together they provide the kind of balance the new investor should look for. Safety and balance will create a portfolio that will shine in a good market, but will also weather the recessions.

ABOUT THE MODEL PORTFOLIO

The model portfolio above is directed toward long-term growth, not income. What income there is, from dividends or interest, would be automatically reinvested in the fund that produced it. The investments are also strongly directed toward safety: the preservation of capital. Except for the small-company funds, all the categories are quite conservative, with a heavy emphasis on blue chip stocks, domestic and international. The overall risk-reward temperature of the portfolio is right in the middle, which is a good place for it to be for the new investor.

We are emphasizing long-term growth here. The investment categories we have chosen have done extremely well over the years, but these years have included many ups and downs.

Investing in these same categories with the intention of buying and selling for short-term profit would send the readings on all of the risk-reward thermometers right to the top. Even bonds, despite their safe and secure reputation, can fluctuate sharply in value over a few months or a year. And stocks (and stock mutual funds) must be considered risky investments in the short term. They go up and down according to the economic winds and the whims of fickle investors. The only factor that lowers their risk is that, as a whole, the trend in their value has always been upward over time.

The Rule of 10%

New investors are often confused about what rate of return to expect from investments. This confusion is not helped by the ads that promise a safe return of 50% a year—or by Uncle Joe, who boasts about how he doubled his money in three months with a hot stock.

From 1995 through 1998, stocks showed returns of 20% to 30% a year. This was due, in large part, to the continuing strength of the American economy, particularly the technology sector. The prosepects still look good, but economies and stock markets can be laid low by other factors, among them, failing economies in countries that purchase our exports, and increased international competition. Investors should not expect these unusually high returns to continue indefinetely.

A 10%-a-year return on your money, averaged over time, is still a good place to start. Don't be discouraged if you make less. Some years may simply be bad ones for the securities in your portfolio. You may show a growth of only a few percent, or even a minus; during the 1970s, for example, there were several years of negative returns and only a few years of small, positive returns. The bad times, like the 1970s, however, are usually balanced out by times of exceptional growth, like the 1990s.

Your eventual goal is to make more than 10%, while maintaining the same level of safety. As you get more experienced in managing your portfolio, this goal can become a fine challenge. But 10% is a good benchmark to start from.

Be aware, then, that the risk-reward thermometers you see in this chapter are for investments held for a number of years.

Modifying the Model

As we will see in Chapter 16, it's very easy to modify the model portfolio to provide an income and even greater safety—or to emphasize more growth. And because we are investing in mutual funds, it's easy to vary the amounts invested to fit the needs of large or small investors.

As new investors evolve into experienced investors over time, these categories can also be modified to satisfy socially conscious criteria. For example, for our international category, it's now possible to find socially responsible mutual funds based in foreign countries. If you become comfortable with international investing, you may want to move in this direction.

If you decide to use all or parts of the model portfolio, you will find in Appendix A a list of appropriate, high-performing mutual funds in each category. You should be

The risk-reward thermometers you see in this chapter are for investments held for a number of years.

aware, however, that funds change over the years—and promising new ones come into existence. For this reason, you should check each fund carefully before you buy. The sources and advisers recommended in this book should help you to make your own informed, up-to-date choices. In the next chapter, we'll go into how to choose the best funds in more detail.

Resources

Richard Young's Intelligence Report, Philips Publishing Inc. (800) 777-5005. Monthly. $99/year. Ask for bonuses. Young is your basic conservative investor: His specialties are bonds, utilities, and high-yielding blue chips. He also recommends mutual funds. Young is a good adviser for new investors. He writes clearly and concisely and frequently restates his investment philosophy and methods. And his subscribers have done very well with his recommendations.

CHAPTER 15

BUILDING A SUCCESSFUL PORTFOLIO

An investment operation is one which, upon thorough analysis, promises safety of principal and an adequate return. Operations not meeting these requirements are speculative.

—BENJAMIN GRAHAM, NOTED INVESTOR

Just a few, important elements are required to set up a portfolio that will ensure a good return and will let you weather various financial storms. These are general factors that should go into the building of any successful group of investments.

In setting up the model portfolio, we considered three major factors, and we will add a fourth—performance—in this chapter:

- Design. What purpose is the portfolio designed for?
- Quality. How are the best investments bought?
- Diversification. How do you keep a good balance among your investments?
- Performance. After the portfolio is set up, how do you keep tabs on how it performs?

PORTFOLIO DESIGN

The design of a portfolio depends on your purposes and your goals. The model portfolio in Chapter 14 was designed for long-term growth, with a strong emphasis on safety—the preservation of capital. Though the overall value of the investments may fluctuate with the markets, we are aiming for as rapid an increase of our principal as we can, while still maintaining the necessary safety.

If our purpose was to get more income, while still cultivating some growth, we would buy more bond and utility funds, fewer small-company funds, and fewer low-yielding blue chips. On the other hand, a need for even greater growth—while accepting the added risk— would have us buying just the opposite: more growth and small company funds, fewer bonds, and less cash in the money markets.

BUYING THE BEST—AND HOLDING ON

In Chapter 19, we're going to talk about a few more advanced methods of investing. Right now, though, let's deal with the only buying system employed by the model portfolio: the venerable *buy-and-hold strategy*.

You are in excellent company with the buy-and-hold method of investing. Such noted investors as John Templeton, Warren Buffett, and Peter Lynch all subscribe to this way of building a portfolio. If it seems too boring, just remember that the reason these men are respected

Making money is not usually boring.

is because they made great pots of money for those who invested with them or followed their advice. Making money is not usually boring.

Buy and hold is just as it sounds—though you probably won't hold an investment forever. If, over a period of a year or two years, a mutual fund or a security is not performing as well as the rest of its market category and its prospects don't look good for the future, then you sell it.

The key to a successful buy-and-hold strategy is selecting the best investments. If you choose companies or funds on the basis of their excellent past performance and their excellent prospects for the future, you can afford to watch their prices fluctuate. If your choices are good, these are the investments that will recover the quickest after a recession and appreciate the most in good times.

Choosing the Best Funds

In Chapter 6, we discussed a few ways of choosing the best-performing mutual funds. Spending enough time to select the best ones will pay off handsomely in the long run.

Using one of the books or journals recommended in the Resources section of Chapter 6, find the three funds in the category you want that have performed the best over the last five years. Then check out what the funds invest in (the books will have this information, too).

Say you're looking at international funds. After finding the three funds with the best records over the past five years, you see that the two top funds are heavily invested in Japan. Now, suppose that when you are looking, the Japanese economy is having a bad time, with no immediate prospects for recovery. The third fund, on the other hand, has diversified investments all over the world. This is the one you want.

The next step is to call the fund's 800 number (listed in the books and journals) and ask for a prospectus. This prospectus will give you all the details about investing in the fund; it will also describe the fund's investment policy and the securities it owns. If you like what you see, then you're ready to invest.

While the buy-and-hold strategy means generally ignoring the ups and downs of the market once you own a security, you *do* need to be aware of market conditions when you are buying. If the stock market appears very shaky, keep your money in cash until things improve.

You also need to be aware of future prospects. If there is good evidence that the Japanese economy is recovering—and that the stock market is beginning to reflect that improvement—then you will want to take another look at those first two international funds.

DIVERSIFICATION

The model portfolio was set up with diversification as a primary objective. Whatever your portfolio looks like, diversification gives it balance and stability. If some of your investments go down in value, they will be balanced by others that don't go down, continue to give you income, or even go up.

For example, if stocks should fall and your stock funds lose value, you would continue to get income from the bond funds. The funds investing in utility companies will also most likely continue to pay dividends. And the international equity funds may not go down with the American market. The total value of your portfolio may be reduced, but you should ride out the storm easily until the stock market turns around.

When it *does* turn around, it is sometimes the blue chip stocks that go up the fastest, sometimes the small-company stocks. This is why it's a good idea to have a blue chip fund *and* a small-company fund in your portfolio.

Chapter 14 lists the various categories of funds, their investment objectives, and their risk-reward thermometers. It's a good idea for the new investor to build a portfolio of funds with temperatures that *average out* to the middle of the scale. A low-risk bond fund, for example, would balance out a higher-risk small-company fund.

Your choices, however, need to be high-quality investments. Buying three risky, high-temperature funds, such as a junk bond fund, a small-company biotech fund, and a precious-metals fund, is *not* the kind of diversification that will help you ride out the storms.

Even if you have only a small amount to invest, it's still important to diversify. If you have $5,000 , you can put $2,500 each in two different funds, then add a couple more funds as you get more to invest. Anywhere from five to twelve funds is a reasonable number for the new investor to own. (See the next chapter for a low-income portfolio.)

PERFORMANCE

It's a good idea to check the value of your funds at least once a week, and do a major evaluation of your portfolio once every six months. If your portfolio is being managed, then you will want to talk it over with the manager every six months.

If the stock market appears very shaky, keep your money in cash until things improve.

The *Portfolio Simplifier* recommended at the end of this chapter is an excellent way of keeping track of your various investments. Alternatively, if you are comfortable with computers, you can buy one of the many software programs that help you organize your finances (see Resources in Chapter 22).

What you are watching for is the increase or decrease in value of your funds compared to other funds in the same investment category. Even though the share price of a fund may have increased, if it is doing noticeably less well than other funds in the same category it may be time to sell yours and buy a better-performing one.

For example, if your aggressive growth fund has gained 8% over two years, but the average gain for the category of aggressive growth funds has been 15%, it's time to consider selling, and buying one of the funds that topped 15%. (The financial papers publish quarterly retrospectives on the performance of different categories of funds and individual funds.)

If, on the other hand, your fund has done brilliantly but the economic situation has changed, it may also be time to think about selling. Suppose, for example, your European small-company fund has appreciated an average of 18% a year during the last three years. Recently, however, tensions in the Middle East have aroused fears of an interruption in the oil supply. The resulting higher oil prices could throw Europe into a recession—and small-company stocks are usually the most vulnerable in recessions.

So . . . it may be time to let go of your prize fund. You could sell it all, or you could sell 70% or 80% of it and hold on to the rest. This would lock in a good profit, but allow you to keep at least some of the fund, in case the political tensions evaporate.

Though buying and selling should generally be based on performance over a period of at least a year, there are times when you may need to move faster. For example, if

> Though buying and selling should generally be based on performance over a period of at least a year, there are times when you may need to move faster.

it were clear that the political situation in the Middle East was deteriorating rapidly, you would not want to wait for your six-month review to sell your European fund.

Unless your investment objectives have changed, you need to maintain the original balance of investment categories in your portfolio. For example, if your small-company funds have been such star performers that they now account for 25% of your assets instead of the original 15%, it's time to think about taking some profits. It may be difficult to bring yourself to sell such winners, but remember that small-company funds can also be big losers in any recession.

How *much* you sell depends on the economic climate and whether the funds are continuing to rise. If they still look good, you could sell enough to bring this category down to just 20% of the whole. If the trend upward has stalled, though, sell more and spread the proceeds around to your other funds, so that the original balance is regained.

Resources

Profitable Investing Portfolio Simplifier, by Richard E. Band. Philips Publishing Inc., 7811 Montrose Road, Potomac, MD 20854. (800) 777-5005. $25. *Band's Profitable Investing* newsletter is listed in the Resources for Chapter 4. If you subscribe to the newsletter, you get the *Portfolio Simplifier* free ($99/year, including telephone hotline).

Unless you plan to use your computer to organize your portfolio, you will need something like this booklet. There are five sections: Getting Organized, Tracking Your Portfolio, Year-End Tax Planner, Targeting Your Retirement, and Sources and Records. It's all laid out very clearly, and the author gives some useful advice in each section.

Morningstar Mutual Funds reports will help you choose the best funds (See Resources, Chapter 6).

Setting up a portfolio online is simple, whether it's mutual funds or stocks. You can track your funds daily and see clearly which ones are performing well and which ones are not. Chapter 22 will show you how to do this.

CHAPTER 16

INDIVIDUAL PORTFOLIOS

O ne advantage to the model portfolio presented in Chapter 14 is that it's easily modified to suit individual needs. In this chapter, we're going to look at a few financial scenarios and how the model can be tailored to each one.

The model is presented simply as a place to start from. As you will see, some people include real estate as part of their portfolios; one woman invested heavily in the stock of the company she worked for; another used small amounts for speculation. By comparing the situations of these people to your own, you should begin to see more clearly what your own portfolio might look like.

Whether you use the model as a starting point, however, or set up your own portfolio, you need to ask yourself a few questions:

1. To what extent do you want to manage your portfolio? There are basically three kinds of investors: those who give the management of their assets to

a financial professional; those who manage their own portfolios, but minimally, adopting a long-term buy-and-hold strategy and reviewing their portfolios only occasionally; and the "hands-on" investors, who keep tabs on things daily, and trade more often.

2. What personal goals do you want your portfolio to help you reach? College for the kids? Retirement? Extra income? Deciding on these goals will determine the design of your portfolio. For example, do your goals mean investing for long-term growth only, or do you need income from your investments?

3. How much risk are you willing to take? Risk comes with the territory in the World of Investment, but you need to determine the amount that seems right for your situation—and for your nervous system. If you're lying awake nights worrying whether International Skeet Management is going to drop another 10 points, then perhaps you need a less risky investment.

The portfolios described below are the result of each person or couple answering these questions. I hope that pondering these examples will bring you closer to deciding what your own portfolio will look like. There's no reason to rush it, though: the World of Investment isn't going anywhere, except up and down.

JIM: EXTRA INCOME AND LONG-TERM GROWTH

Let's start with my friend Jim, the sculptor. After moaning for years that American society doesn't support the artist, Jim finally sold a major work for $25,000. We'll forget the few hundred he spent to celebrate and assume he has $25,000 to invest.

Now, one of Jim's complaints was that he had to do odd jobs to earn a living, which took him away from his art. So he wanted to invest the $25,000 in a way that would give him some income and keep the principal safe. (Jim already has $5,000 set aside in a certificate of deposit for emergencies, and he has health insurance.) Jim, who is 35 and single, is also interested in establishing a fund that might grow over a period of years. Artists don't get pensions.

Proposed portfolio: Two no-load bond mutual funds, one investing in high-yield securities yielding 10.5%, the other in corporate bonds yielding 7.5%—$10,000 in each.

This is $20,000 with an average return of 9% a year = $1,800 a year, or $150 a month. This might not seem like much, but to Jim, who makes a business of living as cheaply as possible, it's one-eighth of his total monthly living expense of $1,200. The extra $150 means he can avoid odd jobs for two or three more days each month and concentrate on sculpting.

These two or three days mean more than just the satisfaction of working at what he loves; they also mean Jim has more time to produce art that might sell. So by investing in funds that give him extra income, he is essentially investing in himself—in his own business.

The remaining $5,000 was divided equally among two no-load stock mutual funds, the first a socially responsible index fund tracking large companies, the second, a high-performing small-company fund. As the $5,000 grows, he will diversify into other funds, but the thrust of the portfolio will be aggressive growth. Jim would like to see growth of 15% a year on the average, but accepts that it may be closer to the historical average of 12.5%.

If Jim's investments grow at the rate of 12.5%, in 10 years he will have about $16,200; in 20 years, $52,750; and in 30 years, when he will be thinking about retirement, a nice sum of $171,000. If he gets lucky, or skilled at choosing the right mutual funds, a 15% average growth rate would give him $331,000 in thirty years.

Jim will invest the $5,000 in a Roth individual retirement account (IRA) account over the next three years. This means he will pay taxes on the $5,000 now, but will not pay taxes when he begins to withdraw money from the account after age 65. Another advantage is that the capital will be able to grow tax-free. (There is more about IRAs in the next chapter.)

In addition, Jim will still have the $20,000 in the bond funds. While the value of these funds may fluctuate over the years, it will probably not increase or decrease by any appreciable amount. The amount will not grow because Jim is using the income, not reinvesting it. Of course, if his sculpture becomes the rage, he might not need the income from those funds and could invest more for growth.

Jim says artists never really retire, but that it's good to have some money put away for old age. If all goes well, he will have about $170,000, plus the $20,000 from the bond funds. Because of inflation, the income from this $190,000 won't go as far as it does today, but it will still be a very nice addition to a Social Security check. And the total amount will give Jim some backup funds for any medical emergencies or long-term care.

SUSANNA: GROWTH AND EARLY RETIREMENT

Jim needed the income to live on. But let's look at investing the same amount in a very different scenario. Susanna, 28, has done well as an assistant buyer for a chain of clothing stores. With her salary and occasional bonuses, she has accumulated $25,000. She doesn't need extra income, so she would like to invest the entire $25,000 for growth over the long term. Susanna is not particularly interested in managing investments on a day-to-day basis; she would like to invest the money and just check it occasionally.

Susanna has an insider's knowledge of the company and thinks its future looks promising—and that she can contribute to its success. So she invests $8,000, which buys $10,000 worth of stock, under the company's plan.

Because she is young and the prospects for future earnings look good, Susanna is willing to invest some of her portfolio in riskier mutual funds, with a likelihood of growth. She would also like to retire early—in 15 or 20 years.

Proposed portfolio: Susanna's company has an attractive stock ownership plan for its employees. For every four shares an employee purchases, management kicks in an extra fifth. Susanna has an insider's knowledge of the company and thinks its future looks promising—and that she can contribute to its success. So she invests $8,000, which buys $10,000 worth of stock, under the company's plan.

The remaining $17,000 is placed as follows: $5,000 in two international growth funds (investing all over the world); $2,500 in a European aggressive growth fund; $5,000 in two U.S. environmental funds, one specializing in large companies, the other in small companies; $2,500 in a utility equity fund; and $2,000 in a corporate bond fund, currently yielding 7%. All the funds are no-load and all dividends and interest are to be reinvested.

Let's suppose that, overall, Susanna's funds, and her company's stock, grow at an average rate of 12% a year—not an unreasonable expectation if all the income is reinvested. Ten years will see her $25,000 grow to $78,000; 20 years, $241,000; and 30 years, about $750,000.

The income from $241,000, after 20 years, would not be enough to support the kind of lifestyle Susanna would prefer. She would like to have at least $500,000: this amount, invested for income at 10%, would give her $50,000 a year to live on, which she considers the absolute minimum.

With the help of a compound-interest table (see Appendix D), Susanna figures that if she can invest an additional $800 a quarter, or $3,200 a year, in 20 years she will have $257,000, assuming the same 12% growth rate. This, added to the $241,000 from the other account, will give her almost $500,000. If, in the meantime, her earnings continue to go up, she will be able to invest more, thus pushing her retirement closer to 15 years away.

Just to illustrate the importance of a few percentage points, if Susanna had invested the $25,000 in government bonds with a return of 6%, the total would amount to only $80,000 in 20 years and $143,000 in 30 years. If, on the other hand, her company's stock and the riskier growth funds do well, causing her portfolio to grow at an overall rate of 15% a year, she would be looking at $410,000 after 20 years, and $1,655,000 after 30 years. This last figure is more than double the amount at the 12% rate—such are the wonders of compound interest.

One last note: because Susanna plans to retire in her forties, she will not invest her $17,000 in an individual retirement account. This is because there are stiff penalty taxes for withdrawing money from an IRA before age 59 $\frac{1}{2}$. However, Susanna's earnings are good enough that she will pay taxes on income from the investments out of her salary, instead of withdrawing money from the account. This will allow all of the income in the account to be reinvested and compounded.

JANET: LONG-TERM GROWTH AND SPECULATION

Janet is doing well as a cardiovascular specialist, though up to two years ago, the majority of her earnings went to supporting her three children and putting them through college. Now, however, they are grown and earning incomes of their own.

Janet is 52 and divorced. She has accumulated $100,000 in savings, and the prospects for continued earnings look excellent. She has backup savings and all necessary insurance, and she will almost certainly continue to generate a surplus that she can continue to invest. Fifty thousand dollars are in an IRA that she has contributed to over the past twenty years. The amount has grown, but very slowly because it was invested only in the money market. Now Janet would like to invest it for more aggressive growth. The other $50,000 she wants to invest and manage herself.

Proposed portfolio for the $50,000 in the IRA: the model portfolio, as portrayed in Chapter 14. This long-term-growth portfolio provides the kind of growth and safety Janet wants for her retirement fund. This $50,000 Janet will essentially leave alone, just checking every month to see whether the funds she chose are performing well.

Now for the other $50,000. Janet has purchased a data-retrieval service for her computer that gives her real-time quotes from the various markets (see Chapter 22). She has the computer at her office and checks her investments during lunch hour and occasionally between patients. (Now you know why you had to sit so long in the waiting room.)

She invests $35,000 in twenty growth stocks she chose from the newsletters she subscribes to and then researched further on her own. She is especially partial to small pharmaceutical and medical research companies, because she has an educated feeling for what products will be successful. She also places $5,000 in rare coins, after carefully researching the market. She checks on the stocks every day, though she may buy and sell only a few over the course of a few months. She hopes the rare coins will appreciate over a few years.

Janet uses the remaining $10,000 for pure speculation. After caring for others for 25 years, as a wife, mother, and doctor, she has suddenly discovered a financial speculator emerging as part of her personality. She trades stock options, index options, a few junk bonds, and futures options on gold. These she buys and sells from day to day, finding the process absorbing enough to divert her attention for a while from arteries and heart valves.

PETE AND MARILYN: BUILDING A PORTFOLIO

Pete and Marilyn, both in their early thirties, are anxious to build up a college fund for their son, age two, and daughter, age 6 months. They also want to start investing for their retirement. Pete works as an estimator and carpenter for a construction firm; Marilyn works part time in a day-care center and full time as a homemaker. Their combined earnings come to $42,000 after taxes, and almost all of this goes for living expenses.

By saving $250 a month ($3,000 a year) for ten years, they were able to get together a down payment on a three-bedroom house. Now, even though there are added expenses with the two children, Pete's salary also goes up a bit each year. So they decide they can still invest $250 a month.

Part of this $250—$140 a month—goes into the 401(k) plan set up by Pete's employer (more about 410(k) retirement plans in the next chapter). The employer contributes an additional 25% (of $140) to this plan, bringing the monthly total to $175. Because the 401(k) is a "tax-advantaged" account, Pete and Marilyn can deduct the amount contributed from their income on their tax statement.

The other $110 goes to paying down the mortgage on their house. According to an agreement worked out with the bank that holds the mortgage, when Marilyn makes the mortgage payment of $1,003 each month, she will add $110 to it.

This additional $110 a month means that their 20-year mortgage of $120,000 will be paid off in 16 years. Over the years, this will save a total of $37,700 in interest on their mortgage.

In 16 years, their firstborn will be ready for college, followed in two years by his sister. By that time, Pete and Marilyn will no longer be making house payments, which means they will have extra cash to contribute to both children's tuition and expenses. If they need to, they can also take out a small loan against the house. They hope to contribute about $10,000 a year to each child for four years, for a total of $80,000.

Real Estate

Some investors may want to include real estate in their portfolios. Many people already own real estate in the form of a home; a few may own income properties. For those who are unable to own real estate, or don't wish to, a real estate mutual fund is a good way of including this category in your portfolio. These funds (as discussed in Chapter 11) invest in the securities of real estate brokerage companies, real estate investment trusts (REITs), and property development companies.

As far as the risk-reward balance of your portfolio, the real estate funds are about three-quarters of the way up the risk-reward thermometer. But *long-term* investments in high-quality homes or income properties should be seen as a relatively conservative investment (the thermometer would stand just at the one-quarter mark). Short-term investing for a quick profit, however, especially in lower-quality properties, sends the thermometer right up to the top.

For further ways of investing in real estate without actually buying property, see Chapter 11.

This amount of money will not be enough to pay tuition and expenses at a private college (especially with the expected increases during the next 15 years). At the state university, though, $10,000 will amount to a large percentage of the children's expenses, with student loans and summer jobs making up the remainder. A less expensive alternative would be for them to start out at the local community college, while living at home, and transfer to the state university after two years. Or, if either child excelled in academics or athletics, scholarships might be available at the expensive private colleges.

Pete is a very conservative investor uncomfortable with the ups and downs of the stock market. He placed the funds in the 401(k) account in a bond fund and planned to buy a few other bond funds over the years. Marilyn finally convinced him to buy at least one balanced fund and a utility fund to add some diversity and growth to the portfolio.

Conservative investments mean conservative growth rates: Pete and Marilyn's funds should grow at about 10% a year. At this rate, $175 a month, contributed over 20 years, would grow to $133,000, or $400,000 in 30 years. After the house is paid off in 16 years, of course, Pete will probably want to contribute more to the 401(k) plan, thereby causing it to grow at a faster rate.

When they no longer have to pay for college expenses, Pete and Marilyn will use their extra cash to build another fund. They would like this money to go toward a down payment on a house or small apartment building. Either Pete will fix it up and sell it, or they will hold on to it as part of their portfolio.

There are a couple of noteworthy points in Pete and Marilyn's story. The first is that by contributing a small amount each month, you can accumulate a healthy sum over a number of years.

The second point is that if you are a homeowner, you have invested in real estate and your home should be considered as part of your portfolio. By putting the $110 toward paying down the mortgage, Pete and Marilyn were investing more in their home.

For them, the house is a good diversification of their portfolio—but not absolutely necessary to their plans. If they had lived in an area where a house was too expensive for them to buy, they could have started another account with the $110 a month. At the end of 20 years, at a growth rate of 10%, this account would have been worth $83,500; in 30 years, almost $250,000. They could have used—or borrowed against—this fund for their children's education.

MIKE AND SARAH: INHERITANCE USED FOR INCOME AND STARTING BUSINESSES

Mike and Sarah have inherited a total of $1 million from their respective families. Because neither of them particularly likes their jobs, they want to leave them and use their inheritance to give them a living income. Mike wants to write a novel and Sarah wants to start a dress shop. They are both in their early forties.

Because they are aware that novels and new businesses are chancy things, they want to set aside a large percentage of the money to provide an income while they work on their new projects.

Sarah's inheritance came only recently, from her father, so she is in mourning and realizes that she is in no shape to make important investment decisions right away. Mike, on the other hand, had inherited a year earlier from a distant uncle, so his emotions are not involved, but both of them realize they need time to acclimate themselves to their new lives.

With this in mind, they buy six-month CDs at their bank and let the money sit there gathering interest. Sarah leaves her job, but Mike stays on at his for six months, providing an income during this period. In the meantime, they start reading books on investing and asking their friends and relatives for advice.

At the end of six months, they have come to some conclusions. Their main decision is that because they want to concentrate on their various projects, neither of them is particularly interested in managing their investments. So, on the recommendation of a good friend, they make an appointment with a woman in a reputable financial-planning firm, first agreeing between themselves that they will *both* have to like this person and agree on her recommendations before working with her.

The planner goes over all of Mike and Sarah's financial needs, from various kinds of insurance to tax considerations, from retirement planning to investment possibilities. The process is time consuming, but both of them agree that it is worthwhile.

In the end, the planner, having gotten a good idea of Mike and Sarah's investment preferences, recommends a

Their main decision is that because they want to concentrate on their various projects, neither of them is particularly interested in managing their investments.

portfolio of diverse stocks and stock funds for growth, and bond funds for income. Because both of them have strong social concerns, emphasis is placed on funds investing in socially and environmentally responsible companies. The planner recommends that they meet again in six months to review the portfolio.

At the same time, Mike's father asks him to invest $100,000 with him in an apartment complex. Because Mike's father has several successful property investments, the planner approves this, saying it will provide more diversity and good growth. This investment will generate $5,000 in cash each year, plus whatever growth the building brings over time.

From the $800,000 invested with the financial planner, Mike and Sarah get a yearly income of about 6% from dividends from the stock funds and interest from the bond funds. This comes to $48,000 ($800,000 × 0.06 = $48,000). This is income only—it does not count any appreciation in the value of the funds. They get an additional 5% cash from the $100,000 real estate investment $5,000—so their total yearly income comes to $53,000.

Sarah takes the remaining $100,000 to start her dress shop. Although she has high hopes, she realizes that she shouldn't expect any net income from the shop for at least a couple of years. The $53,000 is enough for them to live on in the meantime, although after taxes they will hardly have a sumptuous lifestyle. For the present, though, they are more interested in following their dreams.

For more information on investing in yourself by starting a business, you can look at Chapter 23. For now, it's important to note that Sarah and Mike have enough that, if worst came to worst, they could afford to lose the $100,000 going into the dress shop. They have their finances worked out so that they don't need the $100,000 to live on. I mention this because starting a business should be considered a high-risk investment. Ideally, it should be done with money that you are not depending on for income.

It's also important to realize that, except for the apartment building, the couple have not locked themselves in to any long-term investments. If their situation should change and they should want more income, some of their growth stock funds could easily be sold and reinvested in higher-yielding stock or bond funds. Or if Sarah's dress shop became a hit and Mike wrote a best-seller, they would not need as much income from the portfolio. In that case, they would want more of the portfolio in growth investments with the possibility of greater long-term gain. In any case, they have left their options open.

LOW-INCOME INVESTING: CREATING A PORTFOLIO

Except for Jim, the sculptor, everyone else described in these scenarios was fairly well-off. (We will present a scenario for a retired couple in the next chapter.) Pete and Marilyn were certainly not rich, but they could contribute $250 a month to build their portfolio.

Many people, however, have incomes too low to invest more than a few dollars above their monthly expenses. If they are able to contribute these small amounts to an investment plan, however, the money can grow into much larger amounts over time. I have developed a program for low-income investors that combines safety with growth.

The first thing any investor needs to do is to set up an emergency fund. As described in the box on the previous page, this fund is considered as savings, not investment capital.

Any amount you can save—$50 a month, $75, $100— should go into this fund. If you can't find any money at the end of the month, try thinking of it as a tax and set it aside when the paycheck first comes in. Another way is to set aside a dollar or two each day.

Your goal is to build up a savings account equal to at least three months of expenses. Suppose your total monthly expenses came to $1,350; your savings would need to amount to about $4,000 ($1,350 × 3 = $4,050). This money is left in the bank or credit union to earn interest and be at the ready for any future emergency. The money should be in a money market account or a CD in an institution that is insured by the Federal Deposit Insurance Corporation (FDIC), or the credit union equivalent, the National Credit Union Administration (NCUA).

Savings Versus Investment Capital

You will want to keep a certain amount of extra cash accessible and safe from market fluctuations in case you need it for an emergency. One way of determining the amount is to figure how much you (and your family, if you're married) would need in monthly expenses if something should happen to the major wage earner. It's a good idea to keep at least three months' expenses on hand in readily available cash.

The first two months' worth of this amount should be in a money market account at your bank where it is immediately accessible. Make it a joint account, with both you and your spouse able to write checks. Further amounts can go into one-year certificates of deposit (CDs) at your local bank. This money is also readily accessible, though the bank will charge you a fee if you withdraw it before one year.

Extra money in these amounts should be looked on not as investment cash but as backup money. There are a couple of reasons not to invest this money in stocks or bonds. First, a sale of securities can take up to a week to clear and you may need the cash immediately. Secondly, your securities may be down in value when you have to sell; you could easily come out with less money than if you'd left it in the bank.

When you accumulate more than you need for emergencies, that is the time to start thinking about investments. Carefully chosen investments will almost always appreciate, but they need time. Investment capital, therefore, should be money that you can leave for at least several years.

You will have some help in building up this fund from the interest earned from your savings. Without interest, $50 saved every month would amount to $600 a year, or $2,400 over four years. Adding in a 5% compounded interest rate on what you save, however, will give you $2,650 after four years, $3,400 after five years. Seventy-five dollars a month at 5% would give you the needed $4,000 after four years

Once you have the necessary savings for emergencies, *then* you can begin to make the money work for you. While the principal amount—in this case the $4,000—has to stay in the bank, the interest earned by the $4,000 can now go toward investing. Four thousand dollars at 5% will earn you $200 a year. If you can continue to put aside $50 a month, you will have $800 to invest each year: $600 from your continuing monthly contribution of $50 plus $200 in interest from your emergency account.

As soon as you accumulate $500, you can start a Roth individual retirement account and invest in a mutual fund. Mutual funds allow smaller initial investments for IRAs and some are as low as $500. Start out with a balanced fund, one that includes stocks and bonds, then as you add more money to the account, you can buy an index fund that follows the S&P 500 Index. Over the years, you can tailor your account to fit the Model Portfolio, oriented towards growth.

In less than four years, you will have $3,500 invested in four or five different funds—and probably more than that, if your funds have increased in value. When you achieve eight to twelve funds, you can send your money to each fund alternately, every month or every quarter, whichever is easier. Your $800 a year would come to about $66 a month or $200 per quarter.

Here's how your investment would grow if the markets act as they have in the past: At a growth rate of 12% a year (with all dividends and interest from the funds reinvested), after 5 years, $200 per quarter would amount to $5,375; after 10 years, it would be $15,000 ; 20 years, $64,275, and after 30 years, you would have a grand total of $225,000 . Not bad for an out-of-pocket outlay of $50 a month.

This chapter opened with some questions you need to ask yourself before setting up a portfolio of investments: your management style, goals, and risk tolerance. If, for example, you need an income, like Jim, the sculptor, you will need more bond and utility funds. If you are well-off and are investing for long-term growth only, your portfolio will look more like the Model Portfolio. But if the whole idea of putting your hard-earned money in stocks

> The other things that make a portfolio work are always the same, whether you start with a million dollars or invest a dollar a day: designing your portfolio based on your goals, taking care to choose the best investments, diversifying, and keeping tabs on your portfolio.

makes you cringe because your grandfather lost everything in 1929, then you may want to invest more in real estate and bonds, like Pete and Marilyn.

The other things that make a portfolio work are always the same, whether you start with a million dollars or invest a dollar a day: designing your portfolio based on your goals, taking care to choose the best investments, diversifying, and keeping tabs on your portfolio.

Ideally, this chapter has helped you to focus on your investment goals and the best ways to achieve them. The situations described above, while certainly not identical to your own, may be similar enough to help you organize your investments.

When you get ready to invest, the Model Portfolio—or your personal variation of it—is a good place to start. Some will choose to stay with mutual funds and manage their investments in the manner described above. But even if you plan to be a more active investor, the model is a good place to begin. You can get your footing and develop a feel for different areas before you start trading in more complex markets.

If you do begin to buy individual securities, starting with the model will help you keep your portfolio balanced and diversified. You would simply substitute individual securities for a mutual fund in the same investment category. For example, you could sell a utility fund and buy stock in three utility companies. To maintain diversity you might buy into a gas company, an electric utility, and a telephone company.

CHAPTER 17

RETIREMENT

O ur culture has traditionally divided life into the working phase and the retirement phase. Many people, though, have begun to rethink this artificial division. Quite a few younger people don't want to wait until age 65 to be free to pursue interests other than their work. And many older people enjoy continuing to be productive. Ideally, it should be possible to be productive at things you enjoy, while still having plenty of time to pursue other interests. Time to read, play music, travel, or be with your children or grandchildren should be available at any age—35 or 85.

Some people are happy with their jobs; others simply like the security of working until the normal retirement age. Still others, however, would like very much to retire early and pursue a different lifestyle or cultivate new interests. At the end of this chapter, these people will find a resources section created especially for them.

INCOME AND INVESTMENTS

In Chapter 16, we suggested several ways of building up a portfolio for your retirement years. The earlier you start, the more you will have when you get ready to retire. Either by investing a lump sum, putting away a certain amount each month, or both, you can build up quite a large amount in 20 or 30 years.

The total return on your investments will be much greater if you invest as much as you can in a tax-deferred retirement plan. These plans are explained later in the chapter.

You can get income from your retirement account; if you are a later retiree, you may also have a pension, and you will get Social Security. To find out how much you will get from Social Security, you can ask for a Personal Earnings and Benefit Estimate Statement (Form 7004-PC) from your local office. This is a record of your earnings and an estimate of your retirement benefits based on your past and expected future earnings.

Investment during retirement is really not that much different from before. There is simply a greater emphasis on income and on safety—more bonds, more utilities, fewer small-growth companies. Even if you are retiring in your mid-sixties, however, it's a good idea to keep at least 25% of your portfolio in growth stocks. There's a good chance that you may live at least another 20 years, and you need the growth to counter inflation.

GLEN AND ALICE: A WELL-PLANNED RETIREMENT

Let's look at a portfolio for a newly retired couple who have planned carefully for their retirement. Even though they are retiring at 65, their portfolio is pertinent to anybody on a fixed income. The difference, of course, is that early retirees wouldn't have a pension or Social Security. They would, therefore, need a larger amount to invest to give them an income—unless they plan to live very modestly.

Glen and Alice have just retired at age 65. They have Glen's Social Security (Alice worked as a homemaker), his pension, and $100,000 in savings. The pension and the Social Security provide a comfortable income, their house is paid off, and they have health insurance. They also have long-term-care insurance, in case either of them has to go into a nursing home (see box on page 231). If they decide to live in a retirement community in a few years, they will sell their house and buy in with the proceeds.

They would like to have extra income to travel, and they want to set up a fund to help with college expenses for their four grandchildren. The oldest won't be ready for eight years, so they have a little time to work on this.

Proposed portfolio: First of all, $5,000 goes into a money market account for readily available emergency cash. In addition, they purchase a certificate of deposit with another $5,000. Glen's pension and Social Security would continue to support Alice if he should die, but this CD they have earmarked for expenses surrounding either of their deaths, such as the cost of a funeral.

Of the remaining $90,000, $70,000 goes into a mix of bond mutual funds and high-yield stock funds, with an emphasis on utilities. The average return on the $70,000 is 7% or $4,900 a year. Of this, Glen and Alice will take $4,000 a year for traveling and other extras and reinvest the remaining $900. They could get a slightly higher yield by investing exclusively in bonds, but they expect the stock funds to appreciate over time.

Glen has decided to manage the remaining $20,000 himself in an attempt to increase the contribution to the grandchildren's college fund. He starts reading the books recommended in this book, talking with friends, and subscribing to a few of the best newsletters. He also makes a move that many people his age find difficult: he gets

> Glen and Alice are securely set up for their
> later years. In addition to handling their
> money well, they have prepared for
> eventualities like death or the need for long-
> term care.

online. After a few months, with a little instruction and plenty of practice, he is navigating the investment web sites like a pro. He finds he enjoys this, and within a year he is fully invested in stocks of well-established companies with good growth potential and a record of secure dividends. Because of the importance of the fund and the limited amount of capital, Glen avoids the smaller, riskier growth companies.

Glen and Alice are securely set up for their later years. In addition to handling their money well, they have prepared for eventualities like death or the need for long-term care. Each one has also taken care to make a detailed will, so that the survivor—and, eventually their children and grandchildren—will inherit their estate with minimum interference from the state.

Many people who are retired or approaching retirement, though, are not so well prepared. The following vignette is, unfortunately, a common story.

TED AND LINDA: STARTING LATE

At age 45, Ted and Linda realized that their retirement was a disaster in the making. Like many of their cohorts in the baby boom generation, they didn't begin to think about retirement until they were well into their forties. Their one son, Josh, had just finished college and found a good job, so they were relieved of any further expenses related to his support and education. It was at this point that they realized, with growing panic, that they had nothing saved for the future. Ted had bounced around from job to job, most recently as an insurance estimator, and was presently unemployed. Linda's job as a medical technician was steady, but the pay was not that good and the one salary barely met their monthly expenses. Under the pressure of helping Josh through college, they had maxed out their credit cards and now owed $23,000; to make matters worse, they had already missed a few payments on the cards and were worried about their credit rating. Although they dreamed of owning their own home, they had never been able to gather enough for a down payment.

It was time for a long, hard look not just at the prospects for retirement, but also at just where they were in their lives and where they wanted to go. Linda took a week of her vacation time and they began to take stock and make plans. Even though Ted felt pressure to start earning money, he was hesitant to return to estimating. He believed that if he was going to bring in a decent income, he had better find something that he enjoyed doing. Because he liked working with young people and had skills in math and science, he decided to investigate tutoring as a profession. Linda was supportive of this, even though she was stressed at being the sole provider and at having so little money.

The next thing Ted and Linda agreed to do was to see a financial adviser. The adviser took one look at their credit card debt and immediately sent them to Consumer Credit Counseling (CCC). CCC, with branches in major cities, is set up to help people with a debt load beyond their ability to pay. In Ted and Linda's case, the counselor at CCC was able to convince the three credit card lenders to lower the amount owed to a total of $18,000, in return for immediate payoff. Then she helped the couple negotiate a bank loan for the $18,000; this five year loan had a much lower interest rate than that of the cards and a monthly payment amount that was easier to meet.

Next, the financial adviser looked at saving for retirement. Linda had a 401(k) plan at her job, but had been unable to put very much into it; the total amount only came to $6,500. The couple agreed to start increasing Linda's contribution to the plan as soon as Ted was bringing in a good income.

This story has a happy ending. Ted was able to establish a business as a tutor and in a few years was earning good money. The bank loan was paid off in four years and the couple was able to contribute $700 a month to Linda's 401(k). Linda had a choice of mutual funds in the 401(k) account and chose the growth funds with the best records. Counting the $6,500 that was already in the account and an average growth rate of 12% a year, Ted and Linda will have about $300,000 by the time they're 65. Income from this, added to their social security benefits, will assure them a decent retirement.

TAX-DEFERRED RETIREMENT PLANS

Elsewhere we have recommended using tax-deferred investment plans wherever possible. Now we're going to talk about why. The benefits of these plans can be dramatic, as you will see.

Over the years, the federal government has created various ways of encouraging people to save for retirement. The incentives are centered around taxes: If you contribute to a retirement plan, you will get a break on your taxes. The incentives have worked. Hundreds of billions of dollars are now invested in different kinds of retirement plans.

It's interesting to note that the benefits of these savings work not only for the individuals who own them but also for the national economy. Whether invested directly in stocks and bonds or in bank savings accounts, the money is used as capital for economic growth.

There are various plans that will give you tax breaks if you put away money for your retirement. There are individual retirement accounts (IRAs), Keogh plans for the self-employed, simplified employee pension plans (SEPs), and 401(k) plans for employed people. The basics of these plans are all similar: You are allowed to put a certain amount of money away each year and deduct that amount from your taxable income.

You not only save on your yearly taxes by this deduction, you also save on taxes on the income from the account you set up. *Any interest or dividends on these monies is not taxed on a yearly basis.*

These are called "tax-deferred plans" because when you eventually withdraw the money, you do have to pay the taxes on it then. But the idea is that you will withdraw the money in small increments over a period of years when you retire—and you may well be in a lower tax bracket at that time.

Are these plans good? They're terrific! First of all, they provide a real incentive to set up a solid retirement savings plan. If you need further incentive, though, take a look at the box "Double Your Money." This shows the difference in return between a tax-deferred 401(k) plan and a straight investment plan.

While the idea behind these plans is simple enough, the rules surrounding them are quite complex (the Internal Revenue Service is involved, after all)—and they keep changing. For example, the money you invest in a tax-deferred retirement plan must be *earned income*: no Social Security, interest, dividends, or money from rentals. You may consider that your business is in managing your investments, but it's no go. The IRS considers any money you make to be investment income, not earned income.

Double Your Money

Suppose you are able to put $500 a month into a 410(k) plan at your job. That adds up to $6,000 you can deduct from your yearly income. If you are in the 28% tax bracket, this amounts to a savings of $1,680 every year ($6,000 × 0.28 = $1,680).

If your investments grow at a rate of 10% a year, compounded monthly, in 20 years you will have $379,684. This is assuming that all interest and dividends will be reinvested.

If, on the other hand, you invest the money without the benefit of a retirement plan, the $6,000 will be taxed as income. This means you will start off with only $4,320 to invest yearly: $6,000 minus $1,680 (the 28% tax on the $6,000) = $4,320. In addition, any interest or dividends generated by the account will be taxed at the 28% rate. (We are assuming here that money would be withdrawn from the investment account to pay the taxes.)

How much slower would a taxed account grow? Well, $4,320 divided by 12 months = $360 a month. The tax cuts into the amount you have to reinvest each month, so the fund grows at a slower rate. At the end of 20 years, you will have $192,157, roughly half what you would have in the 401(k) account.

How much you can contribute yearly is strictly controlled. At present, you can put $2,000 a year into an IRA, though as this book goes to press, there are proposals to raise this to $2,500. Depending on how much you earn and whether you have other retirement plans, you can deduct this $2,000 on your tax return. If your yearly earnings are over $50,000, you will not be able to deduct your contribution from your income (this earnings amount is subject to change, so you will need to check the current earnings limit). However, you can still contribute to an IRA and the investment earnings will not be taxed until you withdraw them during retirement.

There is a new variation of the individual retirement plan, instituted in 1997, called the Roth IRA. The Roth IRA allows you to contribute $2,000 a year, but this money is not deductible from your taxable income. However, the funds in the plan grow tax free, then, when you retire: Surprise! You pay no taxes on your withdrawals! For most people, this plan is preferable to regular IRAs. True, you don't get to deduct the $2,000 a year from your taxable income, but consider that this $2,000 may grow by ten times over the years. This means that you will have $20,000 worth of assets that you can withdraw tax-free.

If you already have a large amount in a regular IRA, it's generally not worth it to transfer it to a new Roth IRA. But I recommend starting a Roth account and contributing to it from now on (you can have as many IRAs as you want, even though you can only deduct a total of $2,000 a year from your income). You will thank yourself when you retire.

The manner in which you can withdraw money from your retirement plan can be quite complex. If you withdraw money before you reach the age of $59\frac{1}{2}$, there are penalties—except in certain cases. I encourage you to find out all you can before you invest in any one of these plans.

Mistakes can cost you money. For example, after you reach the age of $71\frac{1}{2}$, the IRS says you *have* to start withdrawing a certain amount from your IRA. If you don't, you get socked with a penalty of half of what you should have withdrawn! So do read the recommended tax book and or consult with a tax adviser. The money you save will be your own.

Where to open an IRA account? You will find that banks, credit unions, brokerages, and mutual funds will fall all over themselves for the privilege of managing your

IRA. There is nothing financial institutions like better than money that stays with them for a long time! You can contribute to the account in any manner you wish—monthly, quarterly, yearly, or whenever you feel like it.

You can buy CDs at your bank, or you can invest in securities at a brokerage in an IRA account. Buying and selling stocks goes on just as it would in a regular account. The only difference is that you can't take any money out without the IRS charging you a penalty.

If you open an IRA account at a mutual fund office, you can invest in different funds within that family of funds. However, all the financial institutions will charge you a small yearly fee for managing your IRA account. It is, therefore, worth your while to keep your IRA at one or two fund offices instead of opening a lot of IRA accounts in different places. A number of those fees could put a dent in your yearly return.

Keeping your IRA at a brokerage allows you the greatest amount of investment options—and you will be charged only one management fee.

Insurance companies sell tax-deferred savings plans called *annuities*. These are similar to mutual funds and resemble IRA accounts in that the *earnings* from the investments in the account are not taxed until they are withdrawn. However, *contributions* to deferred annuities are *not* tax deductible. You can, however, contribute as much as you want each year.

Deferred annuities will pay you a certain amount monthly once you retire—how much depends on how much you have contributed over the years and how well the investments have done.

The financial soundness of the insurance company is a critical factor here. Some large insurance companies have been experiencing difficulties in the last few years. Investigate carefully before you buy. You might do better setting up a retirement account on your own with the help of a financial consultant.

Extended-Care Insurance

One important kind of insurance that is often over-looked is extended-care insurance. This will pay for care for a long-term disability such as Alzheimer's disease or rehabilitation from an accident or stroke. Many health insurance plans pay only for intensive hospital care and a minimum of rehabilitation. But continued rehabilitation or quality nursing home care is extremely expensive. Long-term care for many couples, therefore, has meant the loss of all their assets.

Extended-care insurance is not expensive if you start at age 40. But even though the expense is greater later on, it is still a vital thing to have. There is quite a bit of difference between policies. Some are very expensive but limited in their coverage (some provide for home care, for example, while others do not). You need to compare policies very carefully.

To learn more before you buy, contact the American Association of Retired Persons (AARP), 1909 K Street NW, Washington, DC 20049, (202) 434-2277. Ask for their two booklets *Making Wise Decisions on Long-Term Care* and *Before You Buy: A Guide to Long-Term Care Insurance.*

PLANNING—AND A LITTLE CAUTION

No matter what your age, there are various things you can begin right now to make your wishes come true. In the preceding chapter, we dealt with how to set up various portfolios so that they will grow over time, and we discussed how one person might achieve an early retirement. The number of things to consider, however—for an early or later retirement—go beyond the scope of this

book. For further information, I believe you will find the
material listed in the Resources very helpful.

Retirement—early or late—should be a time of fulfillment. Getting your finances squared away can leave
you more time to do the things that really interest you.

One last word. Older, retired people are often seen as
easy marks by con artists or unscrupulous advisers. You
have probably read stories about crooks who convinced a
group of retirees to put their money in a "surefire investment"—and then disappeared with the money. In a recent
version, someone persuaded a number of people that his
company could convert the black sand of a Caribbean
island into gold!

Sometimes, the villain may not even be dishonest,
but rather an incompetent adviser or manager. This is
one reason you are reading this book: to be able to recognize such people. If you are an older retiree, caution is
even more important, because you may not be able to
earn more to replace the losses. You will find information
on how to choose a good investment adviser or financial
manager in Chapter 9.

Resources

The Retirement Letter, Peter Dickinson, editor, with Philip
Springer. Philips Publishing. (800) 777-5005. Monthly. $49.95/
year. This is the newsletter written specifically for those in
retirement or actively planning for it. Dickinson has also writ-

**Retirement—early or late—should be a time of
fulfillment. Getting your finances squared
away can leave you more time to do the things
that really interest you.**

ten some useful books and pamphlets, some of which you get as subscription bonuses. Philips offers a money-back guarantee, so you can take out a subscription and see whether you find the newsletter useful.

The Wall Street Journal Guide to Planning Your Financial Future: The Easy-to Read Guide to Planning for Retirement, by Kenneth M. Morris, Alan M. Siegel, and Virginia B. Morris. Light Bulb Press, 1998 (the Wall Street Journal Guides are usually updated every year or two). $15.95 (paperback). This guide comes complete with lots of pictures and diagrams. It is easy to read, as the title suggests, and will give you more details about the various types of retirement plans—IRAs, Keoughs, SEP IRAs, and 401(K) plans—as well as general advice on retirement. It also covers such topics as wills, trusts, estate taxes, health insurance, and long-term care high-risk investing.

Your Money or Your Life, recommended in Resources, Chapter 3, contains excellent information on how to retire early. Even if you retire later, if you would like to know how to live well on a low income, this is your book.

How to join the American Association of Individual Investors (AAII) is described in Resources, Chapter 1. Not only does the AAII monthly journal run useful articles on retirement, the group organizes seminars covering such topics as estate planning and investment strategies for retirement. Joining is also a good way of contacting other investors. If you plan to be an active investor, you may want to join an investment club.

Many companies still have pension funds that employees depend on for their retirement. But just because your company has hired professional managers to invest your pension fund doesn't necessarily mean they are doing a good job. There are other dangers too: occasionally, when corporations are taken over by new owners, the pension fund is raided to procure extra cash. Know your rights and be aware what goes on with your pension! The Pension Rights Center is a private watchdog organization that keeps tabs on pension funds. Contact them if you believe your pension is in danger. 918 16th Street NW, Suite 704, Washington, DC 20006-2902. (202) 296-3776.

The Pension Rights Center has published a handbook called, *Protecting Your Pension Money: A Pension Investment Handbook*, which is available for free from the U.S. Department of Labor: (800) 998-7542. The Labor Department will also direct you to a regional information center, if you think your pension might be in trouble.

CHAPTER 18

GOING FURTHER
WITH STOCKS

B efore you take the plunge and begin investing in individual stocks, there are a few more things that you need to know. We're going to cover them in this chapter.

PREFERRED STOCKS

If you consult the stock listings in the financial pages, you will occasionally see two listings for a stock; the second will have a "pf" after it. (Occasionally a company will show a list of "pf" stocks at varying rates of interest.) These are so-called "preferred stocks" (in contrast to the regular "common" stocks), so named because the dividends are given preference, or priority, over common-stock dividends. In other words, if a company is having a bad year, it must reduce its dividend on its common stock before it does so on the preferred.

This sounds good, until you realize that, like bonds, preferred stock has a fixed dividend payment. Common stock dividends fluctuate according to the fortunes of the company. With preferred stock, however, you will get a certain amount of income each year. If the stock sells for $50 a share and the dividend is set at 8%, you will get $4 per share—no more, no less.

This means the price of the preferred stock will stay pretty much the same, unless overall interest rates change. The reason for buying preferred stocks, then, is not that you think they will increase in value, but that you want a steady income and a higher dividend than most common stocks provide.

As you look through the "pf" listings, you will see some with spectacular dividends: 15%, 18%, and more (normal return from preferreds is 3% to 6%). These are usually companies in trouble. The investment community believes there is a good chance the company will default on its payments to the preferred stockholders, so the price of these shares has gone down (as the share price goes down, the percentage of return to a buyer goes up—*if* the company continues to pay the dividend).

So this is yet another instance where you would have to decide how speculative you want to be. Remember that even though owners of the preferreds will be paid before holders of common stock, they come after the bondholders.

One more thing about preferreds: Most of them are "callable"; that is, the company can tell you at any time to turn in your shares at a set price. This price is something to be aware of should you buy this kind of stock—especially if it is lower than the market price of the stock.

In my opinion, there are safer ways for the new investor to get a steady income and better ways of speculating. An exception are the *convertible preferred stocks*. These are preferred shares that you can convert into shares of common stock in the same company at any time. Because of this factor, these "convertibles" go up and down with the market price of the common stock. The dividend rates are not as good as those for straight preferreds, but substantially better than for common stock.

Like convertible bonds, convertible preferreds are a good way of getting substantial dividends, but also investing for growth.

ODD LOTS

Brokers like to trade stock in denominations of 100 shares. If you buy less than 100 shares of an equity, you will be buying what is called an *odd lot*. This should not dissuade you from buying, say, 10 shares of IBM at $120 a share, if it looks like a good buy (100 shares would cost $12,000—too much for some people).

But if you can afford it, it's generally better to buy 100, 200, or 500 shares at a time, rather than 162 or 305 shares. This makes it easier for you to figure the value of your holding, as well as easier for the brokers to make a trade. Two hundred shares of a $36 stock, for example, is simply $2 \times 36 = 72$, plus a couple of zeros, or $7,200.

STOCK PRICES

The price range of stocks over about $10 a share is not necessarily related to the underlying value of its company. IBM at $180 a share is not worth three times as

> With preferred stock, however, you will get a certain amount of income each year.

much as Ford at $60 a share. . For reasons of their own, different companies prefer to have their stock trading in a certain price range. IBM has been an expensive stock for a long time.

If the price of a company's shares increases over a period of time, perhaps doubling in value, often the company will engineer a stock split.

STOCK SPLITS

When a company splits its stock, it will ask you to send in your shares; it will then send you twice as many shares in return, each worth half as much. General Electric split its stock several years ago when it was selling for about $120 a share. If you had owned 100 shares, you would have traded them in and received 200 shares, each worth $60.

A stock split is generally welcomed by shareholders. They see it as an indication that the company is doing well, and the hope is that the lower price will attract more buyers, thereby sending the stock up again. Splits of 3 for 1, 4 for 1, or higher are not unknown, though not as

> The important thing to remember with both kind of stock splits is that the dollar value of your holdings will not change—only the number of shares you hold.

common as the standard 2 for 1. Occasionally, a small company wanting to increase the dollar amount of its shares, will engineer a reverse split, giving one share for two at double the value. If the stock is selling for pennies, they may do a reverse split of one for five shares or even one for ten.

The important thing to remember with both kind of stock splits is that the dollar value of your holdings will not change—only the number of shares you hold. But it is also true that a two-for-one stock split is generally a good sign; stocks often rise after a split. Conversely, a reverse split can often bring about a loss in dollar value. For example a small company whose stock is selling for 10 cents a share might engineer a one for ten reverse split, raising the stock price to $1.00 a share. A month later, however, the price has gone down to 50 cents; stories like this are all too common.

EX-DIVIDEND

As you read through the stock tables, you will occasionally see an "x" in front of a stock. This means the stock is about to issue a dividend. About a week before the dividend is issued, the stock, in market lingo, "goes ex-dividend." If you buy the stock during this time, you will not receive the dividend. You will pay less per share, however; the stock price will be lowered during that week by the amount of the dividend. If the dividend were a dollar per share, the stock price would be lowered by a dollar.

LIMIT ORDERS

In Chapter 5 we described how to buy and sell stocks, using what is called a *market order.* To buy or sell "at the market" means you are simply asking your broker to get you the best possible price.

You can, however, specify the price at which you want to buy. "I want to buy a hundred shares of AT&T at no more than eighty dollars a share" is what you would tell your broker. This is called a *limit order* and you can make it just for the day (a "day order"), or specify that it is "good till canceled" (GTC). If you make it GTC, the order will stand unless you cancel it; the broker will buy the 100 shares as soon as the stock goes down to $80 or less.

Similarly, you can sell stock with a "limit order to sell." For example, you might tell your broker you don't want to sell until AT&T reaches at least $90 a share.

STOP ORDERS

Say you succeed in buying AT&T for $80 a share. You chose well, because over the next few months the stock climbs to $95 a share. You hope it will go higher, but at the same time, you don't want to lose what profit you have. You're a busy person and don't have the luxury of keeping track of the hour-by-hour changes in the stock. So you tell your broker to sell your AT&T stock if it goes down to $90.

This is called a *stop order* (short for "stop-loss order"—you are stopping any possible loss). Like the limit orders, it can be a day order or good till canceled. With your stop order at $90, you have locked in a profit of $10 a share, should the stock start to go down from $95. If the price should continue to rise—say, to $105—you should also raise the stop price, in this case, to $100. It's important to know that a stop order is not always a sure thing. If a stock suddenly plummets, your broker may not be able to sell at your specified price, and you will be sold out at a lower price.

SELLING SHORT

Suppose you have it on good authority that Consolidated Bobsleds is about to go downhill fast. What you want to do is sell it, of course, but the trouble is that you don't *own* any Bobsleds stock. Difficulties like selling something you don't own, however, have never hampered people in the Wonderful World of Investment.

All you have to do is call your broker and say that you want to "sell short" Consolidated Bobsleds stock (or, simply, to "short" it). The broker then "borrows" the stock from someone who owns it and sells it to a buyer at the market price. You are obligated to buy it back sometime in the future; this is called "covering your short position." The broker will then "return" the stock to the lender. (You don't have to understand these machinations—all you need to know is that you make money if the stock goes down and lose if it goes up.)

If the stock goes down, you can buy it back at the lower price and keep the difference. If it goes up, then so do you—up the creek! At some point—it's your decision when—you will have to buy back the stock and take a loss.

Selling short is more complex than buying stocks. You have to have a margin account with your broker, for one thing (see the next section). You have to pay the stock dividend to the lender of the stock, and your broker will hold onto the money from the short sale and charge you interest on it.

MARGIN ACCOUNTS

Now wait, all you people who believe you can't understand anything involving arithmetic, don't space out! I have tested this chapter on people who started spacing out in math class in third grade, and they gave it a thumbs up. So hang in there!

You may not be aware that if you own $10,000 worth of stock, you can purchase $10,000 more for free. Well, not exactly for free; the brokerage will charge you interest on the $10,000 you borrow. Low interest, to be sure—these days it is around 7.5%—but interest nonetheless.

When you open an account, the broker will ask you whether you want a *margin account*. "Margin" in this case simply means collateral; the broker will hold your shares of stock as collateral for a loan. ("Collateral" is something of value held by a lender in case you can't pay back your loan. Your house, for example, is collateral for your mortgage loan.)

If you have a margin account, you can use your stock as collateral for a loan to buy more stocks or bonds, up to double the amount you own—in this case, $10,000 more. This is called "buying on margin."

It's pretty clear that if you use your margin, or collateral, to buy more stocks, they had better increase in value more than 7.5% over the course of a year (you will have the benefit of any dividends, too, of course, to offset the interest charges). If their price stays the same or goes down, you are out the 7.5% interest on whatever you borrowed—$750 in this case, if you borrowed the full $10,000.

Buying on Margin: An Example

Suppose you own $10,000 worth of General Electric stock and have $2,000 cash in your margin account. You use the stock as collateral to buy shares worth $10,000 more— still GE, for simplicity's sake (the security bought on margin does not have to be in the same company). But GE has a so-so year, and the stock is selling for the same price a year later. You still own $20,000 worth of stock, but you are out $750—the interest on the $10,000 you borrowed from the broker. It has been deducted in increments each month from the $2,000 cash in your account.

The next year, you think things look better for GE; it is expanding its markets in Eastern Europe and the prospects seem promising. So you hold on to your "margined stock" (the $10,000 worth you bought with the borrowed money), and yes, indeed, the stock does go up very nicely—25% by the end of the year. So . . . your original $10,000 is now worth $12,500 and your $10,000 of margined stock is also worth $12,500, making a total of $25,000 worth of stock.

At this point, you decide to sell the whole shebang, and $25,000 is credited to your account. From this is deducted the original $10,000 loan, leaving $15,000. In addition, you have paid a total of $1,500 interest on the loan, $750 each year. This leaves $13,500. You have made a $3,500 profit in two years.

It's interesting to compare this $3,500 with how much you would have made with only the original $10,000 worth of stock. No margin loan—no interest costs. A 25% increase in value would have left you with $12,500, or $2,500 in profits, minus commissions—not that much less than the $3,500, but with less risk.

What these figures say is that you have to believe a stock is going to go up by at least 15% to 20% a year to justify the added risk of buying on margin.

One more note: A stock you can borrow against is called a *marginable stock*. To be marginable, a stock must be selling for at least $5 a share (according to present rules) and be traded on a major U.S. exchange. Most brokers also allow mutual funds to be used as margin. If you own marginable securities, it is possible to use them as collateral to buy nonmarginable stocks under $5, but only half as much. For example, if you owned $10,000 worth of mutual funds, you could borrow $5,000 to buy low-priced stocks.

Margin Calls

So buying on margin is chancy—chancy enough for the new investor to avoid. The value of a stock has to increase quite sharply to make it worthwhile. Your opportunities for a greater profit increase, but should the stock take a real dive, your losses will double. In short, the risk-reward ratio has moved up sharply.

And there is one more thing: Suppose the stock you bought for $20,000, with a $10,000 margin loan, should go down by $7,200 to a new total value of $12,800. The broker is unhappy about this because he lent you $10,000 with your $10,000 worth of stock as margin, or collateral. Now, however, the $10,000 collateral you started out with only amounts to $2,800 ($10,000 minus $7,200). Your broker wants you to bring your collateral up to 50% of the *new* value of the stock, that is to 50% of $12,800, or $6,400. This means a *margin call*, where the broker tells you to send in additional money. In this case, you still

Experienced investors will usually choose to sell, even though the price is down. If the stock has dropped sharply, they feel they don't want to throw good money after bad.

have $2,800 as margin; to raise this to $6,400, you will need to send in $3,600.

Brokerage firms can set their own margin levels, but this level cannot be more than 75%. Most firms set their levels at 65% to 70%. This means you will get a margin call if the value of your stock falls to less than 65% or 70% of its original value.

If this happens, you can now do one of two things: You can pony up the needed $3,600, or you can sell enough of the stock to cover the shortfall. Experienced investors will usually choose to sell, even though the price is down. If the stock has dropped sharply, they feel they don't want to throw good money after bad. Only if they are certain that a rise is imminent will they put up more money.

If you fail to do anything, the brokerage will act for you by selling twice the amount of stock necessary to cover the margin shortfall.

1929

Of course, if the stock price continues its downward spiral, you will get another margin call, because your collateral will have again decreased. A bad situation.

As a matter of fact, this downward spiral is what compounded the disaster of the 1929 crash. In those days, you needed only $10,000 worth of stock to borrow $90,000 more. As you can guess, quite a few people did just this—they borrowed the limit. If they had only $1,000, they borrowed $9,000; if they had a million dollars, well, they borrowed 9 million more!

A $100,000 portfolio with a $10,000 cash outlay looks pretty good—as long as the stocks continue to go up. When they go down, however, watch out! If the value of the stocks falls to $80,000, you have a situation where the total value is less than the $90,000 that was borrowed—$10,000 less, to be exact. So that $10,000 would be the amount of the margin call.

Because so many shareholders had borrowed up to the limit, they had no way of meeting the margin calls with cash. They had no choice, therefore, but to sell some of their stock. Everyone selling their stock at once tended to depress prices even further, leading to *further* devaluation of the stocks—and more margin calls! A deadly spiral. It is easy to see why the Federal Reserve Board now sets the amount you can borrow at a much lower level. (Margin requirements change from time to time. They have been at their present levels for more than a decade.)

Modern Margin Calls: Watch Out!

In addition to borrowing on margin to purchase stocks and bonds, you can also use your securities as collateral for a personal loan. For these personal loans you can borrow up to half the value of your portfolio. If you own $10,000 worth of stocks (or bonds), you can borrow $5,000.

The larger brokerages make it very easy to write checks or use Visa cards as a loan against your balance—too easy, if you're not careful. Brokerage Visa cards are different from the charge cards you are accustomed to. They are called *debit cards*. If you have a cash balance in your account, your brokerage Visa purchase will be charged against that balance—*it will not be a loan*. Only when you have no cash in your account are your card charges—and the checks you write—lent against the collateral of the securities in your account.

A loan with such low interest can be very seductive, especially since you need *make no payments*. The 7.5% interest is automatically deducted each month from the cash in your account—or added to the amount owing, if there is no cash (the actual interest charged may vary, depending on the prevailing interest rates).

Another difference from regular bank loans is that if you should sell some stock, the resulting cash will immediately go first to pay off any outstanding margin loan.

The main thing to watch for here is borrowing too much, because, just as in the case of buying stocks on margin, you can get a margin call for this kind of loan, too. Suppose you owned $10,000 worth of securities, and that you borrowed your limit, in this case half the $10,000, or $5,000. Now, if the value of the stock goes down to $7,000, you will get a margin call asking for $1,500. With a collateral of only $7,000, your borrowing limit has decreased to half this $7,000, or $3,500. You are being asked to come up with the difference between the $5,000 you borrowed and your new $3,500 limit. This can be a very nasty shock if you're not prepared for it.

To prevent this kind of upset, if you do borrow, a good move would be to set your borrowing limit at half your actual limit. In this case, with $10,000 worth of stock, that would be $2,500. This allows quite a bit of leeway and should prevent margin calls in all except truly disastrous dives by your stocks or bonds.

Resources

National Association of Investors Corporation. P.O. Box 220, Royal Oak, MI 48068. (810) 583-6242. <www.better-investing.org>. Membership: $39/year. Includes subscription to *Better Investing* magazine and a manual: *Starting and Running a Profitable Investment Club*.

Some 26,000 investment clubs are members of the NAIC. If you are interested in getting together with other folks and pooling your money and investment savvy, this is a good place to start. Even if you're not interested in joining a club, the organization's magazine is one of the best I've seen for new investors. It even runs a monthly "Beginner's Corner." The clubs and the magazine are mainly for investors in individual stocks.

CHAPTER 19

BUYING METHODS

In 1973, an economist named Burton Malkiel planted a bomb on Wall Street. No, not a terrorist bomb, but something much worse, as far as the stockbrokers and professional money managers were concerned. The bomb was a book titled *A Random Walk Down Wall Street.*

According to the Random Walk theory, a portfolio of stocks picked at random has just as much chance of success as one selected by most stockbrokers. In other words, a group of chimpanzees throwing darts at the *Wall Street Journal* would hit as many winners as most professional advisers (or individual investors).

The reason is what Malkiel terms the "efficient market." The idea is that any information about a company will be immediately picked up by the market, causing the stock price to rise or fall too soon for most investors to profit from the news.

Malkiel has since revised and updated his book, but he has changed few of his assertions. During the 1970s

Yes, Ma'am, we have our latest stock picks right here.

and 1980s, according to Malkiel, the stock market as a whole, as measured by the S&P 500 Index, outperformed two-thirds of the managers of large institutional funds.

The implications of these figures for the individual investor are quite dramatic. They say that in selecting winning stocks, in the majority of cases, you are better off investing in a stock index fund that covers the overall market than in giving your money to a manager or listening to a stockbroker's recommendations. And the same may be true, according to Malkiel, of trying to pick stocks on your own.

The professionals might give you other useful advice, of course—the chimps won't know about your tax situation or the balance in your portfolio. Our model portfolio, for example, takes into consideration more than just increase in value in the stock market—balance, diversification, and safety of principal are weighed. The *Random Walk* theory deals only with stocks that go up in value.

There are, however, exceptions to the *Random Walk* theory—even Professor Malkiel admits this. The advisers who write the books and newsletters that I recommend in this book, for example, beat the averages more often than not—some of them dramatically. There are ways to optimize your chances of coming out ahead.

The buying methods presented in this chapter are among those that have helped investors to beat the averages. These are the kinds of techniques you can use in setting up and working with your portfolio. We'll start out with the famous method of dollar-cost averaging.

DOLLAR-COST AVERAGING

What it all comes down to, of course, is "buy low, sell high." Buying methods are simply various ways of doing this—or trying to. The question is, how do you tell when the highs and lows occur? The first method—dollar-cost averaging—doesn't even try to guess. But it very neatly has you buying more shares at low prices, fewer at the highs.

What you do is invest a given amount each month, say $500, in a security or mutual fund. Over a period of a year, on the 20th of each month the price of shares in a mutual fund might vary like this:

Jan	Feb	Mar	Apr	May	Jun	Jul	Aug	Sep	Oct	Nov	Dec
$12	14	15	14	12	12	10	8	9	8	10	12
41	37	33	37	41	41	50	62	55	62	50	41

The figure below the price per share is the number of shares purchased by $500 (rounded off). Each month, your $500 is divided by whatever the price per share is at the time; the resulting figure is the number of shares you purchased. Over the year, you invested $6,000 ($500 × 12 months), and bought 550 shares of the fund. Notice that you bought more shares in months when the price was down, fewer when the price was up.

Notice also that the fund returned to its original price of $12 a share on December 20. If you had taken the $6,000 and invested it all in January, you would have bought 500 shares of the fund ($6,000 ÷ $12 = 500 shares). By December, after some ups and downs, you would be back exactly where you started: you would own 500 shares at $12 a share = $6,000.

But, using the magic of dollar-cost averaging, by December you would own 550 shares, worth $6,600 (550 × $12 = $6,600), even though you invested the same $6,000. This happy difference is the result of buying more shares when the price was down, fewer when it was up.

Dollar-cost averaging is an excellent way of creating a portfolio if you have only monthly income to invest. As we discussed in Chapter 16, putting in a small amount each month will eventually result in a large amount. We have chosen a time period of a month, but you could, of course, put money in every week or two weeks, or every quarter—whatever is most convenient for you.

Even if you have a lump sum to invest, you may want to do it using dollar-cost averaging—especially if the stock market has been acting like a person on a trampoline. By investing each month over a year, you will avoid putting all your money in at the top of the market, and have a better chance of coming out ahead, as in the example above.

Most brokers make it easy to dollar-cost average. As we mentioned in Chapter 6, brokers have a number of mutual funds that you can buy with no commissions. After the initial investment, you can add as little as $50 a month, commission free.

You will do even better if you make your dollar-cost averaging part of an individual retirement account (IRA), so that your investments grow without a tax bite. The advantages of IRAs are explained in Chapter 17. Most funds allow smaller initial investments and smaller monthly additions for IRA accounts.

The final postscript is that with stock funds, you will do best over the long run by putting in your monthly investment on or about the 20th of the month. The large institutions tend to do their buying around the early part of the month, driving prices up. Around the 20th is when much of the selling occurs, so prices are driven down. This also means that the first two or three days of the month are good days to *sell*, statistically speaking.

Though this will vary from month to month according to market direction, statistically speaking, prices will be marginally lower during the days around the 20th. A small thing, but one that will add up over the years.

Fundamental Analysis

Fundamental analysis evaluates the stock of a company starting with the company's financial statements. You want to know the general financial health of the company as well as its position in its industry, and its ability to cope with ups and downs in the economy. A detailed description of all the methods used in fundamental analysis is beyond our scope here. For active investors, the way to pick the best companies by doing your own fundamental analysis is described thoroughly in the two books listed in Resources.

Technical Analysis

Technical analysts attempt to predict the direction of a stock by studying what is actually happening to it in the market. Forget the financial statements. Are

people actually *buying the stock*? If so, is the daily volume of stock trading going up? What does the graph
of the stock's price over the last year look like? Are
the large institutions buying the stock? In his book
cited below, William O'Neil goes into the most important technical factors in choosing a stock.

Technical analysis can also be performed on the
entire stock market, using a variety of indicators: the
direction of the market, the volume of stocks traded,
the volume of short selling, whether the mutual funds
are buying or selling, what the majority of investment
advisers are saying, etc., etc.

The technical analysts are trying to "time" the
stock market—to ascertain the exact time the market
is going to move, and in what direction. (For more on
market timing, see Chapter 24.)

LOW-PRICED STOCKS

When we speak of low-priced stocks, we are discussing
small companies with good prospects; we are not including larger corporations whose stocks have fallen because
of bad times or bankruptcy. For example, in January
1991, after the international airline, Pan Am, filed for
bankruptcy, you could have bought its stock for $\frac{3}{8}$ (37.5
cents) a share. Buying companies in dire straits, however,

**Unless you have specific knowledge about a
small company, it's generally wise to stick to
those stocks listed on the major stock markets.**

is an entirely different—and risky—buying method (Pan Am eventually went out of business).

During most of this century, stocks of small companies, as a whole, have done significantly better than those of large companies. During the 1990s, returns from the larger companies were greater, but the small companies may reassert themselves in the coming decade. In any case, individual small companies, when carefully chosen, can bring excellent growth to a portfolio.

Unless you have specific knowledge about a small company, it's generally wise to stick to those stocks listed on the major stock markets. As we discussed in Chapter 8, the unlisted stocks in the over-the-counter market are too volatile and uncertain for the new investor's portfolio.

Within those restrictions, though, low-priced, small-company stocks can be an excellent addition to a portfolio. Investors who are just starting out can buy mutual funds specializing in small companies, as recommended in Chapter 14. As you gain experience, however, you may want to buy individual issues. This is, after all, where the Microsofts and Adobe Systems of tomorrow are to be found.

One attractive feature of the low-priced issues is that when they go up in price, the percentage gain is usually greater than for the higher-priced stocks. For example, if you buy a stock in a company for $\frac{3}{4}$ a share (75 cents a share) and it goes up $\frac{3}{4}$ of a point to $1\frac{1}{2}$ ($1.50 a share), you have doubled your money. Yes, it could also go down and you could be a large percentage loser on paper, but you don't have to sell. If you have done your research and the company is a good one, there is a good chance it will go up again.

Another attraction of low-priced issues for the adventurous investor is that it's possible to buy a large number of shares. For an investment of $1,250, plus commission, you could buy 1,000 shares of a company's stock selling at $1\frac{1}{4}$ ($1.25 a share). If this company should hit the big time and the stock go to $10 a share or higher, your 1,000 shares will suddenly look like gold.

It is true that occasionally even the best research doesn't do the job, or a company encounters unexpectedly difficult times. There is risk here—these are small companies, and a couple of bad years can be disastrous.

Most investors are well aware of these dangers, so the stocks tend to be traded much more lightly than those of the big companies. When the demand is low, the price of the stock will stay down. If the company begins to do well, however, you have a situation where investors are bidding for a relatively small number of shares. This can drive the price up quite dramatically.

If a small company catches your eye in a newsletter or elsewhere, you can do your own analysis of the company's fundamentals. Call up the management, ask for recent quarterly reports, and visit their web site. Then, while you're reading the information about the company, follow the price of its stock for a while in order to get a feel for the company and its prospects.

This can be fun as well as profitable. Investing in a small company where you have spoken with the managers and learned about its history and field of operations makes for a stronger involvement in your investment than with a large, impersonal corporation. If you are acquainted with the type of business carried out by the company, perhaps you will make suggestions to the management. This is the way investment used to be carried out. Investors in the 17th and 18th centuries usually involved themselves intimately in the companies they bought into.

Research and diversification will help you tilt the odds in your favor when investing in small companies. Diversification becomes even more important with riskier investments. If you invest in small-company stocks, it's good to own at least a half dozen. This prepares you for an occasional loser in your portfolio.

The third way of limiting your risk is simply to put only 10% to 20% of your portfolio into low-priced issues. That way, the risk-reward thermometer of your portfolio

> While everyone else is following the high fliers—investing in the bright, successful companies that have captured the public's attention—the contrarian is off in a little room studying the companies that have been left behind.

will stay in a comfortable range, but you will have a good chance of seeing some real winners emerge, given a reasonable economic climate.

To further increase your chances of success, try the three small-company newsletters listed in Resources. These will give you a running head start in the field of low-priced stocks.

CONTRARIANISM

Sounds like a political faction, doesn't it? Or, perhaps, the stance taken by your teenager in your last discussion. It's actually the method used by many of the sharpest investors to buy low and sell high. This is one way the less-experienced investor can successfully imitate the pros.

What it means is just what it sounds like: being contrary. While everyone else is following the high fliers—investing in the bright, successful companies that have captured the public's attention—the contrarian is off in a little room studying the companies that have been left behind.

This studious contrarian is looking for the success stories of the future: companies with great balance sheets, a large percentage of the market in their field, good management, or perhaps an exciting but unpublicized product.

These companies either have not yet been discovered by the investment community, are currently out of favor because of a bad year or two, or have simply been eclipsed by the high fliers. Their stock, then, is currently trading at a low price relative to earnings or projected future earnings.

Even entire market groups can be food for contrarian diets. Those investors smart enough to buy small-company funds in the autumn of 1990 saw their investments go up by 30% to 50% in six months. These funds had performed poorly relative to blue chips for several years, but some contrarians realized that the small companies were undervalued—and underpriced.

Usually, however, being a contrarian involves buying stocks of individual companies. If you decide to be an active manager of your portfolio, this is one excellent method of picking potential winners.

The good newsletters often recommend stocks for contrarians. One newsletter that specializes in small companies with good prospects is listed in Resources. You can also find such companies on your own by doing the kind of fundamental analysis explained in the recommended books.

Perhaps the most difficult part of contrarian investing is bringing yourself to invest in a currently unpopular stock. We are social animals, often given to believing that the safest course to follow is that of the herd. If you invest in a popular issue and it takes a dive, you will, at least, have a lot of company. If you're wrong with your contrarian investments, you'll be wrong alone. It can seem like a risky business.

Things to Watch For: Overmanaging

Overmanaging a portfolio can cause as much trouble as not giving it enough attention. "Has the stock gone up one point? Perhaps we should sell now before it goes down!" This kind of excessive concern can lead you to sell prematurely.

Appreciation in a portfolio is generally something that happens over a period of years. The more volatile, smaller companies may require more attention. But if you choose quality investments, you are usually expecting them to appreciate over the long term.

Being a successful investor often involves being aware of your internal responses and correcting for them. In this case, you might need to be aware of your tendency to overreact.

This perception of risk is usually a false one, however. Contrarian investors—at least the ones who really do their homework—have traditionally been among the most successful in the investment community. The courage it takes to listen to a different drummer is, more often than not, rewarded.

Resources

Newsletters

U.S. Investment Report. Quickel International Corporation. (215) 862-1313. Bi-monthly. $275/year.

This is one of my favorite newsletters. Editor Stephen Quickel sets an elegant tone, starting off each report with "Dear Ladies and Gentlemen," and continuing with an astute view of the overall market followed by updates of the recommended companies.

This is one of the few newsletters recommending large and mid-size companies whose record equals that of the best small company newsletters. The Conservative Growth Portfolio, started on January 1, 1987 with $100,000, reached a total of $3,600,000 in 1999 (with all dividends and profits from stock sales reinvested). . The Growth Leaders Portfolio, starting at the same time with the same amount, topped $18,000,000 in 1999. This amazing performance has been helped, to be sure, by the strong stock market starting in 1995, but the stocks in both portfolios always manage to substantially outperform the stock indexes, even in bad years. This is done partly by the judicious use of stop orders— gains are protected while big losses are prevented.

Once you are ready to begin trading individual stocks in a serious manner, this is the letter you should subscribe to.

The Acker Letter, 2718 E. 63rd Street, Brooklyn, NY 11234-6814. Published ten to fourteen times per year. $150/year, $40 trial.

The Acker Letter is another of my favorites. Bob Acker puts it out himself, with his wife as business and production manager. There is a kind of capitalist class struggle going on in this newsletter: the individual investor against the "big boys"—the large investors who ignore or look down on the small companies recommended by Acker. With each stock recommendation that succeeds, Acker triumphantly headlines: "Score one for the Good Guys and Gals!"

The "Good Guy" subscribers who buy stock in the companies recommended in the newsletter have done very well over the last few years. Acker is not only a small-company specialist but a contrarian. These are companies with a special product that have been overlooked by most investors, or basically sound firms whose stock has been driven down by a couple of bad years.

The Bowser Report, P.O. Box 6278, Newport News, VA 23606. (757) 877-5979. MiniStocks@aol.com. Monthly. $48/year. If you are interested in small-cap stocks, this is the newsletter you want. *The Bowser Report* is one of the oldest and most successful small company newsletters; it recommends only stocks under $3.00 a share. Not only do you get the letter every month with buy recommendations and articles, you get a very useful booklet on the best ways to buy low-priced stocks. For an additional $2.50, you can buy *Bowser's Notebook,* a glossary of stock market terms and articles geared to the new investor.

Small company stocks have been among the most profitable investments of this century.

The Stewart Report, P.O. Box 3715, Dana Point, CA 92629-8715. (800) 276-6786. <www.stewartreport.com>. There are several things to like about *The Stewart Report.* First, you don't get snowed under with recommendations—you get just a few each year, but each company is researched in depth. Second, you get lots of follow-up on each stock. David Stewart has a phone hotline that he updates either every week or every other week. And, third, I've discovered that these stocks tend to go up, sometimes dramatically. The companies recommended are small, but, perhaps, not for long.

Books

How to Make Money in Stocks, by William J. O'Neil. McGraw-Hill, 1994. $10.95 (paperback). O'Neil is the founder of *Investor's Business Daily* newspaper and a well-known figure in the investment world. This book lays out his methods for choosing stocks in a clear, readable manner. In the process, he gives pointers to new investors and tells stories about his own experience as an investor. O'Neil is a technical analyst, as contrasted with Peter Lynch, who analyzes the fundamentals of a company. A good read for the serious, hands-on investor.

One Up on Wall Street, by Peter Lynch. Penguin, 1990. $13.95 (paperback). Lynch was the manager of the immensely successful Fidelity Magellan Fund, one of the equity mutual funds that consistently beat the market during the 1980s. He advocates investing in areas where you have special knowledge—the subtitle of the book is "How to Use What You Already Know to Make Money in the Market." You will also learn what he looks for in the companies he investigates. This book reads easily—very good for the new investor.

The First Book of Small Stock Investing, by Samuel Case. Prima Publishing, 1998. $12.95 (paperback). Small company stocks have been among the most profitable investments of this century. This book tells you how to get on board: how to research and choose the best small companies, how to set up a portfolio of inexpensive stocks, and how to accomplish all this with a minimum amount of risk.

CHAPTER 20

BAD TIMES

IRAQ INVADES KUWAIT! . . . MIDDLE EAST IN TURMOIL . . . OIL PRICES SOAR! . . . DOW LOSES 300 POINTS.

Who could forget these headlines in early August 1990? Investors are not likely to. The Dow Jones Industrial Average, which had been as high as 3,000 in July, lost 20% of its value in a matter of weeks. And this was just the average loss of the blue chip stocks; many of the smaller, over-the-counter stocks went down by 30%, 40%, or 50%. Many analysts had felt that the market was due for a "correction" (a move against the upward trend), but the prospects of war and high oil prices turned the correction into a rout.

A downturn in the stock market does not necessarily mean that the economy will fall into a recession, but in this case, a number of factors, including the stock market, did bring about a recession. Businesses began to cut back, consumers slowed their spending, and many workers suddenly found themselves without a job. Real estate prices began to turn down in most areas, to the dismay of homeowners and speculators alike. Younger property owners were especially distressed; for those who had started buying in the mid-1970s, it had seemed as if real estate went in only one direction: up!

What is the individual investor to do in a case like this? Many stockholders sold at a loss and got out of the market entirely. This was particularly hard on the investors who had watched stocks climb during the bull market earlier in the year. They had decided in June or July that they should get on board, even at inflated prices, lest they be left behind altogether. So they ended up doing what investors are always warned against— that is, buying at the highs and selling at the lows.

But what were the alternatives? Some analysts were talking about a possible 50% drop in the market and were even raising the specter of the crash of 1929. Wouldn't it be better to preserve what capital was left and get out?

This, as you might guess, is a source of much disagreement among investment advisers. Some will tell you to sell and then buy again when the market reaches its lows. Others will tell you to grit your teeth and hold on; don't sell while prices are declining.

"HARD TIMES, COME AGIN NO MORE . . ."

Before we get into practical measures to deal with economic downturns, let's look at how bad times have manifested themselves since the Second World War.

The fear of another 1929-type crash and subsequent depression has colored the thinking of individual and professional investors for 60 years. Perhaps this fear goes back even further in the common memory. Throughout the nineteenth century and into the twentieth, devastating boom-and-bust cycles were commonplace.

Guns and Money

War, despite persistent beliefs to the contrary, is not good for capitalist economies. It disrupts the flow of goods, upsets energy supplies, and directs money and manufacturing away from consumer goods into weapons.

During the nineteenth century, there was more reason for Karl Marx and others to believe that increased government spending on war, or preparation for war, had stimulating economic effects. Nowadays, however, there is already so much government spending that the main effect of increased outlays for defense is simply to add to the national debt.

The enormous government debt in this country is almost entirely related to the massive cost of our defense establishment, which was set up to fight the Cold War. The enormous yearly interest on this debt coupled with ongoing military expenditures makes it extremely difficult to pay down this debt, even in good times. A chief cause for the collapse of the Soviet Union was its economy's inability to carry the burden of its enormous military establishment.

Stock investors all over the world get very nervous when there is a chance of an armed conflict involving one or more of the countries with major economies. And when tensions or conflicts wind down, markets go up.

Although the recessions of the post–World War II era can look grim to those who lose their jobs or see their assets plummet in value, these downturns have actually been very mild compared to the bad times of yesteryear. Modern-day recessions generally last only about six months to a year and are now seen as simply part of the normal business cycle.

Why is this? Economists point to a better understanding of fiscal and monetary policy by government
leaders and central banks. There are various actions a
government can take to revive a slumping economy, and
during the 45 years since the end of the war these actions
have succeeded in smoothing out the old boom-and-bust
cycles in most modern economies.

To John Dessauer, the well-known adviser on international investing (see Resources, Chapter 13), the constant concern about the state of the economy is a good
sign—when the concern is coupled with positive action.
He points out that the Great Depression of the 1930s came
about partly because of the general consensus in the 1920s
that prosperity was here to stay. The few economists who
disagreed not only saw their warnings go unheeded, they
were accused of being unpatriotic! Dessauer believes that
our ongoing anxiety about the economy makes an economic catastrophe less likely to happen.

From this point of view, the doomsayers who write
books with titles like *How to Profit from the Coming
Collapse of Western Civilization* are actually performing a
useful service. At least some of the failings in our economy that they describe so graphically are indeed things
we should be concerned about. But the new investor
needs to know that so far, the great majority of such
books have been mistaken in their predictions of major
economic disasters and great depressions.

There have been 14 major bear markets in stocks
since World War II ended. Some of these downturns lasted
several years, some only a few months. The average

**Some investments will go down sharply during
a recession, others will weather it better, and
some may even go up.**

decline in value of the overall stock market during these times was 25%.

The market traditionally rises substantially, then goes to unrealistic limits where stock prices reflect speculative rather than real value (Alan Greenspan, the Chairman of the Federal Reserve calls this stage, "irrational exhuberance"). A "correction" inevitably follows and the market goes down anywhere from 7% to 30%. A bottoming-out process then occurs in which stocks stay at roughly the same low prices for several months. And, finally, a new rally begins. This pattern has been repeated over and over throughout the years.

The stock market usually goes up and down with upswings and recessions in the economy. Stocks are often a good predictor of a downturn: prices will head south before the other economic indicators point to a recession. And they will usually start back up in advance of a recovery. The crash of 1987 was an exception to this link—that was a solo performance by the stock market. The recession that many analysts predicted never happened, and the market gradually recovered.

After each of the postwar bear markets, the market recovered and went on to make new highs. Long-term investors have done well with a buy-and-hold strategy. Rather than worry about every downturn, many people opt for this strategy of buying stock in quality companies and simply sitting it out.

PLANNING AND ACTION

The key to success with a buy-and-hold strategy is *diversification*. Some investments will go down sharply during a recession, others will weather it better, and some may even go up. In Chapter 15, we discussed keeping your portfolio diverse enough to handle the inevitable ups and downs of the market. A balanced group of investments, such as the model portfolio, is designed to do this.

But what action should you take if you—and the advisers you respect—feel strongly that a fall in the market is imminent? Generally, no action. The model portfolio is designed to be bought and held, not traded or timed with the market. The great danger of selling your stocks or stock funds is that you will be out of the market when it makes a major advance.

If you feel you just *have* to do something, one move is simply to *alter the balance* of your portfolio, so that the risk-reward thermometer goes down a few degrees. This can be easily accomplished by selling a few of the higher-risk investments—like small-company stocks or mutual funds that invest in them—and buying low-risk bond or money market funds. The bulk of your portfolio, however, should remain intact.

Actions like this should be planned in advance of any recessions; it's a good idea to know what you might sell or buy before the time for action arrives. What you need to watch out for is unwarranted panic at a market downturn.

The classic mistake made by inexperienced investors is to panic and sell all their stocks after a market crash. Those who hold on, however, and ride out the storm almost always do better than those who sell. Remember that stocks have always recovered and gone on to new heights. Barring a major change in the economic structure of the country, this pattern of recovery is likely to continue.

DEFENSIVE ACTION IN REAL ESTATE

If you have invested in a home or in income property, you have already chosen a buy-and-hold strategy, whether you like it or not. Real estate is generally difficult to sell fast enough to protect you from a downturn in property values. You can take comfort, though, in the fact that real estate, as a whole, has always recovered its value and gone on to new heights.

The way to avoid trouble from a real estate bear market is by exercising as much foresight as possible. When you buy a home or income property, do your best to arrange things so you won't have to sell at a loss. Obviously, this may not always be possible, but imagining a few worst-case scenarios could help you avoid them—or, at least, prepare for them.

INVESTMENT WORLD ANOMALIES

As a new investor, you are, perhaps, beginning to follow news of the economy more closely. Suppose that over a period of a few weeks, the newspapers report grim news. Many of the major economic indicators look bad: The negative trade balance is getting worse, consumer spending is down, and corporate earnings have not been good. Then the unemployment figures come in, looking even worse than expected . . . and the stock market responds by going *up* 200 points! What's going on here?

This is one of those things that can leave the newcomer to the World of Investment wondering whether she's ever going to get back to Kansas. In this case, because unemployment is up sharply and the economy is hurting, investors believe that the Federal Reserve Bank will now be forced to lower the discount rate—the interest rate at which it lends money to member banks—in order to stimulate the economy. With cheaper money being lent to them, banks will then be able to make loans to corporate clients and consumers at lower rates—and this usually stimulates the economy.

See? It's all very clear, isn't it? Bad news is really good news. . . .

Now that we've cleared up that little matter, let's go on to individual stocks. Say you bought some shares of International Widget Software a few months ago and the stock has taken off. You're up 25% from your purchase price and feeling pretty good. You feel even better when you read that earnings are up a dazzling 20% from the previous quarter—until the next day, when the price of the stock goes down 15% in heavy selling. Over the next week, it drops even further, until it's close to where you bought it.

Wha' hoppen? Does somebody know something you don't about the demand for widget software? Probably not. More likely, IWS disappointed traders with an earnings increase of "only" 20%. The price of the stock had gone up over the last few months as these traders anticipated a truly stupendous earnings gain. So in this case, good news is really bad news.

What do you do? Hold on! You're an investor, remember, not a trader. You think in terms of years, not weeks. You buy on value and you researched IWS carefully before you bought it. You didn't buy it just because the price was going up and everyone said it was a "hot stock" (did you?). Its earnings have been increasing for several years; the company has sound management and a good position in the widget software market.

So hold on. Don't let the strange doings of the market get you down. The people who make money, ultimately, are those who are aware of the fluctuations in a market, but hold fast to their method of buying and selling.

AWAKE AND AWARE

So what's ahead for the new century/millennium? As you might guess, there are roughly an equal number of bulls and bears speculating on the United States and world

In 1997 and 1998, a number of large, growing economies crashed and burned. Russia, Brazil, Thailand, Korea, and Indonesia, all of which had appeared very promising during the early part of the 1990s, experienced severe declines when investors suddenly withdrew their money.

economies. In the same newspaper, you can find predictions of the stock averages doubling in the next five years right next to predictions of total disaster. The disaster scenarios usually include a collapse of the banking system and a debt crisis, brought on by the massive amount of private, corporate, and government debt.

The new investor should be aware that there *are* serious economic problems in the world. In 1997 and 1998, a number of large, growing economies crashed and burned. Russia, Brazil, Thailand, Korea, and Indonesia, all of which had appeared very promising during the early part of the 1990s, experienced severe declines when investors suddenly withdrew their money. These investors were reacting to concerns about continued prospects for growth, but the withdrawal of their capital turned economic slowdowns into routs. Governments attempted to remedy the situation, but the problems ran much deeper than simply a lack of capital.

Regulations of markets in these countries was generally lax, speculation was encouraged, and the economies were generally controlled by a moneyed elite with little concern for anyone but themselves ("crony capitalism"). All these shortcomings were ignored by most analysts as they wrote glowing reports about these growing economies earlier in the decade. These reports, coupled with speculators' and investors' desire to make a killing, ran markets up to unrealistic levels.

Recovery in these countries will come about only when proper controls and reforms are in place—and when analysts and investors alike take a more level-headed view of the risks and rewards inherent in growing economies. In the meantime, as of this writing, the major economies of Europe and the United States have continued strong in the face of these disasters. Bearish analysts would say that even though they have continued strong so far, there are certain to be repercussions from the recessions abroad. Bullish advisers, on the other hand, will argue that there have always been serious problems, and the trend has been upward anyway. This may be true, but the job of the individual investor is to stay awake and aware. In addition to the dangers we know of, unforeseen events, like the 1990 war in the Middle East, or the 1999 crisis in Kosovo, can happen at any time, sometimes with devastating effects on the economy.

The keys, to dealing with bad times then, are preparation, preparation, and . . . more preparation. A well-planned, balanced portfolio will help you ride out the storms. Deciding in advance what to buy and sell in a downturn will allow you to act quickly, if you need to. And, most of all, resolving to stick to your plans and remain cool during any bad times is the kind of preparation that will help you act like a seasoned, successful investor.

Why Do Markets Go Up and Down?

What makes the stock market—or any financial market—go up and down? This has been the subject of an extravagant amount of research, speculation, and fancy mathematics. Much of this research has been directed at trying to discern the exact time a market is going to move; if you know this time, you can then get in or out before the crowd. When the crowd gets in or out, the market reacts to the massive buying or selling, the law of supply and demand kicks in, and the market goes up or down, often violently.

Traditionally, the stock market goes down in times of recession and up in good times. Other things tend to drive it up as well: buying by foreign investors, lower energy prices, lower interest rates, good performance by an important sector of the market, and (in the short term) program buying by large investment firms (buying large quantities of stocks according to signals generated by computer programs).

The opposites of the above things tend to drive the market down; in addition, wars are generally bad for the market, as are political upheavals. Even the U.S. President being in ill health can send the market into a tailspin.

It's not just real situations that affect investors, however; *rumors* of any of the above can send the financial markets up or down. The futures markets are especially sensitive to rumors, but the stock and bond markets are vulnerable too. Sad to say, these rumors are occasionally started by unscrupulous people for their own trading reasons. The effects of such rumors are usually short-lived, but they illustrate how easy it is to frighten investors and traders, and how important it is not to buy or sell on rumor.

As you can readily see, there is much more at work here than the calm, rational assessment by experienced investors that, perhaps, their money might earn more in another place. The main focus of attention is not on the problem—the economy, for example—but on the *perception* of the economy by other investors. Is the news bad enough that people will get scared and start to sell?

I see the financial markets as excellent examples of self-fulfilling prophecies. If people *think* other people are going to sell, then *they* will sell, and the market will indeed go down. It is a situation where everyone is doing his or her very best to figure out what everyone else is going to do.

It reminds me of army ants—the jungle ants that go out in hordes, devouring everything in their path. For years, entomologists tried to discover which of these ants were leading this march of destruction. They were finally forced to conclude that there *were* no leaders—that the ants in front were simply being pushed by those behind!

The key to understanding markets is that there is a limited amount of capital in the world. This capital flows to whatever market looks the most profitable at any given time. If it appears that the stock market is going down, many individuals and institutions will sell much of their holdings.

These shares, of course, are bought by other buyers, who take advantage of the lower prices brought about by the selling. But soon, the buying and selling slows down and the prices stay at depressed levels. The majority of stocks and the market as a whole are now worth less than before, because so much capital has been withdrawn.

Where has all the capital gone that was invested in these stocks? It has gone into anything that appears safe: savings accounts, money market funds, or so-called "cash equivalents," like government bonds. Some may go into corporate bonds, certain foreign stock markets, or currencies, thus driving these markets up. If investors perceive the stock market to be a bad bet over the long term, some money may go into real estate, sending prices up there.

Finally, when whatever situation scared people out of the stock market looks to be improving—an economic recession starts to turn around, for example—then the owners of capital begin to look at stocks again. This process, wherein investors try to decide exactly when to start buying, is wondrous to observe. It's like a cat getting ready to spring—quivering with anticipation, but waiting till just the right moment!

Everyone is keyed in to the slightest indication that everyone else might be ready to make the plunge, but no one wants to buy first and expose himself to another downturn. Some market analysts warn that it may not be quite the right time yet—that the bear market has a ways to go yet; others urge buying while the prices are still low.

Finally, the buying begins, the market reacts to the increased demand, and the prices go up. Before long, the speculation will turn to whether investors will be bothered by the speed of the advance and start selling . . . and the cycle goes on.

CHAPTER 21

BONDS

Bonds are also known as fixed-income securities, debt securities, debt instruments, or debentures. You don't need to remember all these terms, but be aware that the writers in the financial papers will sometimes use them.

In Chapter 7 we talked about what bonds are and why they are useful investments. Now we're going to discuss the different kinds of bonds. This chapter is not just for those who may invest in individual bonds. Those who plan to buy bond mutual funds still need to know about what kind of bonds the funds are investing in.

CORPORATE BONDS

In order to raise new capital, corporations can issue stock, or they can borrow by selling bonds. These "issues" of bonds are available for purchase through your stockbroker.

You can buy them when they are first issued by the corporations, or later on, on the open market (the so-called secondary market).

Corporate bonds are almost always issued in denominations of $1,000. Most of these bonds are called *debenture bonds* or simply *debentures*. Debenture bonds are not backed by any tangible assets (as, for example, a home mortgage is backed by the tangible asset of the house). They are backed only by the good credit and financial strength of the issuing corporation.

The safest, highest-rated bonds currently return about 5% to 7% to the investor. This would mean a return of $50 to $70 a year on a $1,000 bond. The return on corporate bonds is generally higher than that for government securities, because they are considered a little riskier. Historically, however, the top-rated bonds issued by the major corporations have been extremely safe.

Corporate bonds have terms of anywhere from 1 to 20 years until they "mature." At that time, the holder of the bond receives the $1,000 back from the corporation.

U.S. GOVERNMENT SECURITIES

Treasury bonds, or *T-bonds*, can be purchased in denominations of $1,000 up to $1 million. T-bonds have terms of 10 to 30 years; the 30-year bond is called the long bond.

You can buy T-bonds through your broker or through your bank. The income from all the government securities is exempt from state and local taxes, but not from federal taxes.

Treasury notes (T-notes) have shorter terms than T-bonds—from 2 to 10 years. Like corporate bonds, all the government securities can be bought and sold on the open market and, like corporate bonds, they will rise and fall in price with the prevailing interest rates (why fixed-income securities rise and fall in value is explained later).

Treasury bills (T-bills) are issued for periods of three months, six months, and a year. They come in large sizes only: $10,000 and up, with $10,000 being the standard amount. T-bills don't pay interest in the same way as other bonds; instead, you buy them at a discount and then receive the full $10,000 when the bill comes due. For example, a T-bill may be quoted at $9,400. If you buy it, you will receive $10,000 when it matures (comes due), for a profit of $600. On a 12-month investment of $9,400, $600 would mean a return rate of 6.38% ($600 divided by $9,400 = .0638 = 6.38%).

The main advantage to all the federal securities is safety. Regardless of what you might think about the size of the national debt, the government has not yet defaulted on any of its bonds. In return for this safety, you get less return than from the corporate bonds, though this difference can vary a good deal.

Another advantage is that the market of buyers and sellers is large. Some corporate bonds can be difficult to sell because there aren't enough people wanting to buy them. This feature makes government issues "liquid." Liquidity can be an important thing to consider in any investment; if you want to get out for any reason, ease and rapidity of sale are an attractive feature.

MUNICIPAL BONDS

Municipal bonds, also known as "municipals" or "munis," are issued by your own city hall, often for a specific purpose, such as new schools or sewers. These are the "bond issues" you vote on in your local elections. The majority of these bonds—the so-called *public purpose bonds*—are *tax free*. The interest income you receive is free from federal income taxes and, in many cases, from state and local taxes as well (be sure to check this out before you buy). State governments issue public purpose bonds, too.

The yields on the tax-free bonds are less than for other types of bonds, but the tax-free aspect makes them attractive to individuals in high tax brackets. By not paying taxes on the income from the bonds, you effectively receive 2% to 3% more income from munis. Whether they would be right for you is something to discuss with your tax accountant.

Munis come in a few different forms. The most common are general obligation bonds and revenue bonds.

General obligation bonds are repaid from tax revenues. If a municipality has a good tax base, these are considered the safest bonds.

Revenue bonds are issued by states and cities to fund income-producing projects, such as toll bridges or sports stadiums. The interest and principal will be paid by income from the project. These bonds are somewhat riskier; if the project doesn't produce the expected income, the bondholders may be out of luck.

Municipal bonds as a whole have become a little chancy in recent years. A few cities have actually defaulted on their bonds. You need to take note of the bond ratings (explained below) before you buy.

Alternatively, you can put your money in a mutual fund specializing in municipals and let the fund managers worry about such things. Depending on the kind of municipals the fund owns, the income is free from federal

Zeros are cheap, especially those with maturity dates 20 or 30 years away. This makes them attractive to small investors.

taxes and sometimes state taxes, just as with the individual bonds.

ZERO-COUPON BONDS

Remember how we have discussed reinvesting all the income from an investment when growth is the only objective? Zero-coupon bonds do this for you. The interest is simply added to the principal twice a year. You get the face value (usually $1,000) when the bond matures.

Zero-coupon bonds (also called simply "zeros") get their name from the fact that they pay out no yearly interest in cash—all the interest is reinvested. Bonds used to have detachable coupons (a few still do), which the holder clipped and sent in when the interest payment was due. "Coupon," therefore, has become synonymous with "interest" in bond jargon. Zero yearly interest payment = zero coupon.

The interest is nevertheless subject to taxes each year, even though you don't get this income until the bond matures. This makes zeros good for tax-deferred accounts like IRAs and Keoghs (see Chapter 17). They are also good presents for a child with college education in mind, since up to $1,000 of the interest is tax-exempt until the child reaches 14.

Zeros are cheap, especially those with maturity dates 20 or 30 years away. This makes them attractive to small investors. A 30-year zero, for example, might cost as little as $50 to $60, depending on the going interest rates. In 30 years, you would receive the full $1,000 face value of the bond.

Zeros are bought and sold on the open market, but their prices are even more sensitive than those of regular coupon bonds to changes in the prevailing interest rates. And some may be redeemed—"called"—by the issuing company before they mature, at less than face value. This is an important thing to check ("calling" a bond is explained later).

CONVERTIBLE BONDS

The trouble with owning bonds instead of stocks is that if the corporation issuing them starts to do well, you will get no benefit from this success—you just continue to get your 7% a year. If the company does poorly, though, and the rating on your bonds goes down, the bonds and your portfolio will lose value; if the company goes bust, you can lose it all. Convertible bonds attempt to remedy at least part of this situation.

Convertible bonds are similar to other coupon bonds in most ways, except that their interest rates are not as high. The dramatic difference is that at any time you can convert the bonds into the common stock of the corporation at a fixed rate. For example, your bond might be convertible into 50 shares of company stock. If the stock is selling at $25 a share, your bond will be worth at least $1,250 (50 × $25). This is called the *conversion value*.

The bond will probably be worth a bit more than its conversion value because it gives a higher interest rate than the common stock. It is hardly ever advisable, then, to actually make the change. If the stock goes up, the price of the bond will rise right along with it. If the stock price should go down, the bond will also, but you will continue to get your 4.5%, or whatever the interest rate is.

Convertibles are a neat way of dealing with the risk-versus-return dilemma. They are safer than common stocks in that their interest payments always take precedence over the dividend payments of the common. They give a good return, so in bad times you might not fret so much if the price is down. And in a bull market, their prices will rise with that of the common stock.

Naturally, you need to research a company in the same way you would if you bought its common stock. Even convertibles can lose their interest payments if a company is on the skids. To lessen your risk, there are—you guessed it—mutual funds dealing only in convertible bonds.

JUNK BONDS

Junk bonds are also called "high-yield" bonds—just to confuse new investors. "High-yielding" *stocks* are in companies that pay a high dividend and are among the safest and best stock investments. High-yield *bonds*, however, have acquired a negative connotation, because so many of them are risky investments.

High-yield bonds were formerly issued by smaller companies that used the higher yields to attract investors. Because these yields were usually several percentage points higher than those of the top-rated bonds, some investors were willing to take a chance. There was always the danger, however, that the company might not be able to meet the interest payments, and this caused the bonds to be graded very low by the ratings services (hence the "junk" label).

In the 1980s, larger, more established companies began to issue high-interest bonds as a way of paying for takeovers of other companies. This method of financing takeovers was developed by a former Drexel Burnham executive, Michael Milken, about whom you may have heard in connection with other creative (and illegal) manipulations of large sums of money.

These so-called leveraged buyouts were not illegal, but they were often ill-advised, as corporations were left with troublesome amounts of debt in the form of their high-interest junk bonds. When the recession hit in 1990, many companies were unable to meet the payments on these bonds. In that year, 8.5% of the junk bonds, with a value of $24.6 billion, were in default.

When a class of investments, such as the junk bond market, starts to look shaky, investors begin bailing out. This selling then drives down the total value of the whole market—even the better-quality investments. This happened to the junk bond market in 1989 and 1990, leaving many portfolios worth substantially less than a few years before.

This kind of loss can be very hard on individual investors. When the junk bond portfolios belong to large institutions, however, you have the makings of a world-class crisis.

The collapse of the junk bond market made the savings and loan crisis much worse, because many of the S&Ls had bought large quantities of these bonds. Even sections of the insurance industry were in trouble, due to a diet too rich in high yield bonds.

In addition, the massive amount of corporate debt created by the issues of junk bonds left some analysts worried about the ability of many corporations to function effectively. Money that goes to pay high-interest debt is money that is not funding the kind of research and development needed to compete in today's world markets.

These difficulties were part of the legacy of the 1980s, when a certain air of unreality enveloped much of the financial marketplace. This departure from reality resulted, to a large extent, from indifference to the traditional risk-reward ratio by financial managers who were supposed to know better. They believed they could get high returns in junk bonds and still retain the necessary safety. By 1990, the risk-reward ratio had reasserted itself, and the bills had come due for ignoring it.

This bit of financial history underscores the importance of paying attention to the risk-reward ratio, as pictured by our little thermometers throughout the book. For a while,

> **When a class of investments, such as the junk bond market, starts to look shaky, investors begin bailing out.**

in good economic times, risky investments may do well. But the reasons they are known as risky can make themselves apparent with a vengeance when times turn bad.

Yes, there are mutual funds that deal mostly in junk bonds—and no, they are not recommended for the new investor. Returns of 12%, 15%, and higher can look awfully good, until you consider the possibility of default and further loss of value on the part of the junk bonds. You would think that most people would be warned off by the name....

RATINGS

Nowhere are there clearer illustrations of risk-versus-return than in the bond market. From the absolutely safe government bonds to the junk bonds, the story is the same: greater return = greater risk. (Government securities are not even rated—they are considered risk-free.) The bonds that receive a lower grade from the rating services will give you a higher return, but the risk will be measurably bigger. Junk bonds give you the highest yields, but are extremely risky.

So how can you learn which bonds are the most highly rated? For years, Standard and Poor's ratings and Moody's ratings have been the industry standards. You can find their books in the business reference section of your public library, or you can subscribe. The Resources section of this chapter tells how to subscribe to Standard and Poors stock and bond ratings.

Bond Ratings

Moody's	Standard & Poor's	Quality
Aaa	AAA	Highest quality
Aa	AA	High quality
A	A	Upper medium grade
Baa	BBB	Medium grade
Ba	BB	Speculative elements
B	B	Speculative
Caa	CCC, CC	Default possible
Ca	C	Default—partial recovery possible
C	D	Default—recovery not likely

A warning is in order here. Ratings can change—sometimes drastically. A friend of mine was dismayed to find that the AAA top-rated Occidental Petroleum bond he had held for just a year had been downgraded to BBB, a "medium grade" rating. The rating services didn't like the looks of the latest balance sheets at Occidental. Unfortunately, a drop in ratings almost always means a drop in value for the bond, and this case was no exception.

This is another argument for investing in bond mutual funds instead of holding individual bonds. The large quantity of bonds in the funds' portfolios means that any risk is spread out; if one bond loses value, another may rise. For added safety, in this book I recommend buying mutual funds that invest only in bonds rated A or better.

Junk bonds, incidentally, have a rating of BB or lower—almost always lower, in fact. Many are not even graded by the rating services.

UPS AND DOWNS IN THE BOND MARKET

Unlike savings accounts or certificates of deposit in a bank, bonds can increase or decrease in value. This is true of anything you can buy or sell: the markets will determine the price. If you need to sell a bond, there is a good chance it will have gone up or down in price since you purchased it.

A decrease in the value of a bond does *not* mean its interest rate will go down. Your interest payments will stay the same, barring something drastic like a default on bond payments by the corporation—a very rare occurrence in high-rated bonds. (Some bonds have variable interest rates, but these are rare.)

If you are invested over the long term, you don't need to worry too much about market fluctuations; you just hold on to your bond until it matures and continue to collect your interest payments.

Two things can cause a bond to decrease in value: the downgrading of the rating or an increase in the interest rates paid by newer bonds. Even government bonds fluctuate with the prevailing interest rates. The reasons for this decrease are pretty clear. Who wants to buy a bond yielding 6% when the new ones are giving 7%? The only thing that would make a 6% bond more attractive would be to lower its price.

Say you bought a General Motors bond for its face value of $1,000, maturing in 10 years and yielding 6%. This 6% is called the *coupon interest rate* or *coupon rate*. You will be getting $60 a year, or $30 every six months.

> **If you are invested over the long term, you don't need to worry too much about market fluctuations.**

But now suppose that after a year, interest rates on new, comparable bonds have risen to 7%. Your 6% suddenly looks kind of shabby.

How the Federal Reserve Bank Controls Inflation and How This Affects Interest Rates

When credit is easy to get, the large amount of borrowed money tends to stimulate growth in the economy. Businesses have more to spend on expansion, and consumers support business by purchasing more on credit. This growth, however, can also lead to an increase in inflation; with more people buying, the increased demand causes prices to go up. To prevent inflation from getting out of hand, the Federal Reserve Bank (also known as "the Fed") can restrict the total amount of money in the economy. Less money = less borrowing = less growth = less inflation.

One way the Fed accomplishes this is to make loans more expensive. It does this by raising the interest rate at which banks can borrow money from the Fed (this is called raising the discount rate).

Because banks have to pay more for their money, they must charge their borrowers more. As a result of the increased cost of loans, corporations and individuals will borrow less. Less borrowing means less spending, which means economic growth will be slowed down—and this, in turn, will put a damper on inflation.

The increase in the cost of money from the Fed coupled with the decrease in the money supply makes your money more attractive to banks and corporations. They will pay you more if you deposit money in

savings or buy bonds, and will lend this money out at
higher rates of interest.

When the economy is in recession, the Federal
Reserve will lower the discount rate, thus making
borrowing easier and stimulating the economy.
Cheaper money from the Fed means banks can charge
less interest on the loans they give their customers.
But this also means that the banks will pay less for
the use of your money; interest rates paid on your
savings will go down.

But if the price of your bond were lowered to $860 it
would then yield 7% to whoever bought it at this new,
lower price. The bond would still be *yielding* $60 a year in
interest, but this $60 would be 7% of the $860 price to the
new buyer. This new interest rate of 7%, based on the $860
price, is called the *current yield*—as opposed to the *coupon
rate* of 6%. What this means is that having bought the
bond for only $860 , the new holder will continue to get an
effective yield of 7% until the bond matures.

In addition, this new buyer will get the full $1,000
face value when the bond matures. This gives rise to the
term, *the yield to maturity*. This yield adds the extra $140
the buyer will realize when the bond matures.

Conversely, if the new buyer paid more for the bond
than the face value, you would *subtract* the difference to
get the yield to maturity. If the bond was purchased for
$1,100 and was going to mature in four years, the buyer
would receive the $1,000 face value at that time—but this
would be $100 less than was paid for the bond. The yield
to maturity would then reflect this $100 difference.

Yields to maturity are computed according to a fairly
complex formula. Your broker can provide you with a
bond's yield to maturity before you buy it.

Of course, you don't have to sell your bond just because the interest rates change—if you hold on to it, you will continue to get your 6% for the next 10 years. But if you do decide to sell when interest rates have risen, you will get less than you paid for the bond.

And yes, happily, the reverse can be true. Interest rates might fall to 5% in which case you could be proud of your 6%—and the value of your bond in the market would increase.

There is, however, one more thing about bonds that could ruin your delight over any increase in value due to falling interest rates: Corporations don't like paying 7% when the prevailing rate is 6%. They would rather issue new bonds at the lower rate. So if interest rates drop sharply, the company issuing your bond may *call* it—that is, it can tell you to send the bond in so it can pay you the face value now, instead of when the bond matures. This feature, known as *callability*, is something to check carefully before you buy a bond. You will get your original investment back, but you'll have to go looking for 7% elsewhere—and in a 6% market. Even government T-bonds are callable these days.

When you buy a bond on the market, it's a good idea to check out the callability. If you buy a $1,000 bond for $1,100, it will not be to your advantage to have it called at the $1,000 face value in a year or two. Even after figuring in your interest payments, the $100 loss will make your

> **There is, however, one more thing about bonds that could ruin your delight over any increase in value due to falling interest rates: Corporations don't like paying 7% when the prevailing rate is 6%.**

total return look like Wile E. Coyote after an encounter with the Roadrunner.

Again, of course, the reverse could be happily true. Buying the bond at $900 would leave you very content to have it called at $1,000.

HOW TO READ THE BOND
TABLES IN THE NEWSPAPERS

(1)	(2)	(3)	(4) Cur Yld	(5) Vol	(6) Last	(7) Net Chg
PG&E	$6\frac{1}{2}$	09	6.9	70	$94\frac{1}{2}$	+1/8

(1) The name of the company, in this case, Pacific Gas and Electric.

(2) The coupon rate, or yearly interest this bond will pay: $6\frac{1}{2}\%$. A bond with a "par value" (or face value) of $1,000 would yield $65 a year at $6\frac{1}{2}\%$.

(3) The maturity date, when the face value of the bond will be paid back. Only the last two digits are given. In this case, the maturity date is 2009.

(4) The current yield. Because the value of this bond has declined, a buyer will actually be receiving 6.9% on his or her money, rather than the coupon rate of $6\frac{1}{2}\%$.

(5) Yesterday's volume. Add three zeros and a dollar sign. Unlike the stock tables, where the volume refers to the number of shares traded, bond volume is figured in dollar amounts. In this case, there were $70,000 worth of PG&E bonds traded.

(6) The last price at which the bonds traded. This figure is a *percentage* of $1,000—the face value of most corporate bonds. A bond trading at $94\frac{1}{2}$ will cost $945 ($94\frac{1}{2}\%$ = .945 x $1,000 = $945.00). This PG&E bond is

trading "at a discount." Sometimes bonds will trade "at a premium" to their face value. If you see a price listed as "102," this means a buyer will have to pay $1,020 for the bond.

(7) The net change in price from the previous day. If you look at the bond tables on any given day, you will usually see either a great majority of plus signs, or of minus signs. The price of bonds is very sensitive to changes—or rumors of changes—in the interest rates. A few bonds will run counter to the majority, because of a revision of their rating, or good or bad information about the company that issued them.

(Occasionally, you will see an "s" between the coupon rate and the year of maturity: for example, "7s99." The sole function of the "s" is to separate the two numbers, so you don't read them as "799.")

So . . . are bonds a good investment? Bonds are good for investors who need a safe source of income over the long term, or those who need to balance and diversify their stock portfolios. And again, the bond mutual funds are probably the best bet for safety and stable return.

This is a good time to assess again the amount of risk you are comfortable with. If you want no risk at all, you will buy Treasury bonds or notes, or mutual funds that invest in them. A little more risk tolerance will put you into corporate bonds, then convertible bonds, and finally common stocks.

Or perhaps by now you're bored with bonds and blue chips and are ready to consider Cousin Jack's Australian gold mine. . . .

Resources

Standard & Poor's Bond Guide, Standard & Poor's Corp., 25 Broadway, New York, NY 10004. Monthly. $284/year (ask about discounts). To subscribe, call (800) 221-5277. The Bond Guide is a quick reference booklet to over 7,000 bonds, mostly corporate, but some foreign and municipal bonds are also included. An essential reference for anyone wanting to invest in individual bonds.

For bond mutual funds, check Resources, Chapter 6. The books listed contain not just stock mutual funds, but also bond mutual funds. The statistics on past performance will help you choose the best funds.

CHAPTER 22

INVESTING ONLINE

The key question here is: "Do you need to be online to be a successful investor?" The answer is a qualified "no." No, you don't *have* to be online, but you don't have to have a word processor to be a successful writer either—it just makes things infinitely easier. If you are not online and want to invest in stocks, bonds, and mutual funds, I recommend that you seriously consider taking the plunge. This book is written for those who wish to take control of their money and there is no better way of doing this than being on the Internet. The ease and low cost of trading, the vast amounts of information available, and the ability to see what you own and what it's worth at any moment—all this is why eight million individuals have online investing accounts (this number is expected to triple in the next two years).

Millions of investors online have brought about an explosion in the number of businesses anxious to capitalize on this new opportunity. All the major brokerages now have online capabilities, and dozens of new brokerages have started up. Similarly, there are ever-increasing numbers of information providers, quote servers, and online newsletters. In addition, every publicly traded company now has its own web site. With all this, is it any wonder that "overwhelm" is a common problem among new users of the "Net."

With this in mind, what this chapter is going to do is tell you the best ways of dealing with this mass of information, so you can get what you need. You will be directed to a few of the most useful sites and instructed on how to find new sites on your own. In spite of its mass of information, you can look at the web as simply another tool which, when used cleverly, can greatly enhance your investment capabilities. Once you learn the basics of this tool, you will begin to discover new ways of using it.

Hardware

First, here are a few pointers for those of you who do not yet have computers—and for those who are computer-literate but not yet online. Computer technology has made great strides in the last few years: the amount of memory has increased many-fold and the speed of operation has likewise gone up. As far as the ease of operation . . . well, the programmers have certainly made the operating systems—the software—easier to use, but they still have a ways to go. New users need to be aware that they are communicating with an alien mind; computers do not *think* the same way that humans do. The programmers do their best to create an *interface* between person and machine so that they can communicate, but novices are often frustrated that the computer doesn't seem to understand exactly what they want to do.

In ten or fifteen years, these problems will certainly evaporate: by then, you will be able to *speak* to the com-

> **What all this means is that to facilitate your online operations, you should buy computer hardware that is as up-to-date as possible.**

puter and tell it exactly what you want it to do, just like Captain Kirk on Star Trek. Right now, however, new users need to be aware that computer technology is roughly comparable to automobile technology in the 1930s when electric starters were becoming common and automatic transmissions were being introduced. Just like the cars of that era, computers are no longer in the "Model T" phase, but real ease of operation is still a dream of the future.

What all this means is that to facilitate your online operations, you should buy computer hardware that is as up-to-date as possible. Buy the most advanced machine you can afford, along with the latest software. What you are mainly after is *speed of operation.* Browsing on the Internet (going from site to site) and downloading information (transferring the information from a web site to your computer), can be extremely time consuming. More powerful hardware coupled with the fastest "modem" available will keep you from sitting around cooling your heels between sites. A modem is the device that allows your computer to communicate over the telephone lines. Modems are rated by speed; the fastest can deal with 56 kilobits per second, which is abbreviated to 56K. This 56K modem is the one you want.

If you have never owned a computer, the best way to start is to talk to a computer-literate friend. He or she can help you translate digital jargon into English and discuss with you what kind of hardware you need. Once you own the hardware, however, the best thing to do is to *get instruction*: take a class or hire an individual teacher to show you the ropes. Do not try to do this on your own unless you enjoy high levels of frustration. My feeling is that computers should come with a warning label like a pack of cigarettes: *"Warning! May cause excessive stress and tension! Use carefully!"* In this case, you can avoid much of this stress by having the number of someone you can call with questions. Make a list of everything you don't understand as you work, and then phone them as often as you need to—their fee will pay for itself many times over in the time you save and the headaches you avoid.

Getting Online

Once you have all the necessary equipment, and are able to find your way around Windows, or whatever operating system you're using, you will be ready to get online. You will need to sign up with an online service provider, one of the companies that provide access to the Internet. I recommend going with one of the larger service providers at first, like CompuServe or America Online (AOL).

Because there is a good deal of information at these sites alone, they are a good place to start practicing being online. Then, when you've learned how to navigate through one of these home sites, you will be ready to log on to the World Wide Web (www) and start visiting the sites that catch your fancy.

This is not the place to go into everything you need to know about the web. Again, I recommend getting some help when you first start. Once you know the basics, some of the beginneris manuals in bookstores can be very helpful (these are generally much clearer and easier to read than the manuals that come with the software). For the rest of the chapter, we're going to assume that readers know their way around the web and are familiar with basic computer terminology.

Free Information

One of the keys to successful investing is accurate and timely information. Until recently, investment professionals had much better access to key information than non-professionals. The Internet has begun to close this gap, but it has created a new problem for investors: an information glut. There are now hundreds of sites—many of them free—where you can get all kinds of data on stocks, set up a portfolio, and do your own research. Combine this with enticing ads, promising free this and free that, and you have a good recipe for *new online investor overload.*

This is an excellent reason to sign on with a major service provider, as suggested above. This way, you aren't exposed to the entire World Wide Web all at once. America Online (AOL), for example, has a very useful investment section that is quite easy to use. There is enough similarity among investment sites that the skills you can learn in navigating this site will stand you in good stead when you expand to other sites. Even if you subscribe to another service provider, you should have no trouble following the steps listed below.

From the AOL "Welcome" page, simply click on "Quotes" and you have entered the online World of Investment. The "Quotes" page, also titled "AOL Personal Finance," has a menu from which you can go to a number of sites providing various kinds of information. First, however, notice the small, oblong box in the upper left with the flashing cursor. You can type in the symbol of any stock in this box—say, AMZN, for Amazon.com—and get the most recent price, the daily highs and lows, and the total number of shares traded so far. If you don't know the stock symbol, click on the "Company Name" circle, and type in the name in the box.

You discover that Amazon.com is trading at 155 right now ($155/share), down from a closing price of 165, yesterday. But is this decline connected with a drop in the overall market, or is Amazon stock having troubles of its own? If you click on the "Market News Center," you find a graph showing that the Nasdaq Stock Market is down 50 points. This means that the majority of the tech and Internet stocks like Amazon are probably down. The commentary to the right of the graph confirms this: there is a sell-off in the Internet sector.

We now know that Amazon's price drop could have been caused by the selloff, but we still want to know how the present price compares with the price of the stock for the last month? Is it on its way up or on its way down? In the menu on the right, click on "Historical Quotes," then type in AMZN in the box with the flashing cursor. You then have a choice of graphs at the right; choose "Daily for One Month," press the "Enter" key and voila!—a complete graph appears showing the daily price for Amazon.com during the last month. The little green bars on the graph show the extent of the price range on each day. For example, on the 17th of April, AMZN had a low price of 155 and a high of 192 (Amazon.com is a very volatile stock, like many of the Internet stocks). The small horizontal line through the green bar represents the closing price for that day. A quick view of the entire graph shows a high for the month of 219 and a low of 150.

With a few clicks, we have learned some very important information, that is, that the present price of 155 is near the lows for the month. Furthermore, it's easy to see from the graph that the stock has been on its way down for the last few days—that 219 high was just last week. To get a broader view of the stock's performance over the last year—or two years—you can create a custom graph from the choices on the "Historical Quotes" menu page.

Now, you wonder, is the sharp decline in price over the last week due simply to investors turning away from the high-flying Internet stocks, or did Amazon.com release some bad news recently. To find out, return to the "Quotes" menu and click "News by Ticker." At that site, type in

AMZN and a list of titles of articles about Amazon will appear below. Scrolling down that list, we find a May 3 article stating that Amazon plans to increase spending on promotions and new services. Investors are concerned that this spending will cut into the company's earnings, and further on in the article we see other concerns about increased competition for Amazon's online music business.

Another article, however, states that Internet stocks are unpopular with investors right now; there is a broad sell-off of many of the high-flyers. This means that the decline in the price of Amazon's stock is probably related *both* to the projected drop in earnings *and* the sell-off in Internet stocks. (In this case, there was enough investor concern to drive the price down to 131 before the stock recovered.)

The stock prices in the "Quotes" section of AOL (and other service providers) are so-called "delayed quotes." This means that the price you are seeing is fifteen or twenty minutes old. "Why can't I get up-to-the-minute price quotes in this age of instant communication?" you might ask. The answer is, because you haven't paid for them! The stock exchanges want service providers to pay them for up-to-the-minute quotes—also known as "real-time quotes." To obtain real-time stock quotes you are going to have to pay a monthly fee to an online *quote server* (see "Real-Time Quotes" below). When you get an online broker, you will also be able to obtain real-time prices at that site. But at the "Market News Center" on AOL, only the quotes and graphs for the indexes are real-time.

We will leave Amazon.com for now and go back to the "Market News Center" where the graph for the Dow

Jones Averages is displayed. Notice that the graph and the numbers above it do not change, even though it is the middle of the trading day. This is because this window is a "snap" display (for snapshot); it will not change until you leave the window and come back to it, or click the "Refresh" icon (this particular graph is updated every two minutes). If you click "NASDAQ" at the top of the graph, a graph of the Nasdaq Composite Index will be displayed. Then, when you return to the Dow graph, it will have been magically updated. Only when you pay for real-time data at a quote server web site will the information be automatically updated. This continuous updating each time a price changes for an index or a stock is called "streaming" data or streaming quotes.

Also at the "Market News Center" are links to other investments such as bonds, futures, international stock markets, and currencies. It can be interesting to explore these sites even if you are not about to invest in these areas. For example, you will find out that on this particular day that the U.S. markets have lost value, most major stocks markets around the world also went down. More and more, the financial world is interconnected.

But why are world markets down? To discover this, we can click on the "AOL Business Day." There we find numerous articles concerning the U.S. and international economies. There is one article about the recent, sharp rise in oil prices; investors around the world are concerned that higher energy prices will raise costs for businesses

It's all part of the game: you get free information, and the creators of the financial site get their money by selling space to advertisers.

and cut into profits. This concern—the writer concludes—is bound to be reflected in the financial markets.

On the opening page of "AOL Business Day" is a link to "Bloomberg News." Bloomberg's used to be available only to investment professionals, but now the web site is accessible to individual investors. Give it a try—it's like a constantly updated financial magazine with articles about such things as home mortgages and car buying, as well as stocks and bonds.

Many links on Bloomberg's, as well as other financial sites, are commercially oriented. You think you're going to get information on the latest interest rates for home refinancing and you suddenly find yourself being urged to actually fill out an application for a refinance. You will learn to recognize these kind of links very quickly. It's all part of the game: you get free information, and the creators of the financial site get their money by selling space to advertisers.

Mutual Funds

There is plenty of good information about mutual funds online. Let's start with the AOL Market News Center that carries reports from Morningstar Mutual Funds. From the "Quotes" page, select "Mutual Fund Center" and, on that page, fill in the symbol for the fund you want to know about. If you don't know the symbol, there is a choice called "Lookup Funds by Name" where you can get the symbol. Once you have the symbol, click on the "Get Report'" button and, at the next window, select "Mutual Fund Reports."

The report starts with basic information about the fund: the Morningstar rating (five stars is the highest), the load, the yield, the total assets held by the fund, and the net asset value. A brief description of the fund follows, then the performance figures for the last few years and the average percentage gain or loss for the last three years and five years. The three-year and five-year figures are averages—the percentage gain or loss for each year is added up and divided by three or five. Finally, the top ten holdings of the fund's portfolio are listed.

The performance figures are the most critical. Has the fund performed consistently or are the gains sporadic? Does it have a good five-year average? These figures are, as they say, no guarantee of future performance, but they do give some indication. The more complete Morningstar Reports have some analysis of each fund's past performance and prospects for the future. These are not yet online, but you can get the hard copy at the address given in Resources, Chapter 6.

Want to choose your own mutual funds? Go to <www.quicken.com/investments/mutualfunds> and click "Fund Finder" from the list on the left. Then select "Full Search" from the menu and a window will open where you can choose criteria for the kind of fund you want to invest in. Again, the performance figures are the most important in this search. What you want to screen for is a fund that has performed well over the last several years, not necessarily a high flyer that made a big gain by investing in Internet stocks in 1998.

In the next section, we will discuss how to set up personal portfolios in the AOL Personal Finance section. Once you know the symbols of all the mutual funds, you can set up a portfolio of mutual funds much the same way you set up stock portfolios. The portfolio window will display the fund symbol, the net asset value (NAV), the gain or loss for the day and the gain or loss since you bought the fund. This enables you to check on how your funds are doing at any time.

The only danger with up-to-the-minute information is that you might be tempted to sell if one of your mutuals is down for a few days or weeks. With mutual funds, the time frame for review should be months, rather than days or weeks. If, after three months, your fund is down substantially more than other funds in its class, then you might consider selling (some investors do a review only every six months). One of the biggest mistakes that new investors make is selling too soon. If the fund is down a little, give it time; if you chose wisely, there's a good chance it will go up again.

Portfolios

Okay, now let's have some fun. Start thinking about some companies whose stock you might like to buy. When you have a list, click on "My Portfolios" and then click the box for "Create." You need a name for your portfolio, like "Sky's the Limit" or "Double in Six Months," or you might want something more mundane to differentiate this portfolio from others you may set up, like "Large Growth" or "Small Caps."

Once you've named it, then click "Add," and you will be asked for the symbol of the stock, the number of shares you are "buying," and the cost per share. Remember, you can get the symbol and the current price by returning to the "Quotes" window. Once you have filled in the blanks, click "Add to Portfolio." The portfolio will then be displayed showing the stock symbol, the number of shares you own, the last price the stock traded at, the change in price since the closing price yesterday, the price you bought the stock at, the gain or loss since you bought it, and the present value of your shares.

You can now add further stocks from this portfolio window—simply click the box for "Add" at the bottom of the screen. Say you have placed five stocks in this portfolio; above the portfolio display you will see the total value of your stocks and the change in value for the whole portfolio since you purchased them. If the trading day is still going on, this amount will have already shifted up or

> If you're truly interested in the company,
> make a list of questions as you go through the
> site and call the investor relations person
> again.

down. Remember that the portfolio display will not change on its own—it is not "streaming" data; to see the changes in your stocks, click the "Refresh" box at the bottom left.

To your delight, you see that one of your stocks is already up a whole point since you "bought" it just fifteen minutes ago. Zebra Technologies (ZBRA) is now at 34, up from your purchase price of 33. To find out the reason for this rise, first highlight ZBRA by pointing the mouse arrow at the symbol in your portfolio display and clicking once. Then go down to the bottom of the page and click on "Details." This will give you information similar to the windows on the "Quotes" page, showing the high and low for the day, the number of shares traded so far, and the average number of shares traded daily for the last thirty days. You quickly notice that the number of shares traded today is already double the average.

In addition, underneath this display, there are a list of articles and news releases pertaining to Zebra. The very first one is an eye-catcher: "Zebra Technologies announces record sales for last quarter." Clicking on that article, you read how the company sharply improved profitability in the most recent quarter. The article also presents a chart showing earnings for the last quarter compared to earnings in the same quarter one year ago. At the end, there is a brief description of what Zebra does: their main business is bar codes—making the printers and decoders for automatic price checking systems (let's see, black and white striped labels . . . zebras . . . okay, okay, you already got it . . .). There are also a phone number and e-mail address for the investor relations person at Zebra, in case you want to know more about the company.

The investor relations person will give you the address of the company web site—or you can find it by going to "Ask Jeeves" at <www.ask.com> (see Resources for more about "Ask Jeeves"). In the question box, simply type in "Zebra Technologies, Inc." and Jeeves will find the site for you. Company web sites contain great quantities of information: the history of the firm, what the products are, what the prospects are for growth, all the latest news releases, etc., etc. If you're truly interested in the company, make a list of questions as you go through the site and call the investor relations person again.

Just a couple more things about the "Portfolios" page: in the upper right is a box labeled "Customize Columns." Clicking this will open a window where you change what is displayed in your portfolio. For example, you can display the closing price from the previous day, or the commission you paid to buy the stock. However, you will have to delete one of the columns to add another; in my opinion, the choices made by AOL are the best ones—they show all the pertinent information.

"Select a Broker" at the bottom right of the menu is a commercial link. The brokers listed when you click on that box hope that you will sign up with them. Choosing an online broker should be done with care, however; there is a section later in this chapter on how to do this.

As we stated above, you may set up a number of different portfolios. The "List All" box will give you the menu of your various portfolios and you can double-click onto whichever one you want.

I have gone into some detail demonstrating how to navigate and take advantage of all the features in the AOL Personal Finance section. This is because you will find that most of the free investment web sites bear a good deal of similarity to this one. The formats may look different, and they may offer slightly different features

(some offer real-time quotes), but you should now be able
to navigate these sites quite comfortably. For the purposes of the new investor, these free sites, coupled with a
good, online broker, are all you will need. If you decide
later on to trade stocks and, perhaps, options, you will
want a site with real-time, streaming data. In addition,
you may want to do some number crunching of your own
to find the most promising stocks. For now, we will look
just briefly at a few of these sites and software, so that
you will know what's available.

Advanced Online Information Gathering

Some people reading this book will probably go on to trade
securities and other markets more intensely. Those people
are the ones who will read this section with special interest because it describes the kind of tools available for serious investors and traders. Let's go directly to one of the
best online data providers and see what they offer.

The Data Broadcasting Company (DBC) provides a
variety of services. No matter where you are or what you
kind of data you need, Data Broadcasting intends to see
that you get it. DBC offers—as do a few other quote
servers—information via several different mediums:
cable and satellite dish as well as the normal Internet
connection over the phone lines. Cable connection comes
over the same line as your TV signal; in a few years, all
Internet traffic will go by cable, making long waits and
service interruptions a thing of the past. DBC's cable
service and satellite dish can handle more information
than the Internet connection, but for most users, their
Internet "eSignal" carries more than enough. The only
other advantage to the cable and dish is that you don't
have a phone line tied up.

The basic service on DBC is similar to that of other
quote servers. You get real-time quotes in as many stock

markets as you pay for; you can set up a portfolio of your stocks and, because this is streaming data, their value will change as you watch. You can also set up portfolios of bonds and mutual funds. When deciding which server to go with, it's important to check exactly which stock markets they carry; some will give quotes on Canadian and over-the-counter stocks, others will not. A few will add on international stocks for an additional fee.

DBC serves professional investors who may do quite a bit of trading in different markets. Hence, in addition to American futures and options markets, they offer data on such arcane markets as the London Metal Exchange or the Singapore International Monetary Exchange. You are now in the realm of the international trader, whose livelihood depends on up-to-the-minute information in all sorts of different places.

DBC clients also can subscribe to daily, online reports on options, bonds, currencies, initial public offerings, or a number of other subjects. These run anywhere from $20 to $90 a month. There is also, however, a large amount of free information from a number of financial news services. You can also make charts and graphs of the performance of individual stocks, intraday or interday, and use various kinds of stock screening software (explained in the next section). One nice feature is a connection to your broker that allows you to trade directly from your portfolio as viewed on DBC.

Just to give you an idea of what you might pay for DBC's eSignal Internet service, real-time, streaming quotes on the New York and American Exchanges and Nasdaq will run you about $95 a month, when paid on a yearly basis. Other markets will cost extra. Delayed quotes are $79 a month, while end-of-day data for all U.S. markets is only $195 a year.

There are other services that are somewhat less expensive. In particular, a server called Bull Session gives you real-time quotes for stocks at about $37 a month, with options an extra $13. You can see what they offer at <www.bullsession.com>.

If you're on the move, but have to be in touch with your investments, you can have a wireless modem hooked up to your laptop. You can then be in touch with your quote server on the Internet just as conveniently as at home. DBC will also rent you a hand-held, wireless device called the "QuoTrek," which will display your portfolio and individual quotes. You can learn more about DBC at <www.eSignal.com>.

Okay, so now you have information. But what about choosing the best stocks? There are any number of different software programs that will enable you to do sophisticated analyses of stocks. For a simple demonstration of this, go to <www.stockstuff.net>. From the main menu, click on "Find Your Next Investment." When you get to that page, click on "Basic Stock Screening," where you will be asked to pick eight criteria for the kind of stock you want. Suppose you want to find companies with a market capitalization (market cap) of over 50 billion (these are giants like IBM, Microsoft, and General Motors), a one-year growth rate of 10% to 25%, and a current dividend yield of 2% to 4%. Fill in these choices, plus a few others, and click "Search Database." You will then be presented with a list of stocks that meet your criteria.

There is a 30-criteria screen at the same site, but this is still kid stuff. The more complex software will give you many more choices and allow you to fine-tune your criteria much more exactly. This software will use data from a quote server, like Data Broadcasting's eSignal, so that

> **If you're on the move, but have to be in touch with your investments, you can have a wireless modem hooked up to your laptop.**

information is always current. A good place to find screening software is in the American Association of Individual Investors *Computerized Investing* magazine (see Resources in Chapter 1).

Brokers Online

In Chapter 5, we went over the difference between full-service brokers and discount brokers: full-service brokers give advice, but charge higher commissions, while the discounters give no advice, and charge substantially lower commissions. By trading online, you can give yourself yet another discount—in this case, a big one. Buying and selling stocks has never been cheaper for the individual investor.

Which is the best online broker? There seem to a number of "bests" these days; each rating service and financial magazine has its favorite. But trying to find the best broker is much like trying to find the best breed of dog. In neither case is there any "best"; instead, you need to consider what your needs are. Some brokers will serve these needs better than others. Indeed, in order to establish an identity and serve a market niche, online brokers are busy establishing their own specialties.

Suppose, for example, that you plan to buy only mutual funds and will do very little buying and selling once you have your portfolio set up. In this case, you may want to go with a broker that carries many mutuals, like Charles Schwab or Waterhouse. Most brokers have a number of funds that you can buy and sell for nothing—no commissions and no loads. Larger brokers tend to have more of these kind of no-commission funds than smaller brokers. This is something you need to inquire about when deciding on a broker; ask them how many mutual funds they carry and how many of these are commission-free.

On the other hand, if you plan to buy and sell stocks regularly, you will want a broker who charges very low commissions *and* gives good service. The difference between the $30 commissions charged by some of the larger discount brokers and the $8 to $12 commissions offered by many of the smaller ones can add up to substantial amounts. Suppose, for example, that you make a hundred trades in a year. At an average of $30 a trade, you'll be putting out $3,000 in commissions. If you're paying $10 a trade, however, the total commissions will come to only $1,000, a saving of $2,000 a year.

A few brokers charge no commission at all for most trades. Should you sign up with them? Not necessarily, because they make their money by routing your orders to certain market makers who pay the brokerage to send orders their way. These individuals specialize in trading certain stocks, but the prices they offer for your stocks may not be the best you could obtain in a more open market. Even though zero commissions sounds awfully good, you are probably better off with a low-fee broker who deals with multiple, competitive market makers.

If you want to trade low-priced stocks, you will often need to buy thousands of shares at one time. Certain brokers will make you pay through the nose for transactions such as these, while others will charge just a single, low fee for any number of shares. Be sure to read the commission schedules carefully and ask questions if you have any doubts.

Let's take a look at some of the largest brokerages:

Charles Schwab ranks consistently high in customer service. They have the largest number of local offices, where customers can get individual attention and a variety of information services. Schwab has positioned itself as the broker for conservative investors who may trade infrequently, but want good service and help on financial planning. A visit to the Schwab web site reveals a menu with topics like "Planning," "Retirement," "Estate," "College," and "Tax." Schwab sells over 3,000 mutual funds, about 1,400 of which are no fee, no commission.

Schwab charges relatively high commissions compared to many other online brokers: $29.95 is the basic fee for trading online, while broker assisted trades cost $39 and up, depending on how many shares you buy or sell. At Schwab, it can be very expensive to trade large volumes of stocks. Customer criticisms center around these high costs, delays in reaching brokers by phone on busy days, and occasional disruptions of online services. These criticisms are mild, however, compared to those directed at other large brokers. <www.schwab.com>.

Fidelity also receives gold stars from its clients for good service. They also mention good phone support and good market research and fund screening at the web site. Fidelity sells more than 3,500 mutual funds, of which about 1,000 are no load, no commission.

Commissions at Fidelity are about average if you make at least twelve trades a year ($14.95-$19.99 online). If you buy and sell very infrequently, however, you will pay $25 to $30 per trade. Broker-assisted rates are high: $59 and up. <www.fidelity.com>.

Datek is one of the "bare-bones" brokers, meaning that they don't offer the kind of extras you will find at Schwab and Fidelity. However, their commissions are substantially cheaper: $9.99 for up to 5,000 shares, market, or limit orders; $25 with broker-assist. The price of each stock in your portfolio is updated during the day and there are real-time, streaming quotes. You can trade low-priced stocks at the same commissions, but only if they are listed on Nasdaq; no OTC or Canadian stocks.

Like many of the large brokerages, Datek has been overwhelmed by new customers and the volume has led to complaints about the service, both online and by phone.

By the time you read this, it may have been cleared up, but be sure to check (see the online rating service for brokers described later in this chapter). <www.datek.com>.

Ameritrade is one of the least expensive brokers, charging only $8 to trade any number of shares. Limit and stop orders are $13 and broker-assisted trades are $18. If your account amounts to $10,000 or more, you can pay a flat fee of $800 a year for a maximum of 240 trades (this comes to just $3.33 a trade). Ameritrade offers a number of extras, including detailed company financial reports and stock charts. They also offer "StockQuest," which will screen 10,000 stocks with more than 50 parameters.

Ameritrade has been aggressively—and successfully—attracting new customers, but this has led to complaints about slow service. If they can get these problems cleared up, however, this broker offers some of the cheapest commissions combined with useful services. <www.ameritrade.com>.

E*Trade advertises that its new Power E*Trade will offer extra-fast execution of trades. Fees are $14.95 for up to 5000 shares traded online, then .01 per share for the entire order; broker-assist by phone is $15 extra. You can trade Canadian stocks for about $19 a trade, a service that many brokers either do not offer or charge high commissions for. Like all the online brokers, you can try out E*Trade's virtual web site before signing up. This would be especially wise in this case, because E*Trade's web site is quite complex and difficult to navigate. <www.etrade.com>.

Waterhouse Securities has recently acquired other brokerages like Kennedy-Cabot and Jack White. This means that they carry an enormous number of mutual funds—more than 7,000, with at least 1,000 of these being no load and no fee. Commissions for stock trading are $12 online for up to 5,000 shares, and $45 for broker-assisted trades. Waterhouse has many branch offices in the United States and Canada and offers services like free checking and debit cards (most large brokerages offer these services). You can also get company reports from S&P and Zack's.

Waterhouse has many loyal customers who give it good reviews. Complaints from other customers include slow phone service and difficulties with the web site. <www.waterhouse.com>.

Merrill, Lynch, the giant full-service broker, has decided to go after the online trading business. For $1,500, you can buy an unlimited number of trades for a year. Or, if you need advice, you can still consult a broker. Merrill, Lynch wants to offer both kinds of services—full-price trades with broker advice and assistance, and low-priced online trading.

I expect other full-service brokers will follow Merrill's lead, and, as discount brokers offer an increasing number of online services, the old distinctions will begin to fade. Before long, most brokers will offer a full range of low-cost services to their customers.

Investors should be aware that the online technology for trading stocks is still fairly new. All the exasperating things we mentioned about computer technology at the beginning of the chapter are present here. Some brokerages, however, have the technology down much better than others. It's important to try out the virtual web site

> I expect other full-service brokers will follow Merrill's lead, and, as discount brokers offer an increasing number of online services, the old distinctions will begin to fade.

of the broker you are considering and see if you can navigate it easily.

New investors need to know that service is not what it used to be—or should be—at many of the large brokers. In their race to compete and sign up as many new clients as possible, these brokers have neglected the basics of customer service. As a result, if you should need to contact a broker by phone, you will often find yourself waiting thirty minutes or more. Online service is often disrupted, many web sites are slow and difficult to navigate, and tech support is hard to contact. You should not accept this state of affairs as simply the costs of doing business online. There is more at stake here than simple inconvenience, particularly when trading profits are jeopardized by the delays. You can send a message to the offending brokers by not signing up with them, by registering complaints if you are already a customer, or by switching to a new broker.

Some of the smaller brokers, like Quick and Reilly and InvestTrade, have avoided the rapid expansion that has degraded customer service at the larger brokerage houses. Investors at Schwab and Fidelity also have fewer complaints about service. It's the large, low-cost brokers that are in trouble right now. By the time you read this book, they may have corrected many of these problems, but like your Mama told you, you better shop around!

But how do you decide which broker might be best for you—and which are the ones to avoid? In addition to the information above, there is an extremely useful web site for all investors, experienced or novice, at <www.sonic.net/donaldj/>. Here you will find a list of online brokers, their commission schedules, services, *and* commentary from users. This is great information. For example, you may discover that the broker you are leaning toward has attracted a number of complaints about the speed and reliability of their web site. I have had personal experience with a faulty web site; I was foiled several times when I was in a hurry to make trades (I have since changed bro-kers). This is the site to go to before you make a final deci-sion about any online broker; a half-hour spent reading the reports will save you a lot of grief later on. And once you have a broker, you are encouraged to give feedback of your own at this site.

After you have signed up with an online broker with a good, workable web site, you will find that using the service is simple. To make a trade, simply click on "Trading." You will then be presented with a short list of questions about the trade: Are you buying or selling? Which company (be ready with the stock symbol)? How many shares? Are you willing to take whatever the going price is for the stock (a market order), or do you want to specify a price (a limit order)? The instructions at the site should be straightforward and, as long as the site is work-ing properly, you should have no trouble navigating through it. If you do encounter any problems, you can contact the tech support either by phone or by e-mail.

Day Trading

The ability to trade quickly and cheaply online has led many individuals to try *day trading*. While a num-ber of investors may buy and sell a few times a day, a *day trader* has come to mean an individual who makes it a full-time job. Because of the high risk and large amounts of cash required, day trading used to be practiced only by professional investors. It involves buying and selling stocks within a very short time-frame, often just minutes or less. If the stock a trader just bought ticks up a quarter of a point, he or she might sell at a small profit; if it goes down an eighth, the trader might sell at a loss. The technique is based

on a large volume of trades with a small profit or loss
on each one; a day trader might make dozens, even
hundreds, of trades in one day. The goal, of course, is
to make more profitable than unprofitable trades. As
you might imagine, this is a frenetic, nerve-wracking
occupation.

Large amounts of money can be—and are—gained
and lost by day traders, with the novices generally on
the losing side. In spite of all the enthusiastic ads
that describe how much money you could be making,
this is yet another case where the real money is made
by the people giving the classes—and by the brokers,
who make commissions on every trade. So don't quit
your job just yet. Only if you become a full-time, professional trader, will you possess the skills and know
the risks of day trading; as a beginner, you're better
off starting out slowly.

Message Boards

If you are already online, you are certainly aware of the
various message boards and chat groups where you can
discuss almost any subject you can imagine. It will come as
no surprise to you, then, that there are a large number of
message boards for most publicly traded companies where
investors can chat about the prospects for the company.

If you are a tender soul, sensitive, and easily offended,
however, you may wish to avoid the financial message
boards altogether. For many people, the boards are simply
places to exchange information about a company. For others, however, they are arenas to vent their spleen against
what they view as inept management, push their own
favorite stocks, or carry on about whatever their current
gripe is. They often do this in very colorful language,

cursing with equal fervor the managers who are ruining the company and any other posters on the board who disagree with them. If a company's stock is not doing well, the postings grow even more shrill, reaching an ever-higher pitch as the stock descends.

Having said this, however, I also want to say that I have found some very useful information on these boards. A number of different servers carry them, with postings for almost any stock on the market. Only the extremely small start-ups have, as yet, no group of investors interested enough to start a chat group.

Yahoo provides message boards—also called "threads" —for stocks in its investment section. Go to <www.yahoo. com> and click on "Stock Quotes." Then fill in the stock symbol of the company you want to discuss in the "Get Quotes" square. Allow a few seconds for the stock to be found, then scroll down and you will see the symbol with its daily statistics. In the area to the right, you will see a number of choices, including "Msgs" (messages). Click "Msgs" and you will open up the message board for that company. All you need now is a pseudonym like "Aardvark" or "Goforbroke" and you're ready to do your own postings.

A few more warnings about the boards: Remember the section on *short selling* in Chapter 18? Short sellers make money when a stock goes *down* in value; it would, therefore, be in their interest to make other investors believe that a company is doing poorly, so that they will sell their shares and drive the price down. And this is just what some short sellers, or "shorts," do; they post dire warnings about the imminent collapse of this or that deal, rumored lawsuits against the company, or anything else that might push anxious shareholders into unloading their stock. This is why you will see messages railing against the "shorts" trying to drive the price down.

Not all negative news comes from shorts of course. Sometimes, the boards contain timely warnings about

impending troubles for the company, or, on other occa-
sions, you will hear about good news that may drive the
share price up. The times you should be especially wary is
when a poster is touting some other stock that he or she
expects to go sky-high any day now. The poster may be
doing you a favor—or this may be simply an attempt to
drive the stock price up so the poster can unload 10,000
shares at a profit. (I'm certain that I recognized Cousin
Jack touting a gold futures company. . .) If you stay on a
certain thread for a while, you will begin to recognize who
is on the level and who isn't.

Conclusion

If you really want to be a hands-on investor, there's no
better way than by taking advantage of all the opportunities on the Internet. An online investor, once he or she
knows how to navigate the various sites, is an informed
and empowered investor. Whether you plan on owning
only mutual funds or decide on a career as a stock trader,
being online will make it all easier.

Resources

As you pursue investments online, you will inevitably come
upon many interesting Web sites on your own. I have mentioned a number of sites in this chapter, but here are a few
more to get you started.

Ask Jeeves. <www.ask.com>. One of the best search engines,
Jeeves can direct you to many investment sites, especially company home sites (yes, there actually is a picture of an English
butler ready to do your bidding).

InvestorGuide. <www.investorguide.com>. Need some help in
finding new sites? Here you will find links to thousands of
investment-oriented web sites.

StockTools. <www.stocktools.com>. A useful site with many inventive services.

Silicon Investor. <www.techstocks.com>. This is another good, all-round site, but I especially like its message boards.

Raging Bull. <www.ragingbull.com>. Another useful general investment site with good message boards.

PART 3

HIGH-RISK INVESTING

sometimes think, the answers to these questions are not obvious.

First: *Why do you want to be in business for yourself?* Because it somehow seems more secure than working for someone else? If so, forget it—the great majority of new businesses fail. Because you like the idea of taking an hour (or a day, or a week) off any time you feel like it? Forget that reason, too. Entrepreneurs as a group work harder than almost anybody. The hours, quipped one veteran, are 7 A.M. to 7 P.M., six days a week, plus worrying time in the evenings and praying time on Sunday (just a *little* help, dear Lord, in meeting the payroll next week).

As for making a lot of money, it's true that starting a company offers a possible road to riches. (Look at Bill Gates, the boy wonder who created Microsoft Corp., who is now the richest man in the world.) But not only is the road risky, it sometimes leads in the wrong direction.

Let's say you open a restaurant because you love to cook. To make big money, however, you'll have to run not

Ladies and Gentlemen, I think it's clear that the market
is trying to tell us something about this product.

Chapter 23

Investing in Yourself: Starting Your Own Business

To some, there is no vision so enticing as starting a business. Just think! (says that small, seductive voice). You'd be doing exactly what you want to do. You'd be your own boss. And you'd make a lot of money besides. Now that you have some capital, moreover, you don't need to wait; you can *Just Do It!* After all, doesn't investing in your own business automatically make more sense than investing in someone else's?

The answer to that question is a definite maybe. Starting a business of your own is a noble ambition, but one that is hard to achieve. This chapter will help you think about whether you really want to pursue it—and if so, what to do first.

Two Questions

For starters, you need to ask yourself two funda mental questions. Despite what would-be entrepreneur just one restaurant but many—a chain. And once you head down that path, you won't be spending much time at the stove. I have a friend who began a cabinetmaking business. It was successful, and pretty soon he had six employees. The employees built the cabinets (a task my friend enjoyed) while he bid new jobs (a task he didn't enjoy at all).

Essentially, there are only two good reasons for starting your own business. One, you have something you really want to do, and you can plausibly imagine doing it in your own company. Two, you think you'd enjoy the incredible variety of tasks involved in starting a business: handling the money, hiring the help, dealing with customers, etc., etc. If neither statement applies to you, you'd better find another place to invest your money.

But suppose you do pass that first test. Now you have to answer the second fundamental question: *How much money do you propose to invest—and is it enough?* No single investment can eat through a portfolio faster than a struggling small business. You set yourself up, and you begin to get a few customers. You're not making money yet, but you think you will fairly soon, so you invest a little more. And a little more. And a little more . . . .

Granted, you can read plenty of stories about entrepreneurs who withdrew their life savings, mortgaged their houses, and sold all their worldly possessions to fund their companies and are now multimillionaires. What you *don't* hear about are the entrepreneurs who withdrew everything, mortgaged everything, and sold everything . . . and wound up in bankruptcy court because their companies failed anyway.

So unless you're the devil-may-care sort (and if you are, then why are you reading this book?), you should figure out what you need for peace-of-mind money—a nest egg, college funds, insurance, whatever—in case your business goes belly-up. After you determine how much you need, the remainder is the amount you have to invest

> After you determine how much you need, the remainder is the amount you have to invest in your business. Now you can begin to research the cost of getting started in your chosen field.

in your business. Now you can begin to research the cost of getting started in your chosen field.

This peace-of-mind money is part of a "Plan B" that all people who invest in themselves should have. If the worst happens and the new business has to fold, will you still be able to pay the rent? Will you be able to get a job similar to the one you had or go back to your old profession?

Despite your best efforts, "Plan A" may fail because of factors totally beyond your control. You may do everything right in starting up your business and then, a year later, suddenly find yourself in the middle of an economic recession. Even well-planned, well-run firms can founder in a turbulent economic environment. A good Plan B can help you conduct an orderly retreat instead of being subject to a rout.

PLANNING

Okay, suppose starting a business of your own really *is* your dream. Your motivations withstand scrutiny; the money you have available to invest seems like enough. So you decide to plunge in. You're going to buy (or create) that restaurant, set up that shop, hang out your shingle as a computer programmer or graphic designer or furniture builder. Maybe you even want to start a company capable of rapid growth, such as a temporary-personnel agency or an environmental consulting firm.

Whatever your business, remember that entrepreneurship, like investing, isn't magic, it's a skill. Like any skill, it can be learned, and like any skill, it's sharpened by experience. To start, what you need is a little information-and-experience gathering. There are three basic steps to this.

1. Immerse yourself in the culture of entrepreneurship. Read books about starting a company (see Resources). Subscribe to *Inc.* and *Entrepreneur* magazines. Talk to people who have started businesses—friends, relatives, neighbors, local shopkeepers. You'll find that most are glad to share their experiences.

2. Learn everything you can about the industry you propose to enter. You wouldn't dream of starting a computer company without knowing something about computers—so don't imagine you can set up a travel agency just because you like to take trips.

   If you've never worked in the business, take a job for a year or two. Subscribe to some of the trade magazines for the industry. Contact the industry's trade association and ask whether they have any materials for new entrepreneurs. Again, go talk with people who have started companies in this field. Some may not give you the time of day, but others will be only too happy to advise an enterprising newcomer how to proceed. After all, they were once in your shoes.

3. Write out a business plan and ask a few knowledgeable people to critique it. Putting your plan down on paper forces you to confront questions that a lot of novices prefer to avoid. Exactly what do you intend to sell, and to whom? Who is the competition, and what will your company offer that your competitors don't? How do you propose to make prospective customers aware of your existence? What do you think revenues will be after

> **Once you've drafted the plan, search out a few sympathetic readers—maybe a lawyer, an accountant, or just friends with relevant business experience.**

six months? After a year? When will you start turning a profit?

You can get guidance on writing a plan from the books and tapes listed in Resources, but the fundamental idea is simple. The plan should explain, in detail, why and how your business can succeed.

Once you've drafted the plan, search out a few sympathetic readers—maybe a lawyer, an accountant, or just friends with relevant business experience. You can be sure they'll poke plenty of holes in it, but it's better to plug them in the planning stage than wait until you've launched the business.

CAPITAL

Since this is a book about investment, we'll leave the details of how to do market research, how to set up a corporation, and so forth, to others. But you should know a little about where to look, aside from your own portfolio, for money for your enterprise.

Venture capital—that is, money from organized venture capital partnerships—is probably not for you. Venture capitalists typically fund new companies that have huge growth potential, and that are managed by executives with substantial business experience. Probably less than 1% of all new companies started in the United States each year are plausible candidates for venture money.

Bank loans are hard for new companies to get. Typically, banks require collateral (a mortgage on your house, for example) or a personal guarantee (you'll pay back the loan even if the company goes broke) or both. In some circumstances new companies may qualify for so-called SBA loans, which are bank loans guaranteed by the federal government's Small Business Administration, or for similar state-guaranteed loans. Consult some local bankers.

Buying a Business

A good way to maximize your chances for success in business is to buy a going concern in a field you already know about—and care about. Consider this example.

Ernie and his brother Jim had each worked in the natural-foods industry for 15 years. Between them, their experience covered most aspects of the field. When a small natural-foods store in their town came up for sale, the two brothers moved fast. With the help of a state-guaranteed bank loan to add to their personal capital, they were able to swing the deal. The state agency was impressed with their experience in the field and this helped in obtaining the loan guarantee.

The store was already profitable, but with their experience, Ernie and Jim improved certain aspects of the business and a year later were bringing in even more customers. One visit to the store shows you why. The produce bins are filled with ripe, flawless organic fruits and vegetables, the shelves are neatly stocked with a variety of fine products, the clerks are friendly and helpful—in short, this is a very pleasant place to shop. It's clear that the store is run by people who care about their customers, and about natural foods.

New entrepreneurs might consider starting off by buying an operating business, as Ernie and Jim did, instead of starting from scratch. If you add experience and a real interest in the field to this equation, you have a formula that can substantially increase your chances of success.

Friendly money—that is, loans or equity investment from parents, other relatives, or friends—is probably your best bet. Sometimes you can even find a successful local entrepreneur (an "angel") who invests in new companies as a sort of hobby. Ask accountants and other businesspeople.

One caution: The same rules apply to investments from parents and friends as apply to any investment. Spell out exactly what they're getting for their money (so much of the company's stock; a loan at 6% interest due in three years—whatever). Ask a lawyer to look over the language. You need to treat them as you would any investor, explaining the risk and keeping them honestly informed of your progress. Families and friendships have been torn apart by business misunderstandings. It isn't worth it.

DREAMS

Dreams, enthusiasm, and a positive attitude are fundamental to any business venture. Some people hesitate to do the necessary planning for fear that cold facts will chill their optimism. "If I think about it too much, I'll never do it!" is the argument. Planning, however, is not the same as worrying. Planning is the process of bringing dreams down to earth—of testing them against reality as thoroughly as possible.

Lest you think we have thrown unnecessary amounts of cold water on your dreams in this chapter, remember that the landscape is littered with business failures that tried to operate on enthusiasm alone. Success in business emerges from a *balance* of positive thinking and careful planning. This is not a guaranteed formula, but it is a powerful one.

You owe it to yourself to treat your dreams with care. Test them well against reality in the planning stage before exposing them to the hard knocks of the real world.

This chapter is by John Case, formerly a senior editor at *Inc.* magazine, who has written extensively on the successes and failures of various small businesses. He has also written several books on more general topics relating to business and the economy, including *Open-Book Management: The Coming Business Revolution.* HarperBusiness, 1995. $23 (hardcover). His latest is *The Open Book Experience.* Addison-Wesley, 1997. $25 (hardcover).

If your business grows to where you are employing even a few people, you will want these books. They demonstrates how to involve employees in the business by opening the company's books—that is, by giving the workers the same information as the managers. A smart, well-informed employee who knows exactly how his or her job contributes to the bottom line is an invaluable asset to any business. In the most advanced, socially conscious firms, the lines between managers and workers are beginning to blur, and everyone involved is becoming happier and more successful because of this.

Resources

Inc: The Magazine for Growing Companies, Subscription Service Dept., P.O. Box 51534, Boulder, CO 80321-1534. (800) 234-0999 $14 for 18 issues. <www.inc.com-incmagazine>.

Inc. publishes articles on start-ups, the ins and outs of running a small company, and many fascinating stories of successful and not-so-successful entrepreneurs.

In addition, it offers a number of books and videos with titles like *Anatomy of a Start-Up, How to Really Start Your Own Business* (book and video), *Inc. Guide to Creating a Successful Business Plan*, and others. Subscribing will bring you a complete list of titles.

In Business: The Magazine for Environmental Entrepreneuring, 419 State Avenue, Emmaus, PA 18049. 6 issues/year, $27.

In Business covers the growing number of small businesses in the environmental field. If your interests run in that direction, this is for you. A recent issue featured articles on the natural-clothing trade, franchise opportunities in the environmental field, Ben & Jerry's Ice Cream (a socially conscious company), retail sales for solar systems, nonpolluting cars, and getting in on the ground floor of the water conservation industry.

Growing a Business by Paul Hawken. Fireside, 1988. $11.00

This book addresses the philosophical side of starting a business—initially of equal importance to the practical. It deals with the mental and emotional work you need to do when your business is in the planning stage. Hawken believes that an idea for a business should start from deep inside you.

There is also a good deal of excellent practical advice. Hawken has successfully started several small businesses himself, so the advice in the book is drawn from experience. Even though it was written in 1987, this book still gets rave reviews from readers, who credit it with helping them to make their business a success (check out the reviews on Amazon.com).

I think every prospective entrepreneur should read this book. My feeling is that one of the main reasons new businesses fail is that their owners don't have a clear idea of what they want to achieve. Instead of the business beginning from a place deep inside of them, it starts from a surface idea: "Video stores seem to be making a lot of money, so let's start one." That kind of thing.

CHAPTER 24

CAVEAT EMPTOR: LET THE BUYER BEWARE

SHORT SKIRTS AND SUPER BOWLS

A lot of people were disappointed on December 31, 1990. For the first time in 23 years, an NFL team had won the Super Bowl in January (of 1990) but the S&P Industrial Average had failed to make a gain for the year. In every other year since 1967, an NFL win had meant an up year, an AFL win a down year. (Well, actually, in 1984, the average went from 184.24 to 184.36, even though an AFL team won, but who wants to split hairs?)

Other "analysts" have noted that in years when women's hemlines have gone up, the markets have also gone up. Investors usually smile when they talk about such theories, but there is always a touch of "who knows, maybe it's true" in their smiles. Many investors are willing to listen to virtually any theory if it has a good record.

Quite a few of them also seem to be willing to respond to the direct-mail solicitations and the ads in the journals for various buying methods and advisers with "systems." I know this is true because the number of these ads and solicitations seems to increase daily.

"230% profit in ONE YEAR!" "Easy to carry out!" "Hasn't failed in 20 years!" And the phone solicitors are even less restrained. In the process of writing this book, I responded to a bunch of ads and solicitations. "Did any of them sound good?" you ask. Let me tell you, they *all* sounded good! Take the silver salesmen (please!).

The silver salesmen called to tell me that the precious metal had reached a new low and that knowledgeable investors were buying. They, of course, had a method for buying silver that would maximize my profits. Every time—*every* time—silver had reached a new low in the past, buyers had made thousands of dollars. Did I want to make thousands of dollars, or was I (they implied) one of those schleps who let great opportunities pass them by?

It sounded terrific. The only thing that gave me pause was that I was acquainted with the silver market, and silver was continuing to go down. I finally got rid of the silver-tongued salespeople and over the next few months watched the price of silver decline steadily: 5%; 10%; it was down 20% the last time I looked.

My father used to say that the more you knew about a subject, the more you realized how biased and inaccurate was the reporting of it in the newsmagazines. This observation translates beautifully to the hard sells aimed at the individual investor. The more you know about a market, the more likely you will see through the sales pitches.

> **Did I want to make thousands of dollars, or was I (they implied) one of those schleps who let great opportunities pass them by?**

Many salespeople depend on the inexperience of the average investor. They are experts at putting out just enough information to make an investment sound unbeatable. If you are acquainted with the market they're working in, you may be able to see flaws in what they're saying. But if you don't know about it, then there's all the more reason to leave it alone. Investing in a market you're not familiar with is little more than gambling.

Don't try to argue with them—just tell them you're not interested and hang up. Salespeople try to make it sound as if there's no tomorrow for the opportunity they're offering. But there are always opportunities in the investment world, and the best ones are caught by those knowledgeable enough to recognize them.

LET'S LOOK AT THE RECORD . . .

Concerning the ads in the journals and the direct-mail flyers, the new investor needs to realize that the majority of strategies for buying and selling have been around for years in one form or another. If you see something that looks really good, it needs to be put to several tests:

1. Is the historical data that supports the strategy real or hypothetical? Anyone can figure out a system and then backtest it with selective historical data. Anyone can, and does—the ads are full of such systems. Buying and selling in the real world, however, is a different proposition. This is not to dismiss these methods entirely—some of them may have value, but they need to be checked out thoroughly, and looked at in the light of the markets of the present day.

   This is especially true at present because the last half of the 1990s saw one of the greatest bull markets in history. Most of the performance

The fact that the admonition "Let the buyer beware!" has been around since Roman times says a lot about sales methods through the ages.

records you will see are based on material from these years. But the systems that do the best under these favorable market conditions are often the ones that will do worst in a bear market.

Whether this amazing market performance will continue is the subject of much speculation, informed and otherwise. Good times or bad, though, the new investor needs to be wary of the winning records displayed so enthusiastically. In this case, past performance is not only no guarantee, it may not even be an indication of future results.

2. How easy is it to carry out the system? Some methods require constant attention to the markets, something not all investors are willing to do.

3. What risks are involved? As you begin to get on mailing lists, you will receive direct-mail flyers advertising futures-related systems. Some of these systems cost as much as $3,000 but promise fantastic returns. In these cases, you have to ask yourself the obvious question, i.e., why do they even bother to sell these systems if they work so well for *them*? By now, they should be buying homes in Acapulco and spending all their time at the beach. The sellers try to anticipate these concerns by protesting that they want to "share" these systems with others. Such generosity! Such altruism! Only $3,000!

So caveat emptor! The fact that the admonition "Let the buyer beware!" has been around since Roman times says a lot about sales methods through the ages. Nowhere do you need to "caveat" more than with solicitations for investment systems and strategies.

THE GREATEST DANGER

The greatest danger for the new investor—or any investor—is not, as you might think, the sharpies trying to get hold of your money or the big, bad bear markets. It's something much closer to home: It is his or her belief that it's possible to attain great returns in a short period with little risk.

After all, you hear about people making a killing in this or that all the time. "So why not me?" you ask. This is the question that leaves you open to the clever salespeople or the occasional dishonest adviser.

The media are no help in this area. Success stories make better copy than failures, unless a spectacular scam is exposed. You're much more likely to hear about the lady who made $50,000 in six months buying distressed real estate than about the guy who bought gold futures on a sure bet and lost $10,000 in two weeks. The media are biased this way—and even your friends are more likely to tell you about their successes than their failures.

Inexperience coupled with this kind of misinformation can lead to investments that are too risky. It's important to point out here that it's not necessarily "desire" or "greed" that gets people in trouble, in spite of what traditional moralists might say. Everyone desires the best return on his or her money with the lowest possible risk. And "greed" is simply desire run amok. The thing to watch for is a tendency to believe that *you* can find an exception to the risk-return ratio and come out a big winner in a short time. With a belief like this, you have already done 90% of the work of the salespeople. All they have to do now is turn you in their direction and give a little push. . . .

The Crash of '87

When Charles II was restored to the throne of England in 1660, he quipped that he was unable to find anyone who wasn't delighted to have him back.

In a similar vein, since the stock market crash of October 1987, it's extremely difficult to find even one adviser who didn't predict this debacle. You will see the ads for these advisers, if you haven't already: ". . . out of stocks in May of 1987 . . . ," ". . . advised readers to get into the money markets in early October . . . ," ". . . sold all equities in August of 1987 . . . ."

So *many* advisers seem to have predicted this crash, in fact, it leads one to the inescapable conclusion that it was actually they who *caused* it. If the accounts you read are accurate, there must have been at least several hundred advisers telling their thousands of readers and followers to get out of stocks—certainly enough to cause the massive sell-off of October 19. . . .

This does not mean you shouldn't ever be adventurous or try occasional investments with some level of risk. What we're talking about is simply putting the odds in your favor—and this happens when you research an investment carefully.

For example, buying stocks of selected small companies, using the methods described in Chapter 19, can bring large returns with a manageable degree of risk. For those who want to go after the "big money," this is the kind of place to look—at least for a part of your portfolio.

GOING BROKE WITH BROKERS

It sometimes seems as if there are quite a few things to watch out for in the field of investing, doesn't it? I think this is because anywhere you find money, you find people who are willing to stretch the truth—or ignore it altogether—in order to get hold of more money.

The version we are dealing with here is stockbrokers who put themselves first and their clients a poor second. As noted in Chapter 5, there are so-called full-commission brokers and discount brokers. A discount broker gives no advice on what to buy, whereas a full-commission broker is like a personal financial adviser specializing in securities.

If you choose a full-commission broker, he or she should have a clear picture of such things as your tax situation, your personal risk-reward ratio, and your goals for your portfolio. The investments the broker recommends should be made taking these factors into consideration. A feeling that these factors are not being considered should set off some alarm bells.

A few other practices that should also set the alarms ringing: Because brokers are paid from commissions on buying and selling securities, some brokers have been known to recommend trades simply to gain those commissions. This practice is called *churning* an account. I knew a broker who would call up a client and recommend that he buy more of a certain stock. When the client demurred, saying he had enough shares of that company, the broker might then recommend that he *sell* some of the same shares. This is churning.

A broker who is constantly coming up with "hot tips" is someone to watch out for. He or she may promise unrealistic returns or ignore your risk-reward ratio by recommending investments that are too speculative for you.

Brokerage houses will sometimes agree to "make a market" in a new issue of a stock; this means they will be looking for buyers. It's a good idea to establish with your broker from the start that whenever he or she is recommending a company in order to make a market, you want to know about it. The company making the new issue may indeed be a good investment, but you have to know where the advice is coming from.

Occasional bad advice is not a basis to sue or go to arbitration. Obviously, your broker isn't going to hit all winners, but if you feel you have gotten consistently bad advice, the best thing to do is to take your business elsewhere.

There are certain offenses, however, for which you should seek recourse. These include the abovementioned churning, as well as lying, or executing trades improperly in a way that hurt you financially.

Most brokerage houses require that you sign a paper agreeing to submit disputes to arbitration. The large stock exchanges and Nasdaq hold hearings to mediate disputes between customers and brokers. These hearings are generally very fair to the individual investor; to ensure impartiality, the majority of people on the arbitration panel are drawn from outside the securities industry. This is your recourse if you feel you have been wronged.

The majority of stockbrokers are honest and most have the interests of their clients at heart. Whether they are skillful at choosing the best investments is something else again; if you are going to pay the extra commissions to get their advice, then the advice had better make you more money.

I know many people who are very satisfied with their brokers and who have developed a friendly relationship with them over the years. If you don't feel comfortable with your broker, however, or feel you've been getting bad advice, you shouldn't hesitate to try someone else—or, perhaps, make your investment choices yourself, buying through a discount broker.

SWITCHING WITH THE MARKET TIMERS

Suppose you could invest in a good equity mutual fund when stocks were going up, sell the fund when the stock market and the fund started going down—and then buy back in at a lower price when things started looking better again. And suppose you could do this at little or no cost.

This is what many investors attempt to do with the help of certain market analysts known as *market timers*. Using every economic indicator known since the beginning of recorded history (including, in some cases, astrology), the market timers perform "technical analysis" of the stock market. They are trying to predict which direction the market is headed and to what degree.

Timing the markets is actually a more respectable method than many of the risky systems you see advertised. Deciding when a market is due to rise or fall is a skill employed successfully by only a minority of advisers—but their recommendations are often accurate enough to be useful to experienced investors.

A lot of high-powered selling of timing systems has been directed at naive investors, however. This is why we include the subject in this chapter. Following the predictions of market timers is not an appropriate tactic for the new investor, but you need to know what all the talk is about. And you need to be prepared for the onslaught of advertisements and direct-mail flyers with rosy-sounding timing statistics.

The goal of investors who follow the predictions of the market timers is to sell their stocks and stock funds when the market has reached its peak, stay out of the market during its decline, and then buy back in at the bottom. This is the opposite of a buy-and-hold strategy: instead of ignoring the ups and downs, the goal is to use the cycles to make as much profit as possible.

Getting in and out of the market, however, can be an expensive proposition if you have to pay commissions on buying and selling a portfolio of stocks. Though many kinds of investors do this, market timing has been especially popular with mutual fund investors, because many mutual funds allow their investors to switch their money, at no cost, from stock funds to money market funds— within the same family of funds, of course.

Thus, if you, or your favorite market timer, felt that the market were about to head south—and take your Fidelity Low-Price Stock Fund down with it—you could call up the Fidelity office and ask to have your money switched to the Fidelity Cash Reserve Fund. Switching simply means you sell your Stock Fund, with its portfolio of small-company stocks, and buy into the Cash Reserve Fund. With your money in this money market fund, you are protected from any downturn in the stock market.

Now you are out of the stock market and are hoping, of course, that the market will go down over the next few weeks or months, so that you can switch back into the Stock Fund when its shares are selling at a substantially lower price.

If, however, the market should confound you and go *up* instead, you will be left behind. The market has a nasty way of doing just this kind of thing—which is why so many people stick to the buy-and-hold strategy. With all their buy and sell recommendations, only about 10 of

As support for the buy-and-hold strategy, however, it's important to note that the majority of these funds—where the managers try to time the market—don't do as well as the overall market, as measured by the various stock indexes. What this illustrates is the great difficulty of timing the ups and downs of the markets.

the prominent market timers have consistently done better than the stock averages over the last five years.

Many mutual funds are becoming less lenient with their switching policies. This is because so many people have been switching their money in and out of equity funds that the managers have had difficulty holding on to the stocks in their portfolios.

Many funds have, therefore, cut back to allowing only a few switches a year, while others have taken to charging a fee. Some timing newsletters, however, still dictate as many as 14 switches a year.

Some investors adopt a *modified* buy-and-hold strategy. If the market timers predict a bear market, these investors modify the balance of their portfolios by switching out of those funds likely to fall the most—such as the small-company funds. They sell these funds and put the cash into bond funds or money market funds.

The managers of most equity mutual funds try to be market timers themselves. They will sell many of their stocks—especially the more volatile ones—in a market downturn. As support for the buy-and-hold strategy, however, it's important to note that the majority of these funds—where the managers try to time the market—don't do as well as the overall market, as measured by the various stock indexes. What this illustrates is the great difficulty of timing the ups and downs of the markets.

GAMBLING

When experienced traders invest in risky markets, they are speculating. When inexperienced investors go into the same markets looking for a quick return, they are simply gambling.

A fair number of investors use the markets as a place to gamble. They try their hand at futures trading or junk bonds or timing the markets—anything for a little excitement. The kind of tried-and-true buying methods discussed in Chapter 20 can seem very staid and boring to them.

If you're well-off and risking only a small portion of your portfolio, a gambling spree won't do much harm. If you're not, then I'd like to suggest the obvious, which is that the World of Investment is not the best place to go looking for thrills. Try the racetrack, or take a few hundred to Vegas or Atlantic City. But keep your capital intact—these days, this is already a venture with plenty of challenge and risk.

The investments described in this section of the book—Part III—are really not suitable for the new investor. Why are they included? A few reasons:

1. General information and interest. You may have wondered about rare coins or the futures markets. You deserve to have them explained in a simple, straightforward manner.

2. Forewarned is forearmed! The riskiest investments are the ones that are sold the hardest. You're going to hear and read a great deal about rare coins, fortunes in the futures markets, and the wonders of options. The salespeople are skillful at their presentations and often depend on your naïveté to sell their product.

3. You may be interested in or have a need for these markets in the future. Many businesspeople and investors use certain futures and options as a way of buying "insurance" on their investments. (This is described in Chapters 26 and 27.) Or you may get interested in a certain kind of collectible at some time in the future.

If and when you do get interested in any of these markets, however, you will probably learn all you can about them before you start buying.

That way you will enter into them as a knowledgeable investor, not a gambler.

Plus ca change,
plus c'est la meme chose . . .

The more things change, the more they remain the same, especially in the case of investment scams. Here we have a time-honored scam that has been updated to the Internet.

In the roaring stock market of the 1920s, it was common for wealthy investors to form groups called "stock pools," to buy large quantities of stock in a company, thus driving the price up. Invariably, other investors would try to get on board, believing that the rise in price was caused by a real interest in the stock. But, as the stock rose, the members of the stock pool would then sell their shares at a profit, getting out before the inevitable collapse of the stock.

These so-called "pump and dump" schemes had been going on long before the twenties, and continue to the present day. The difference then was that the scale of the operations was larger, and they weren't yet illegal. These days, pump and dumps are practiced mostly with small-cap stocks, because it takes less money to drive up the price of a low-priced stock with only a few million shares outstanding.

Now, lo and behold, this ancient scam has made it online. Free Web sites, with names like "Great Stocks" or "Quick Picks," advertise a hot new stock, the identity of which will be released at, say, 10:30 AM. At 10:30, everyone is waiting to buy—except the Quick Picks people, who are waiting to *sell!* (They already own a large number of shares, bought at a low price.) At 10:31, the price of the stock suddenly spikes upward, as the unsuspecting public buys the stock, only to fall again after the scam artists have unloaded their shares.

Most analysts want to be paid for their time and research and will charge for revealing their stock picks. The fact that these picks are free should act as a red flag to any investor, new or experienced.

CHAPTER 25

PRECIOUS METALS, RARE COINS, AND OTHER COLLECTIBLES

GOLD!

Gold, indeed! If this book were being written anytime up to a few hundred years ago, it would concentrate mostly on gold, with maybe a few chapters on precious gems and real estate.

Not only does gold have historical prestige, it echoes through the stories we heard as children. What did the king give the young hero as a reward for killing the monster? What was buried under the witch's cottage?

Gold, then, has an emotional appeal that transcends its real investment value in today's markets. Many new investors feel they "should" own some gold. Doesn't it hold its value? Don't the billionaire sheiks in the Middle East own a lot of it? And isn't it a hedge against inflation or a stock market crash?

The facts are, sadly, that in the last decade, gold has lost much of its allure, at least as an investment. Yes, for a long time gold was used as a hedge against bad times. During wars or great upheavals, the price would be driven up by buyers seeking a safe haven for their money. And gold used to go up when the stock market went down.

But no more. When Iraq invaded Kuwait in the summer of 1990, gold took a brief spurt upward. By September, however, it was declining; by January, the price was down to $365 an ounce—$50 lower than a year earlier. Even a shooting war couldn't get it out of the cellar.

So what has happened to gold? In 1980, gold stood at an all-time high of $800 an ounce, and some advisers were predicting prices of $1,200, $1,500, even $2,000 an ounce! What happened was that high oil prices—and the inflation they were helping to cause—were brought under control. In addition, the large, institutional investors found a new way of hedging against a downturn in the stock market—in a word, *currencies*.

If things look bad for the U.S. markets, the big investors will simply buy Swiss francs or Deutschemarks or Japanese yen—whatever economy looks good at the moment. These transactions are carried out instantaneously by computers—a much simpler process than buying gold, which has to be transported and stored.

A further reason for gold being in the dumps is that while demand has stayed relatively flat over the past decade, supply has increased. Unless gold cuff links come back into style, demand is not likely to increase markedly (jewelry is the largest use for gold). So, barring the return

> **So what has happened to gold? In 1980, gold stood at an all-time high of $800 an ounce, and some advisers were predicting prices of $1,200, $1,500, even $2,000 an ounce!**

of double-digit inflation or serious upheavals in the world economy, the best analysis has the price of gold remaining weak during the next decade.

Buying Gold

You say you still want to put some of your assets into gold? Okay, here are several ways of doing this.

First, you can actually buy gold bullion—bars of gold, like the kind they have in Fort Knox. You can get these in various sizes—up to 25 pounds each—or you can buy thin wafers of gold weighing as little as 1 gram. Banks and gold dealers will sell them to you, with a 3% to 10% commission (!) added on. You can then take the gold home with you and hide it in the mattress or bury it in the back yard (be sure to make a good map!).

If, however, you have a waterbed or live in an apartment without a proper yard, the bank will be delighted to store the gold for you and give you a certificate of ownership in return. This is the preferred method of holding gold these days, as hiding the certificate in the mattress

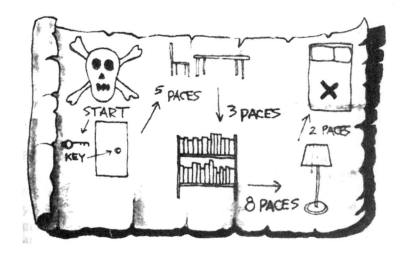

doesn't make for such an uncomfortable lump as the gold bar does. Seriously, the certificate is a safer way of holding the gold. The gold could be lost or stolen, while the certificates are protected by registration.

You can also buy newly minted gold coins at a bank or coin dealer. These so-called bullion coins need to be distinguished from the rare coins discussed below. Rare coins have their own market, whereas the price of the bullion coins goes up and down with the gold market. Coins are easily bought and sold and are a little easier to carry around than gold bars. Commissions range from 2% to 4%.

One of the disadvantages of holding gold is that you don't get any return on it, unless the price goes up. One way around this is to buy shares in companies engaged in mining gold. Dividends from these companies don't usually amount to much, but the stock price will go up if the company makes a big strike in one of its mines. The price will also go up if the price of gold goes up—usually. If the company itself is on the skids, of course, an increase in the price of gold may not help.

Gold-mining stocks are among the riskier ventures, as you might guess. If you want to spread out your risk, try buying shares in a mutual fund owning shares in gold-mining companies. If you must invest in gold, this is probably the least risky way of doing it, though I must warn you that these mutual funds—and the companies they own shares in—are still very high-risk investments.

Finally, if you have it on unassailable authority, like my Cousin Jack, that the price of gold is about to make a meteoric rise, you can invest in gold futures (see Chapter 26 on futures trading). This is combining a very volatile commodity with a very risky trading method, so you'd better be pretty darn sure. As you will discover when you read the chapter on futures, they are generally something for the new investor to avoid. I mention them simply to round out this information on the different ways of buying gold.

. . . AND SILVER

If you have read the section on gold, then you know most of what you need to know about silver. Silver is another metal with a history, not quite so distinguished as that of gold, but just as long.

The silver market is an excellent example of how buying methods that have worked in the past may fail when new situations develop. In the past, when silver fell drastically in price many traders would buy, and eventually the price would rise. During much of the 1990s, salesmen urged investors to buy silver because it had reached new "historic lows." But the silver market responded by making even *lower* historic lows.

The reasons for this are simple enough: The market for silver has changed—demand has flattened out while the supply has increased. And, as with gold, investors who once used silver for hedging against bad times have found new and better ways of doing this.

The various methods of buying silver are similar to those for gold: bullion, coins, stocks in silver-mining companies, and mutual funds. The mutual funds will often buy stocks in both gold and silver mines—it's hard to find a fund specializing in silver only. And, yes, there is a silver futures market.

Unless the world economy and the silver market change radically, however, I would invest only in silver jewelry; there, at least, its beauty is undiminished.

At some point in the next decade, gold and silver will probably rise in value; this will finally give those who have been pushing precious metals a chance to say "I told you so!" Remember, though, that most of them have been predicting a rise for years and years. The increase in value will have to be pretty impressive to make up for all the losses suffered by gold investors during the '80s and '90s.

In the same vein, Harvard economist Robert Reich (the former Secretary of Labor) tells a story about himself.

In early October 1987, he recommended on a radio talk show that his audience sell their stocks immediately. Two weeks later the market crashed, and Reich found himself beset with investors wanting his advice. What they didn't know, as he recounted later, was that he had been predicting a bear market since 1981!

Both these examples should make the reader pause when he or she hears enthusiastic claims of successful market predictions. You have to ask how many times the "guru" was mistaken before finally being right.

RARE COINS

If you read the financial journals, you have seen the ads. Wall Street about to invest in rare coin market! Coins could double in the next year! Only fools and greenhorns are not investing in rare coins!" (Well, they may not actually make that last statement, but it's not hard to catch their drift.)

Even as a new investor, you are probably already aware of the quantity and variety of advertising aimed at you. The investment industry is immense. The people we pay to buy and sell remind me of the people who came to California in 1849 not to look for gold, but to sell mining equipment and other necessities to the miners. It may not have looked as glamorous or exciting, but these people almost always did well.

That fact should give pause to anyone listening to the advertisements. Yes, there are certainly people who make money with investments, but there are also ones who lose. The people selling the picks and shovels, however, make money either way.

This is especially true in the rare coin industry, where the difference between the dealer's price and the customer's price can be as much as 25%. This difference is

> **Even as a new investor, you are probably already aware of the quantity and variety of advertising aimed at you.**

called the *spread*. It means your coin must go up 25% in value before you can sell it back to a dealer for the price you paid for it. There are a few dealers who claim to have smaller spreads, but it's up to the buyer to compare prices.

Just as the merchants to the forty-niners had a lock on the market, the rare coin dealers seem to have a lock not just on the coins, but on information about the rare coin market. It is difficult to find material other than what the industry puts out—though there is plenty of that, and it's very self-serving. You will find a few unbiased sources listed in Resources.

What makes the market in rare coins different from the markets in other collectibles, such as fine art or comic books? The coin dealers have made a big effort to standardize their products.

Since 1986, coins have been "graded" by independent organizations according to their general appearance and lack of blemishes. They are then encased in clear plastic, where they *stay*—woe to any hapless buyer who takes a coin out of its case.

Gone are the days of collectors showing off their precious gold coins to admiring friends. Indeed, it is estimated that true collectors make up less than 5% of the coin market nowadays. Instead, you have the somewhat surreal situation where investors buy a coin encased in plastic, put it away in a dark place, and hope that another investor will eventually pay more for it. It has become a market based almost entirely on perceived value, and while you can argue that this is true of any collectible, at least with works of art you can display and enjoy them while waiting for their value to go up.

The coin market is extremely volatile. It is the kind of investment for only a small percentage of a portfolio—and even then, only for those investors willing to make a real study of the market. Buyers should be prepared to hold coins for a few years—emotionally as well as financially prepared. It can cause a bit of stress to watch the value of your investment decrease by half in a few months. The coin market did well during the 1980s, but its performance in the 1990s has been inconsistent. Don't give up your day job if you decide to invest in rare coins.

GRADING OF COINS

Which coins tend to appreciate in value the most? There are two factors in the value of a coin: its rarity and its condition—its *grade*, in the system set up by the dealers. A coin can have a rating of 1 to 70. The coins most traded are uncirculated; that is, they were never in general circulation and have retained their Mint State condition.

These Mint State (MS) coins have ratings in the mid-60s. The coins you want to buy are the MS64s, MS65s, and MS66s (a rating over MS66 is very rare). Of these, you want the ones with the lowest populations—in short, you want the rarest and highest-quality coins you can afford. These are the ones that increase the most in value. One MS64 1910 Indian head $10 gold piece is worth fifty MS64 1881 Morgan silver dollars, not because of its greater beauty or quality, but simply because there are very few coins of this quality from this particular year in existence.

There are a few things to watch out for if you decide that the rare coin market looks good. Once you start dealing with one firm, the word somehow gets around to other dealers that there's a new dude in town, and soon you're getting phone calls—lots of them. You might be able to prevent this by asking your dealer not to circulate your name, but I have my doubts. It could be that simply subscribing to the *Wall Street Journal* gets your name and number on the mailing and calling lists.

Three Kinds of Valuable Coins

1. Bullion coins. With the American Eagle in 1986, this country joined other countries that mint gold coins. These coins are not used in general circulation as gold was up to 1933. They are bought by people wanting to invest in gold (as we discussed above). There are also silver bullion coins.

   These are not "rare coins." Their value goes up and down with the gold and silver markets.

2. Generic coins. These might be termed "semi-rare." Examples are those silver dollars you've had in your desk drawer for 20 years that you've been wondering what to do with. There are gold coins, too, minted before 1933, which were in general circulation and are not terribly unusual. These coins do have some rarity value, however; their prices are partly tied to supply and demand, partly to the precious-metals markets.

3. True rare coins look pretty much the way they did when they were minted. They were never in circulation, and populations are usually in the hundreds or low thousands. The market for rare coins is not generally tied to the precious-metals markets, though if the price of gold doubled, you would see some movement in rare gold coins.

Aggressive salesmanship is alive and well in the coin market. You will do yourself a big favor by learning as much as you can from independent sources before you start talking to the coin dealers. Their salespeople are fonts of information—torrents! So be firm. Don't let them make you feel like a fool because you don't immediately realize that these recently discovered 1914 Russian gold pieces from the *Czar's personal treasury* will skyrocket in value in a matter of months. They, of course, have only a limited number of these treasures and can't be responsible for what might happen if you should wait till the next day. . . .

Incidentally, speaking of foreign coins, most of the trading in this country is done with American coins. Venturing into foreign coins greatly increases the already speculative nature of the game.

OTHER COLLECTIBLES

If my mother hadn't thrown out my comic books from the 1950s, I'd be extremely rich today. The number of comic book collectors and investors is on its way up. Dealers in the fine arts claim that the arts have outperformed the stock market, but this is another market with extreme volatility. Precious gems are used for investment as well as for decoration.

> **One useful thing to remember, though—and not just in the collectibles market—is that when you come up with a dynamite investment idea, chances are 99 to 1 that a bunch of other smarties came up with the same idea 10 years ago.**

The most recent collectibles are '50s and '60s pop records. The compact disc is turning the old-fashioned 45 and 33⅓ rpm records into rarities; some of the older, more unusual ones are now worth hundreds of dollars; a few are worth thousands.

The tendency of some new investors is to jump at such statistics. Here is something they can understand! No complicated market structures, no research or legwork needed. Just a regular old comic book—buy low, sell high.

One useful thing to remember, though—and not just in the collectibles market—is that when you come up with a dynamite investment idea, chances are 99 to 1 that a bunch of other smarties came up with the same idea 10 years ago. In this case, it's the comics dealers who buy low, sell high—a 50% to 100% spread is not unusual.

Respectable Collectibles

The older, more "respectable" markets deal with art, antiques, and other fine collectibles. Silverware, china, antique dolls, toys, miniatures—there are about 70 recognized categories of collectibles. If you are interested in learning more about a certain type of collectible, several sources are listed at the end of the chapter.

If you have inherited some fine antiques or, perhaps, a collection of miniature animals carved in ebony and are wondering what to do with them, the books in Resources will get you started. Trade associations will help you find a reputable dealer or appraiser; two of these are listed in Resources.

It's a good idea to get clear in your mind whether you are going to be predominantly a collector or an investor—whether you're in it for love or money. It is possible to be both: for example, I have a friend who is a world-renowned authority on Egyptian revenue stamps—but dealing in these stamps is his chosen occupation. For someone to whom it is only an interesting sideline, it's a different game. Do you love those antique dolls for their beauty or because they're valuable? If you're going to spend the kind of money required to have a fine collection, it's something to think about.

If you decide to be an investor, be sure to research how fluid any given market is. The rare coin dealers have made it easy for you to buy and sell (although with a large spread in their favor). But when you come to sell your nineteenth century Shaker rocking chair or your 1958 Elvis album, are there going to be buyers at hand? The ability to move in and out of a market can be worth a good deal if that particular market is going nowhere and you want to put your money elsewhere.

In case you haven't guessed by now, it's probably not a good idea for a new investor to rush out and buy rare coins or other collectibles. You have a much better chance of coming out ahead in the stock market.

I don't like to dismiss a market out of hand, however. When you have gained experience as an investor, you may be drawn to a market because of some interest or expertise in the field. Perhaps your mom didn't throw out your old comics or baseball cards, or you have inherited some beautiful antiques.

If you simply feel drawn to collectibles, the best idea is to pick an area where you have a real affinity or background. Then learn as much as you can about it and start to deal in a small way.

Resources

Coin Dealer Newsletter, P.O. Box 7939, Torrance, CA 90504 (310) 515-7369. <www.greysheet.com>. Weekly. $54/six months, $98/year, $147/two years. The so-called "gray sheet" (yes, its pages are actually gray) will give you the current bid and ask prices for all U.S. rare coins. It also covers trends in the market for coins. The gray sheet is primarily for coin dealers, so the trade language takes some getting used to. If you begin to trade coins seriously, though, this paper is a necessity.

It's easy to find information on the fine collectibles, but harder to find material on things like baseball cards and comic books. One source for popular and fine collectibles is Collector Books, P.O. Box 3009, Paducah, KY 42001. (800) 626-5420. They will send you a free catalog listing the more than 130 books they publish on all kinds of collectibles.

Ralph and Terry Kovel are perhaps the best-known experts on antiques and collectibles. They have written a number of books on different kinds of collectibles. Visit their web site for information on these books and other services: <www.Kovels.com>.

Kovels' Antiques and Collectibles Price List. Three Rivers Press. 1999. $14.95. This price list is updated yearly and contains actual prices from a large number of different collectibles.

Kovels' Know Your Collectibles, by Ralph and Terry Kovel. Crown Publishers, 1992. $16.00 (paperback). A guide to various kinds of fine collectibles. How to buy and sell, determine their value, origin, etc.

If you want to know the value of something you own or have inherited, you will need a good appraiser. The International Society of Appraisers will recommend reputable appraisers in 220 different categories. The ISA may be contacted at 16040 Christensen Road, Suite 102, Seattle, WA 98188. (888) 472-5587. Fax: (206) 241-0436. <www.isa-appraisers.org>. They will send you a pamphlet listing their services and the various categories of appraisers they can recommend. An excellent resource.

CHAPTER 26

FUTURES

T he big, bad futures markets! There seems to be a general consensus about the futures markets: (1) They are absolutely unintelligible; (2) they are of use only to cutthroat speculators out to make a fast buck; and (3) it's possible to make or lose a lot of money in a very short time. Of these assumptions, only the last is accurate.

It takes a little concentration, but futures contracts are not that difficult to understand. No, really! If you have ever made a financial agreement or a business contract, you have made an agreement that something will be transacted in the future. That's all a futures contract is: an agreement to deliver a set amount of a commodity of a certain quality at a given date.

Such contracts started in this country in the mid-nineteenth century as a way for farmers and large buyers of farm produce to stabilize the agricultural markets. Then, as now, the prices of grain and other commodities were always changing as supply and demand changed. This was hard on the producers. One year, a farmer might grow a bumper crop of corn only to find that all the farmers in the region had similar crops. The resulting surplus drove the price of corn way down—often causing much of it to be dumped.

The next year, everyone had learned his lesson. Nobody grew very much corn, and the wholesale buyers couldn't supply their customers. The price was way up, but few of the farmers had much to sell.

It was at this point in one of the cycles that a farmer—we'll call him Smith—saddled up his horse and rode to his buyer's office in the city.

"In one month, I can deliver two hundred bushels of corn to you if you'll give me ten cents a bushel," Smith told the buyer, whose name was Frank Middleman.

The buyer, who had several customers willing to pay him 15 cents a bushel, agreed on the spot. This was a futures contract—not the first one, for the Japanese had contracts for rice delivery in the seventeenth century. But this contract and others like it began to stabilize the agricultural markets in this country.

It's easy to see the benefits of such contracts: Farmer Smith and the other growers had a price they could depend on, the buyers had a supply they could depend on, and the retailers and general public were assured of a steady supply of corn and other grains. Before long, the times of the contracts were extended. Farmer Smith could make contracts in the spring for delivery in the fall;

> **Frank Middleman was happy, not only because he was going to be $8 richer, but because Joe had relieved him of any risk—risk he couldn't afford to take.**

that way he knew how much to plant, not just of corn, but of other grains as well.

"All very well," you say, "but what about the speculators?" Well, after Farmer Smith left, Joe Sharp dropped by his friend Frank's office. Joe was a financial speculator and when he heard about Frank's contract with Farmer Smith, he saw an opportunity. Joe believed that because there was a shortage, the price of corn was going to go even higher.

"Look, Frank," he said, "when Smith delivers that corn, I'll buy it from you at fourteen cents a bushel—twenty-eight dollars for the two hundred bushels. We'll put it in writing, if you like—make a contract."

"But what about my customers?" Frank protested. "I can get fifteen cents a bushel from them. If I pay Smith twenty dollars for his corn and sell it for thirty, I'll make ten dollars."

"If you sell it to me, you'll only make eight dollars," answered Joe, "but it's a sure thing. A lot can happen in a month, you know. If the price of corn goes down to eight cents a bushel, do you think your buyers are going to give you fifteen? You don't have contracts with them, remember."

Frank thought it over. The price of corn might go up, in which case he would make more than the 15 cents a bushel. But Joe was right—it could go down and he was locked into buying from Smith at 10 cents a bushel. He was not a rich man and the prospect of an assured $8 looked good. (Remember, we're talking 1840 here, when a dollar was a day's wages.) "You got yourself a deal," he told Joe, and the futures market was born.

Frank Middleman was happy, not only because he was going to be $8 richer, but because Joe had relieved him of any risk—risk he couldn't afford to take. Farmer Smith was still happy: he didn't care who ultimately got his corn as long as he got his 10 cents a bushel. And Joe Sharp was delighted with his new investment idea. He had enough money to take a little risk for the possibility of a big gain. If the price of corn went up to 20 cents a bushel in a month he could sell the 200 bushels for $40. Subtracting the $28 he would pay to Frank, he would realize a $12 profit.

A few days later, Joe got another brainstorm. He was beginning to worry about the price of corn. If the price dropped below 14 cents a bushel, he would be stuck with a loss.

His bright idea was to go to one of Frank Middleman's customers, a woman named Jenny who ran a bakery. Jenny was greatly in need of corn and Joe was able to make a contract with Jenny to sell her 50 bushels of the corn he was due to receive from Farmer Smith. He simply told her the obvious—that the price of corn was very volatile these days and that locking in a price of 16 cents a bushel was in her interest.

Joe had now made both kinds of contracts that are available in the futures markets: contracts to sell a commodity and contracts to buy it. Both these contracts were based on future delivery of the corn; hence the name *futures contracts* or simply *futures*.

As it happened, the following week one of Joe's other business deals went sour. He now needed the $28 he was going to give to Frank Middleman for the corn. Luckily, he knew another speculator, John, who believed that the price of corn was headed higher. After explaining his agreement with Frank, Joe convinced John to take on the contract—John would now be the one to buy the corn from Frank Middleman.

This kind of transfer is the way futures contracts are traded today. You don't actually "buy" a contract, you take it on, or assume it. You deposit a certain amount of money with a commodities broker in order to assume a contract.

If the price of corn had gone up, the contract to buy Farmer Smith's corn would have become more valuable. Joe would have bought 200 bushels of corn at 14 cents a bushel, and could have sold at least the remaining 150

You don't actually "buy" a contract, you take it on, or assume it. You deposit a certain amount of money with a commodities broker in order to assume a contract.

bushels of it at a much higher price, say 20 cents a bushel, to other buyers (not to Jenny—she has her price locked in at 16 cents on her 50 bushels). Therefore, the value of the contract would also have gone up—and so would the price.

If corn had gone down, on the other hand, the contracts to *sell* would have become more valuable. Joe could have bought 50 more bushels of corn from another farmer for, say, 6 cents a bushel and sold it to Jenny for the agreed-upon price of 16 cents a bushel.

If you think the price of corn, or any commodity, is likely to go higher, you will take on a contract allowing you to buy corn (in market terminology, you will "buy corn" or "go long on corn"). Your contract will specify that you can buy corn at a certain price; then, if the price does indeed go higher, your contract will become more valuable. Conversely, if you believe the bears are in the corn, and the price is on its way down, you will "sell corn"— that is, take on a contract to sell it. This will make you "short on corn." In this case, someone else is agreeing to buy corn from you at a certain price. If the price falls, they are still bound to honor the original price in the contract, so the contract will rise in value. In either case, if you're right in your assessment of the market, the value of your contract will go up and you can sell it for more than you paid.

Those are the basics of the futures markets. Contracts are salable items. Futures contracts may be traded many times before the actual date for delivery. And, no, you don't actually have to deliver or receive 5,000 bushels of corn (the amount of present-day contracts). You simply sell your contract sometime before the last day of trading—the day when the contract comes due. Someone who has the capability will handle the actual delivery. The futures exchanges—the organizations that handle and regulate futures trading—see that delivery is made when necessary.

MODERN FUTURES CONTRACTS

In order to trade futures contracts, you need to open an account with a *commodities broker*; stockbrokers do not handle futures. Depending on which markets you wish to trade, you will be asked to deposit a certain amount of "margin" capital at the brokerage office.

This margin money is not to be confused with the kind of margin required by stockbrokers (discussed in Chapter 18). This margin is "upfront money"—to show your good faith in honoring any contract you may assume. It is similar to the money you might deposit with a title company when you make an offer on a house.

There are full-service commodities brokers, who will give you advice on what to buy, and there are the discount brokers, who will simply execute your trades. Needless to say, the selection of a commodities broker is an important decision. You may be called by commodities brokers looking for new accounts; they will expand on the marvelous profit possibilities in the futures markets. Don't listen to them. Instead, read Jake Bernstein's chapter on how to pick a broker (see Resources).

These days, you can buy futures contracts for any number of agricultural commodities, for metals, and even for currencies. These contracts all have their uses for different people, but their greatest value is in *the transfer of risk to speculators.* In the story above, Frank Middleman transferred his risk to Joe Sharp, who was better able to afford it. The markets may be different nowadays, but the concept is the same.

Suppose, for example, you had a business that dealt in fine china. You have a contract to buy plates from a British firm for $100,000 in three months. In order to actually make the purchase, you will have to change your $100,000 into the equivalent amount of British pounds—you will have to "buy" pounds with dollars.

Now if, during those three months, the pound appreciates against the dollar, say by 5%, you will need more dollars to buy the required number of pounds—$5,000 more, in fact ($100,000 × .05 = $5,000). There is a chance, of course, that the pound might go down against the dollar, in which case you would do well, because you would need fewer dollars to buy pounds. But you are a businessperson, not a speculator. You don't like the risk, so what can you do?

What you can do is "hedge" your purchase by taking on a futures contract for the pound. In this case, you take on a contract to buy pounds, which means you will make money if the pound goes up (you are "buying" pounds—you have taken a "long" position on pounds sterling or, more succinctly, you are "long on sterling.")

Now, with this contract, if the pound should go up by 5%, you will make back the $5,000 you lost by having to buy the more expensive pounds to complete your business contract (actually, you would even make a little more than $5,000—see below).

The contract for the pounds sterling is essentially no different from the contract for corn that Joe Sharp sold to his investor friend, John. In this case, though, instead of 200 bushels of corn for 10 cents a bushel, you are agreeing to buy 62,500 British pounds for $2 a pound. A 5% rise in the pound over three months would mean it would then take not $2, but *$2.10* to buy one pound ($2 × .05 = $.10).

> **In agricultural commodities, the hedgers are the large wholesale buyers and the farmers themselves.**

Your contract would have gone up in value by \$.10 a pound, or \$6,250 (62,500 × \$.10). Sell it!

Of course, the pound could have decreased in value, in which case you would have lost money on your futures contract. You would have gained most of it back, however, because when it came time to pay for the British china, your dollars would buy more British pounds.

So you don't make or lose much either way—and that's the whole point! Your concern is with china, not international currencies. That's the job of the speculators who are creating the currency markets by buying futures contracts in the British pound and other currencies. By assuming a futures contract, you have successfully transferred most of the risk involved in your china transaction to these speculators.

It is also possible to take on a contract to sell pounds whereby you would make money if the pound went down against the dollar. (In this case, you would be "short on sterling.") The manufacturer of the china in England might want a contract like this. It is in his or her interest that the dollar not go up against the pound.

The futures markets, then, are of great importance to individuals or firms wanting to hedge against possible losses in the purchase or delivery of their product. As noted above, one of their main functions is the transfer of risk from businesspeople to speculators. In agricultural commodities, the hedgers are the large wholesale buyers and the farmers themselves.

In recent years new futures markets have been created. Bankers can now hedge with interest-rate futures.

Managers of mutual funds can hedge against large drops in the stock market with stock-index futures.

If you want a fuller explanation of the different kinds of futures markets, see the book cited in Resources. It will also give you the essential details you need to know to invest in futures. My purpose here has simply been to give you some idea of what these contracts are and to demonstrate the importance of the futures markets. If you own a business, you may someday find yourself hedging against losses with futures contracts.

SPECULATION

If you decide to speculate in these markets, you should remember that at least one of the myths about the futures markets is true: It is indeed possible to lose large amounts of money in very short periods of time. You saw, for example, how a profit or loss of $6,250 was possible with just a 5% rise or fall in the value of the British pound.

This kind of percentage change can and does happen much more quickly than in three months—sometimes too quickly to get out of the market soon enough to prevent a big loss. It's very easy to lose thousands of dollars on just one futures contract—it happens all the time. The majority of speculators in the futures markets lose money each year. (Hedgers and businesspeople don't usually lose— just those who trade purely for speculative purposes.)

These markets are attractive to speculators because of the possibility of large profits and because they don't need a large amount of capital to get started. (Cousin Jack *loves* futures!) To enter into the contract for British pounds, for example, the broker would have required only $2,025 to be deposited as "margin." You would get this deposit back when you sold the contract—if you came out ahead. If you lost money on your trade, say in the amount of $3,000, you would sacrifice your margin deposit *and* have to pay an additional $975. The (discount) broker's commission would amount to about $50 to $75 for both trades.

There are ways of minimizing your risk. You should start by reading the book recommended in Resources and then do plenty of practice trading before you think about putting any real money down on futures, either as a hedger or a speculator.

Resources

How the Futures Markets Work, by Jake Bernstein. Prentice Hall. 1989. $17.95 (paperback). This is a comprehensive book on futures. It gives the history of the futures markets and explains how they operate in the present day. It also includes all the practical information you need to get started trading. Clear and well written.

CHAPTER 27

OPTIONS

Anybody who plays the market without inside information is like a man buying cows in the moonlight.
                              —DAN DREW, LEGENDARY TRADER

Options? Options? In my experience, discussing the
concept of "buying an option" tends to draw as
many blank stares as the idea of futures contracts.
But you may have already bought an option of sorts. As a
young man, I bought an option without even knowing I
was doing it.

When I was 21, I decided it was time I found myself
a *real* car, as opposed to the junkers I'd been driving. The
first one I looked at was a red '55 Ford convertible, to my
eyes a most lovely piece of machinery. Having just started
my search, however, I wanted to see what else was out
there. At the same time, I didn't want someone else to buy
the car.

"Look," I said to the owner, "I like the car, but I want
to look around some more. I'll give you twenty-five dollars
to hold on to the car until ten tomorrow morning. If I don't
buy it, you keep the money."

"Okay," he said, "but at ten o'clock, out she goes."

I had just bought an option. And he had just sold an option. As it turned out, there was nothing on the market even close to this paragon; I came back the same afternoon, paid him $300, and drove off at a high rate of speed.

In this case, I got my $25 back. When you purchase an option to buy stock, you're not so lucky; the person who sold you the option keeps the money. What you're hoping, when you put out money for an option, is that the stock will go up enough to cover the price of the option and give you a profit.

CALL OPTIONS

Say you decide IBM is about to make a move upward. The stock has been down recently but their new personal computer looks like a winner, and you think the price will rise maybe 10 points ($10 a share) or more over the next few months. Right now, however, the price of the stock is $120 a share and you can't afford to buy 100 shares. You could buy 20 shares for $2,400, but then a 10-point rise would bring you only a $200 profit, which would just cover your commissions to buy and sell.

In the options section of the financial pages, however, you find an item one day in early January that looks interesting. It's very succinct: "IBM March120 call 9." Translation: For $9, you can purchase an option—a right—to buy 1 share of IBM, or 100 shares for $900 (options are sold in 100-share blocks). "March120" means

> **Why would you buy this option? You would buy because you believe the price of IBM stock is going to go up.**

that at any time before the third Friday of March you have the right to buy these 100 shares at the price of $120 a share.

Why would you buy this option? You would buy because you believe the price of IBM stock is going to go up. Buying a *call option*, or simply a *call*, means you are betting the stock will rise. A call option is a right to buy 100 shares of a certain stock at a given price, at any time during a set period of time.

The seller of the option, also called the *option writer*, is the one who collects the $900 cost of the option. The transaction takes place through your stockbroker, but all the broker gets are commissions on the purchase and sale, paid for by the buyer—in this case, you.

This option writer is hoping IBM stock will not go up—that it will stay at the same price or go down. This is because if you decide to exercise your option, this writer is the one who must sell you the 100 shares of IBM stock at $120 a share. If IBM remains at $120, or goes below $120, it would not be in your interest to exercise your option.

If, on the other hand, the stock should rise to $125, you could buy the 100 shares from the option writer for $120 a share and sell them on the market for $125. This would allow you at least to recoup $500 of your $900, less commissions. The writer of the option would still keep the $900, but he or she must buy IBM stock at $125 and sell it to you at $120—so the writer is minus $500 of the $900.

If the stock should go up to $134 before the option expires, then you would be in great shape. You would have the right to buy 100 shares of IBM at $120 a share, or $12,000, and could sell them at $134, or $13,400. This would give you a profit of $1,400 ($13,400 minus $12,000 = $1,400). Subtracting the $900 price you paid for the option would then leave you $500 to the good, less whatever broker's commissions you paid for selling the stock (you could, of course, hold on to the stock if you wished).

In reality, relatively few options contracts are actually exercised in the manner described above. This is because a rise in the price of a stock will cause an immediate rise in the price of an option based on that stock. Like a futures contract, an option is also a contract and, as such, is a salable item. Salable contracts will go up and down according to the demand for them on the market.

Say you got lucky and IBM went up to $125 just a few days after you bought the March120 option. The next day, the price of the option might look like this: IBM March120 call 13. Your call option has gone up in price by 4 points, from 9 to 13. Four points means a profit of $400, if you should decide to sell the option.

This means some people out there are willing to buy your call option for $1,300 because they think IBM is likely to go even higher before the option expires in March. It also means you do not have to hold on to the option until it expires.

Now you have the pleasant task of deciding whether you want to sell your option and take your profit, or hold on to it a while longer, in case IBM goes up further. If you sell it, you will have made $400, less commissions ($1,300 minus $900 = $400). The commissions will be about $40 each way—$80 in all—with a discount broker, and subtracting the $80 will leave you with a $320 profit. Not bad for a few days, with a $900 investment.

If you decide to hold on to your option for a while, however, watch out! Options usually "expire" on the third Friday of the month listed in the paper—in this case, March. This means that by that date you either have to exercise your option to buy the underlying stock, or sell the option. As their expiration date approaches, options have a nasty habit of "decaying" in price. If IBM stock goes back down to $120 a week before the expiration date, your $900 option will be worth almost nothing. Nobody wants to buy an option that enables them to buy stock at the going market price.

So the best bet would be to sell your option if you get a nice profit in it. If the stock goes down and your option with it, you may also decide to sell before it goes down too far. If IBM goes down a few points below 120 in January, your option will also go down a few, but it will still retain some value—this is called "time" value, because there are still two months wherein the stock might go up.

If the price of IBM goes down in *March*, however, close to the expiration day, the option will have no time value at all. As in most decisions relating to when to buy and sell, there are no rules here. It's up to you and how much risk you want to take.

The advantage to options, then, is that you get the possibility of large profits with a relatively small outlay. The majority of options are less expensive than the IBM options; many cost less than $100. This means your risk is limited. If the bottom fell out of the market and IBM dropped 20 points, a holder of 100 shares of IBM stock would see the stock drop $2,000 in value. You, however, would have lost only your $900.

The advantage of stocks over options is, of course, that the stockholder's loss is only a "paper" loss. He or she could hold on to the IBM shares in expectation that they would go up again (they always have). You, on the other hand, would never see your $900 again.

PUTS

If you believe a stock is about to take a dive, there is a way to invest in that, too. You can buy what is called a *put option* or, more simply, a *put*. This is similar to a call, except that instead of enabling you to buy a stock over the next few months, it enables you to sell it.

"How can you sell something you don't own?" you ask. Don't forget: This is the Wonderful World of Investment.

> **Buying options is a risky business, though. You can make good profits or you can very easily lose your entire investment.**

As in the case of short selling, minor details such as nonownership are easily overlooked.

Puts are listed with calls in the financial pages. They are designated as "puts" or may simply have a "P" after them. For example: IBM March120 Put 8. This means that for $800 you can buy the right to sell 100 shares of IBM at the price of $120 until the third Friday in March.

If you buy this put, and IBM drops 20 points before the third Friday in March, you can buy 100 shares on the open market for the new price of $100 and sell them to the writer of the put option for $120. Profit: $2,000, less $800 for the option, less commissions for buying and selling the stock.

Rather than go through all this, of course, it would be easier to sell the option on the open market. It will have appreciated anywhere from 20 to 30 points depending on how close it is to the expiration date. You will make a very nice profit.

Buying options is a risky business, though. You can make good profits or you can very easily lose your entire investment. Like futures speculators, the majority of options traders lose money over the course of any given year. If you sell or "write" the options, you are also opening yourself up to high risk. In the case above, where IBM dropped 20 points, the writer of the option would have come out $1,200 to the downside ($2,000 less the $800 received for the option).

There are ways of minimizing this risk, but these methods are beyond our scope here. If you're interested, the book listed in Resources explains these methods in detail.

A FEW MORE DETAILS

For now, here are a few more things you need to know about buying options.

You can buy options that have expiration dates anywhere from one to nine months. The most common options you see listed have lives of two to three months. Recently, options called *leaps* have been introduced—options with an expiration date two years away. The longer the life of an option, the more expensive it is, because the stock has a longer period in which to go up or down (the "time value" is greater). Leaps, therefore, are the most expensive of the options.

You can, of course, buy options on the open market that have expiration dates just a week or even a day away. This kind of trading is engaged in by some speculators with a very high tolerance for risk.

The price of the stock at which you can exercise the option is called the *strike price*. In the examples above, the strike price of the options—$120 a share—was "on the money," meaning it was the same as the present price of IBM stock.

The strike price can also be "in the money," meaning the strike price is less than the present selling price of the stock (the stock price is still $120). For example: IBM March 115 call 16. Notice that the price of this "in the money" call option—$1,600—is more expensive than the "on the money" option because you have an additional five points given to you.

An "out of the money" option has a strike price that is higher than the present selling price. These are the options the speculators like to use because they are the cheapest. For example: IBM March 130 call 2. For $200, you can purchase an option to buy 100 shares of IBM at $130 a share. The speculators know it's not necessary for IBM to go up all the way to $130 for them to make a profit. If it only went up to $125 in a few weeks, the option would probably go up a point or two—enough for them to make a profit. (Speculators often buy a large number of a certain option. If 10 were purchased, for example, a rise of one point would mean a profit of $100 on each option, or $1,000.)

Some options are thinly traded. This means you may not be able to sell when you want to—an important consideration. In the options quotes, you will see a column headed "Open Interest": these figures are the number of options traded during the previous day. Occasionally, you will see "No trade," meaning there are options of that kind on the market, but there were no buyers at the price they were offered at.

Warrants are a kind of call option. They give you the right to buy a certain stock at a given price in a given time frame. Unlike most options, however, warrants are created by the companies whose stock they are based on.

Corporations making new issues of stocks or bonds will often offer warrants as a further inducement to buy the securities. Warrants usually have lives of a few years instead of a few months, but they should be considered in the same speculative class as regular options.

Businesses may also offer *employee stock options* as incentives or compensation. These are different from the options traded on the open market in that they are issued to specific individuals and are generally not tradeable. Although they usually have a time limit of a few years, they do not "expire" in the manner of traded options. Like the traded options, however, they give the employee the right to buy company stock at a certain price. If the stock rises above this price, the option holder may decide to exercise his or her options and buy the stock at the lower price specified in the option. Or the option holder may wait in the hope that the stock will rise still further.

If you invest in stocks or mutual funds, and buy and sell rarely, you may still be able to get along without being on the Internet. Not so with options! The rate at which options prices change, coupled with the need for speedy action, make it imperative that you subscribe to an online brokerage where you can get up-to-the-minute price quotes and make quick trades. If you get into trading in any quantity, you will also need a good provider of market data (see Chapter 22).

INDEX OPTIONS

Remember the stock indexes described in Chapter 8—the market indicators based on the prices of certain groups of stocks? Did you know you can buy options that are based on many of these indexes? In fact, the most widely purchased options are those based on the S&P 100 Index and the S&P 500 Index. These are called, respectively, "OEX" and "SPX" options. These are the options you would purchase if you were certain an entire segment of the stock market was due for a rise or fall.

Index options are similar to stock options in that there are puts and calls, different strike prices and expiration dates. When you exercise an index option, however, you cannot buy the stocks that the index represents. These options are settled in cash, the amount of which is based on the value of their index on the expiration date of the option.

For example, suppose you paid $500 for an OEX call option in June, with an expiration date on July 20. The index is currently at $658.50 and your strike price is $670. Because the expiration date is a month away, the option still has time value, which is why it is selling for as high as $500.

By July 20, the index has risen to $672—two points above your strike price of $670. These two points mean you will receive $200 as a settlement. Unfortunately, you're out $300, because you paid $500 for the option.

In actual trading, you would probably have sold your option when it still had some time value. If, for example, the index had gone up to $672 a month before the July expiration date, the value of your option would probably have risen to $700 or $800; this is because the option would still have a month's worth of time value. As with stock options, most people sell their index options before they expire.

These index options are a favorite tool of speculators. Some investors, however, use index options as a kind of "insurance" on their stock portfolios. If they believe the stock market is about to tumble, they can purchase put options on one of the major indexes. Then, if the market does indeed go down, their stocks may lose value, but their put options will gain in value.

OPTIONS ON FUTURES

Yes, you can actually purchase options to buy futures contracts! How about a call option to buy a soybean contract with a strike price of $6.25 a bushel, and expiration date in June? Just as with a stock option, if the price of soybeans goes up, the value of your option will go up and vice versa. And just as with stock options, there are puts and calls, different strike prices, and expiration dates.

To deal in these options requires a pretty fair knowledge of the futures markets. For each commodity there is a different contract, and the options are based on these contracts. As with futures contracts, futures options are purchased from a commodities broker, not a stockbroker.

Futures options as a speculative tool provide most of the profit potential of the futures themselves, but with

> **Even if you choose to have someone else manage your finances, knowing about futures and options will enable you to make informed decisions.**

much of the risk eliminated. You can lose only the price of the option. Like futures, however, they should be considered to be in the realm of the speculative trader, not the investor.

For the businessperson, however, who has a need to hedge some commodity or currency, a futures option is often a simpler, less expensive way of hedging than a futures contract.

Futures and Options—Why?

I include these speculative methods of trading partly for the few who will want to pursue them further. But I also want to dispel the air of mystery that surrounds futures and options, and show their real uses and value in the business world.

My other reason for including such things in a book for new investors is simply that they are important for you to know about. As we mentioned in Chapter 24, much of the high-pressure sales efforts directed at investors describes various techniques for dealing in futures—with promises of enormous profits. You need to know that any "enormous profits" will probably be made only by the sellers of such systems.

Even if you choose to have someone else manage your finances, knowing about futures and options will enable you to make informed decisions. Suppose, for example, your investment manager told you that he planned to invest half your portfolio in futures contracts. You need to know not just that futures are risky, but *why* they are risky, and just *how* risky. Otherwise, the adviser might be able to argue you into it. You need to know enough to immediately take your money out of his control—and, perhaps, notify the agency in your state that licenses such managers.

The above warning is not a fantasy. Every year I hear stories about naive clients whose managers lost their money in futures, gold mines, options, or high-risk stocks. One couple ended up actually *owing* $6,000 on a futures contract—after losing all their money. With a little knowledge and care, such nightmares need not happen.

Resources

Options : A Personal Seminar, by Scott H. Fullman. Prentice Hall, 1992. $26.00 (paperback). This book explains options for the novice, then goes on to lay out more complex strategies for option trading. Full of examples and worksheets, this is a comprehensive overview of the world of options. There are no get-rich-quick schemes here, just solid information, and the new investor can go as far with it as he or she wants to.

Free, free, free! The Options Industry Council is anxious to get you started trading options. To this end, they have created an "Options Education Center" at <www.optionscentral.com> (if you're not online, their address is 440 S. LaSalle Street, Chicago, IL 60605). Free seminars in fifty different cities, free videos, free software, and lists of books and newsletters about options are all available. The enthusiasm with which the Council gives away all these things might possibly lead one to believe that they hope to *profit* from new investors getting involved in options. If you agree that this might be the case, then this is yet another argument for proceeding slowly and cautiously in this fast-moving arena.

Once you are ready to try out some practice "paper trading" with options, go to the web site of the Chicago Board Options Exchange: <www.cboe.com>. Here you can get market information, including price quotes of all traded options. The CBOE will also give you information of various kinds, though not as generously as the Options Council. But this is a very useful, free site for investors getting started in options.

Chapter 28

Starting to Invest

T his book is meant for those who plan to do their own investing *and* for those who decide to hire a professional adviser. If you were undecided when you started, I hope that reading the book has given you a better idea which path is right for you.

Of those who wish to handle their own investments, many will decide to stick with mutual funds and follow the program we presented in Chapters 14, 15, and 16. We laid this out not only as a way of getting started, but also as a continuing method of investing. This program should work very well for those who want to invest in a conservative, buy-and-hold manner.

Once your portfolio is set up, the main task of you conservative investors is to keep tabs on it. Watch for underperforming funds, and buy and sell as necessary at the time of your six-month review.

I hope that those of you who choose to manage your investments more actively will arrive at a method of investing that feels right to *you*. Just as there are no sure things in the World of Investment, neither is there one right way to invest. A close look at successful investors will reveal a different method employed by each.

Much of the investment world is a win-win situation. You buy corporate bonds: you get interest payments and the corporation uses your money to invest. If a market increases in value, everybody comes out ahead—except those who were playing it short.

If you start to trade actively, however, you begin to play zero-sum games in which if you win, somebody else loses. In order to compete with professional investors, you need to improve your odds in any way you can. Playing your strong suits—that is, investing in areas you know about—is the best way of doing this.

If your job makes you knowledgeable in a certain field, then you have an advantage over other investors. You'll be likely to spot the companies that are producing the new products your industry really needs.

Another way to find winners is to get the pros on your side. Learn as much as you can about a field by reading or listening to the experts recommended in this book. Hire some top-notch advisers by subscribing to the recommended newsletters. Go to a few seminars on topics that interest you. The American Association of Individual Investors sponsors some good ones; so do many of the foundations that make up the Funding Exchange (see Resources, Chapter 2).

If Martin Zweig's economic predictions bore you, if the roller-coaster markets make you queasy, or if you simply love your own job so much that you don't want to be distracted (lucky person!)—then forget the whole shebang.

The third way to tilt the field in your direction is to do what the professionals do: Avoid investing in areas you are not expert in. As we have pointed out, investing without knowledge of or a real feel for a market is not even speculating—it's gambling.

Investing is not for everybody. One way of judging whether it's for you is by taking a good look at whether you enjoy it or not. If Martin Zweig's economic predictions bore you, if the roller-coaster markets make you queasy, or if you simply love your own job so much that you don't want to be distracted (lucky person!)—then forget the whole shebang. Find a good financial adviser or manager and let him or her worry about the price of oil, or whether the Federal Reserve will lower the discount rate. Just remember to keep an eye on things.

RECOMMENDATIONS: THE FIRST AND BEST THINGS YOU CAN DO TO START OFF RIGHT

This book was conceived as a way of condensing the vast amount of information about investments so that the subject would be more manageable. Even in this book, though, we have dealt with a pretty sizable amount of material. This section, then, is an attempt to summarize even further. What are the most important things you, as a new investor, can do to get off to a good start?

Because your investment strategy must necessarily depend on your individual circumstances, most of the advice and recommendations for further information in this book are presented for you to pick and choose from. There is much that new investors have in common, however; there are certain things you can do that can greatly improve your chances of success. Here are a few final suggestions.

1. Take a good look at your attitudes toward money
   and finances. What problems do you have dealing
   with them? What are your financial goals? As an
   invaluable aid in considering these questions, I
   recommend *Your Money or Your Life,* by Joe
   Dominguez and Vicki Robin (Resources, Chapter
   3). A good investor needs to know where he or she
   is going and needs to be in a state of internal
   agreement about these goals. If you are investing
   with a spouse or a partner, you need to be in a
   state of external agreement as well.

2. Be sure that your personal finances are in good
   order. The best investments in the world will all be
   for nothing without reasonable spending habits,
   adequate insurance, and good tax planning. If you
   want to do this yourself, consult a book on financial planning. *The Wall Street Journal Guide to
   Understanding Personal Finance,* mentioned in
   Resources, Chapter 3, is a good one.

   If you feel the need of help in this area, financial planners and advisers are available. You can
   find an honest and competent one with the help of
   the information in Chapter 9. Be sure the adviser
   comes with good recommendations and that you
   like and feel comfortable with him or her. It's
   likely to be a long relationship.

3. Give yourself time! If you've just come into some
   money, or just started investing, you need some
   time to get used to this state of affairs. Don't rush
   out and buy the first stock you get a hot tip on.
   Take at least six months to a year to study, talk
   with friends, practice, and generally test the
   waters. It's a good idea to do this even if you plan
   to go to an investment adviser or manager. Buy
   some certificates of deposit at your bank and just
   let the money sit and gather interest. Don't worry
   if the stock market is on a roll or real estate is

skyrocketing. There will always be opportunities, and you'll be much more likely to capitalize on them once you know what it's all about.

If you are anxious or nervous about suddenly coming into money, be assured that you're not alone. If you feel unable to cope with your distress about inheriting or being richer than your friends, try getting together with others in the same boat and talking about it (Resources, Chapter 2).

You can also give yourself the gift of counseling if you are conflicted or confused about dealing with money. You will have to pay for a good counselor or psychotherapist, but it may turn out to be the best investment you will ever make.

4. Start practicing. There's no substitute for actually doing it: buying and selling and watching your purchases—and your emotions—go up and down. This is one great advantage to being online with a provider like America Online. In their investment section, you can set up an imaginary portfolio and do as much paper trading as you like. This is valuable experience because you can try out your skills without the fear of losing money coloring your judgment.

If you're interested in real estate, you can start looking at buildings. With the help of the recommended reading material (Resources, Chapter 11), it's easy to figure out a balance sheet on any given property. How much do you need to invest, how much will the loan payments be, the expenses, the income, etc.?

After doing a number of these balance sheets, and tramping through buildings checking out roofs, foundations, furnaces, and asbestos in the walls, you will begin to get a feel for possible good investments. Or you may decide that real estate is not for you—a decision that will make the time spent no less valuable than if you had gone ahead.

Whatever you decide to invest in, it's a good idea to do it first on paper. Pretend you've bought something, then follow your investment for a few months. If it goes up, don't kick yourself for not investing real money—there are always new opportunities; if it goes down, you can congratulate yourself on your prudence.

5. Start out small. Once you're using real money, it's a good idea to invest relatively modest amounts at first, then build up as your confidence and your feel for the markets increase. Remember the importance of balance in your portfolio, as we discussed in Chapter 15.

6. Don't push the river—let it flow by itself. There is a certain rhythm to investing. It takes time for things to appreciate in value; if you get impatient and try for large profits in a short time, you run a good chance of getting into trouble.

Remember the Rule of 10% (Chapter 14). If you, as a new investor, are getting 10% on your money per year, you're doing well. If you are getting more than that and still investing safely, you're doing extremely well. If you shoot for 50% to 100% or more, however, you've left safety behind and have entered the realm of speculation and gambling.

A SAMPLE SCHEDULE

Here is a schedule for those who like schedules. It is, of course, approximate; some will want to progress faster or slower. But this should give you a general idea of a time frame for getting involved with investing. If the time frame seems slow, keep in mind that this schedule is geared for working people, who can only think about

This schedule is geared for working people, who can only think about investments during their off hours.

investments during their off hours. If you have more free time, you could push things up a bit.

First month: Read this book. Start thinking about what you want from your investments and what your personal risk-reward thermometer might look like. If you have just come into some money—a lot or a little—it's time to get used to having the extra amount. Put the money in the bank and leave it. Talk it over with your spouse and family.

Second month: Now that you know a little, start talking with friends and family about what they invest in—but don't act on any advice yet. Start reading the financial pages in the newspaper. Borrow from the library or buy one or two of the recommended books. If you have inherited real estate, or think you might want to buy a home or income property, subscribe to John Reed's newsletter (Resources, Chapter 11). If you have inherited antiques or other collectibles, look at Resources in Chapter 25 to find the best ways of dealing with them.

Third month: Subscribe to one or two of the recommended newsletters—trial subscriptions, if they have them. Continue to talk to friends and read. Consider joining the American Association of Individual Investors (Resources, Chapter 1). If you don't already have one, seriously consider buying a computer, learning how to use it, and getting online.

Fourth month: Try buying single copies of various financial newspapers and magazines to see whether any of them appeal to you. Sample a few more trial subscriptions to the recommended newsletters, but don't act on their suggestions yet. Advisers in newsletters and magazines have a way of making certain investments sound urgent, but excellent opportunities will always be available. Right now, you are still in the process of taking in information and sorting it out. Actual investing should wait for a while.

Fifth month: Okay, now you're getting ready to test your wings—but without any risk. If you're leaning toward making real estate a part of your portfolio—home or income property—try doing some balance sheets. See how the income and expenses come out on various properties. The recommended books and newsletters will show you how to do this. Start driving around by yourself (no real estate agents yet) and seeing what's available.

Mutual fund investors, start working out your own model portfolio. Without focusing on specific funds, decide whether you want long-term growth or income, or both, and modify the categories of the model in Chapter 14 according to your needs and goals.

Sixth month: If you're now online, set up a portfolio and start buying and selling; this will help give you an idea what it's like to actually risk money. Continue to work on your model portfolio—and read and discuss investing with friends. Start investigating what's available online, beginning with the information in Chapter 22.

Seventh to ninth months: Now we're getting down to business. By now, you have noted quite a few mutual funds recommended in the various magazines and newsletters. Make a note of the ones that look the best to you. Take out a trial subscription to *Morningstar Mutual*

Funds (Resources, Chapter 6). See how they rate the funds you have on your list. Look at their top-rated funds (the five-star list at the front). Generally, you should invest in the funds that are rated four-star or five-star by Morningstar.

You should have an idea by now whether you want to do your own investing or engage the help of a professional adviser or manager. If you feel you want to hire someone, consult with friends and associates and do some research on your own. Remember, you can interview as many advisers as you want to find one you really like.

By the end of the ninth month, you should have your model portfolio pretty well worked out. You should also have come to some conclusions about real estate. If you're leaning that way, ask friends and associates whether they know of a good real estate agent. Start arranging for financing.

Tenth to twelfth months: Investing! Finally! Start out slow. Decide whether to buy directly from the funds or through a broker (Chapter 15). In either case, send for the prospectuses of the various funds you're interested in. The reports in *Morningstar* will tell you most of what you need to know, but you should look over the prospectuses, too.

A good way to begin is to dollar-cost-average your investments (Chapter 19). Start with the conservative funds first and work your way to the riskier ones.

Now that you've done your homework in the real estate area, it's time to engage a real estate agent. By now, you should be able to tell the agent just what kind of property you want, including the price range. Don't jump at the first likely property, but do be prepared to put down money if you find exactly what you're looking for.

First year and continuing: Once you're fully invested in mutual funds, remember to do your review every six months. If you have decided to invest in individual stocks, now is the time to begin your research. When you're ready to buy a stock, you can sell some of your mutual funds in the same category; for example, if you're buying a small company, then sell part of a small-company fund. That way, your portfolio will stay in the same balance you started with. Keep some of your mutual funds—not only is this a good diversification, but you can compare your stock picks against the performance of the funds.

Constant vigilance is a necessary quality of the successful investor. You may give the wheel to someone else—an investment manager, perhaps—but you need to stay aware of this person's state of mind. Is he or she driving well?

Thousands of other people may have driven the road you're on; you may have road maps and the best directions. But this day, a bridge may have washed out and all your directions are no substitute for being alert and quick to react. You need to have a Plan B—an alternate route—for such contingencies.

Awareness is energy well spent. Money may not be able to buy you happiness, but it can mean greater freedom to pursue your goals and interests. And it can provide at least some security in an uncertain world.

Learning to deal with money successfully is the kind of experience that can empower you to handle other areas of your life more skillfully. Willingness to learn, to change, to take some risks, balance, perseverance—the factors that make for success in the World of Investment will inevitably carry over into other fields of endeavor.

Money is a central issue. The money you earn is the physical representation of the life energy you have expended to earn it. If you have inherited or won a lottery, it represents other people's life energy. Investing, then, is a way of making this energy grow so that you may benefit from it—and, perhaps, help others to benefit.

I wish you the best of luck in this important and absorbing endeavor.

THE MODEL PORTFOLIO

T he funds listed here should be considered only as an example of what a model portfolio might look like. Right now, these particular funds have been performing well, but you may be reading this some months later. As we discussed in Chapter 15, it's necessary to choose funds according to their recent performance as well as their performance over the last five to ten years.

Remember, this model is directed toward growth, with all income reinvested. If your goal is more income or a lower risk-reward temperature, you will need to buy more equity-income and bond funds and fewer growth funds. Try to keep some growth funds, though. Even if you're retired, you need the growth to counter the effects of inflation.

Balanced/Equity Income/Utilities

Pax World Fund (PAXWX)	10%
Fidelity Utilities (FIUIX)	10%

Growth

Janus Twenty (JAVLX)	7.5%
Reynolds Blue Chip Growth	7.5%

Index

Domini Social Equity	7.5%
Vanguard Index 500	7.5%

International

Citizens Global Equity	7.5%
Janus Worldwide	7.5%

Small Cap

Robertson Stevens Emerging Growth	7.5%
Citizens Emerging Growth	7.5%

Bonds

Westcore Long-Term Bond	10%
Strong Short-Term Global Bond	5%

Cash

Money Market	5%
	100%

THE SOCIALLY RESPONSIBLE MODEL PORTFOLIO

A few years ago, when I wrote the first edition of this book, a portfolio of socially responsible mutual funds like this one would have been impossible—there simply weren't enough of them. Now, even though the choice is still a bit thin in a few categories, it's possible to set up a full portfolio. Not only that, the overall performance of these funds in the last few years has matched those listed in the Model Portfolio. Socially concerned investors can be assured that all the funds in this portfolio are rated at four or five stars by *Morningstar Mutual Funds* (five stars is their top rating). The same caveats apply about checking the most recent performance data; these funds look good as of this writing, but there may be others that are doing better by the time you read this. *The GreenMoney Journal* is a good place to find a list of SR funds and their recent performance figures (Resources, Chapter 12).

Balanced/Equity Income/Utilities

Pax World Fund	10%
Flexfunds Total Return Utilities	10%

Growth

Green Century Equity	10%
Bridgeway Social Responsibility Portfolio	10%

Index

Citizens Index	10%
Domini Social Equity	10%

International

Citizens Global Equity	10%

Small Cap

Citizens Emerging Growth   10%

Bonds

Citizens Income   15%

Cash

Money Market   5%
_____

100%

APPENDIX B

FRACTIONS INTO DECIMALS

Since the stock market has not yet learned about decimals, here are the decimal equivalents of the fractions in which stocks are traded:

$\frac{1}{16}$	=	.0625	$\frac{9}{16}$	=	.5625
$\frac{2}{16}$	=	.125	$\frac{10}{16}$	=	.625
$\frac{3}{16}$	=	.1875	$\frac{11}{16}$	=	.6875
$\frac{4}{16}$	=	.25	$\frac{12}{16}$	=	.75
$\frac{5}{16}$	=	.3125	$\frac{13}{16}$	=	.8125
$\frac{6}{16}$	=	.375	$\frac{14}{16}$	=	.875
$\frac{7}{16}$	=	.4375	$\frac{15}{16}$	=	.9375
$\frac{8}{16}$	=	.5			

TOTAL RETURNS:
1925 TO 1994

This chart illustrates how $1.00 invested in various ways would have grown from 1925 to 1994. The chart is an excellent illustration of how compound interest works over the years. For example, the average rate of return, compounded annually, for the large stocks of the S&P 500 is approximately 12% a year. The rate of return for small stocks, however, is close to 15% a year. Notice what a difference these three percentage points make in the total returns over 70 years. The term "total returns" means that any dividends paid to stockholders are reinvested in the entire portfolio. Total returns, therefore, include not just the increase in the price of the stocks, but in the reinvested dividends. Likewise, payments made to bondholders are counted as being reinvested. Taxes and transaction costs are not included.

TOTAL RETURNS OF $1.00 INVESTED IN 1925

	S&P 500	Small Stocks	Long-Term Corporate Bonds	Long-Term Government Bonds	Treasury Bills
1994	810.5	2842.7	3801	25.8	12.18

Source: Ibbotson Associates, "Stocks, Bonds, Bills and Inflation 1995 Yearbook," Chicago.

APPENDIX D

COMPOUND INTEREST

Here's how much you $1.00 would grow over the years if the rate of growth was the same every year. Remember, with compound interest the profit from each year is added on to the principal. Then the next year's interest is figured from this new, larger amount. If you take any income out, the charts won't work.

Compound interest is pretty amazing stuff. If you left $150,000 to your great-grandchildren and it grew at a rate of 15% a year, in a 125 years it would be worth some $6.4 trillion. The great-grandchildren could help pay off the national debt and still have enough left over for one of them to run for president. . . .

To find the compounded amount for any sum of money, simply multiply the sum by the proper amount in the columns. Example: How much would $45,650 grow to, if compounded at the rate of 9% for five years? Go to the 9% column and follow it down to five years. Multiply 1.538 by $45,650 = $70,209.

$1.00 COMPOUNDED ANNUALLY

Years	Annual Rate					Years
	5%	**6%**	**7%**	**8%**	**9%**	
1	$1.050	1.060	1.070	1.080	1.090	1
2	1.102	1.123	1.144	1.166	1.188	2
3	1.157	1.191	1.225	1.259	1.295	3
4	1.215	1.262	1.310	1.360	1.411	4
5	1.276	1.338	1.402	1.469	1.538	5
6	1.340	1.418	1.500	1.586	1.677	6
7	1.407	1.503	1.605	1.713	1.828	7
8	1.477	1.593	1.718	1.850	1.992	8
9	1.551	1.689	1.838	1.999	2.171	9
10	1.628	1.790	1.967	2.158	2.367	10
11	1.710	1.898	2.104	2.331	2.580	11
12	1.795	2.012	2.252	2.518	2.812	12
13	1.885	2.132	2.409	2.719	3.065	13
14	1.979	2.260	2.578	2.937	3.341	14
15	2.078	2.396	2.759	3.172	3.642	15
16	2.182	2.540	2.952	3.425	3.970	16
17	2.292	2.692	3.158	3.700	4.327	17
18	2.406	2.854	3.379	3.996	4.717	18
19	2.526	3.025	3.619	4.315	5.141	19
20	2.653	3.207	3.869	4.660	5.604	20
25	3.386	4.291	5.427	6.848	8.623	25
30	4.321	5.743	7.612	10.062	13.267	30

Years	Annual Rate					Years
	10%	**12%**	**15%**	**18%**	**20%**	
1	1.100	1.120	1.150	1.180	1.200	1
2	1.210	1.254	1.322	1.392	1.440	2
3	1.331	1.404	1.520	1.643	1.728	3
4	1.464	1.573	1.749	1.938	2.073	4
5	1.610	1.762	2.011	2.287	2.488	5
6	1.771	1.973	2.313	2.699	2.985	6
7	1.948	2.210	2.660	3.185	3.583	7
8	2.143	2.475	3.059	3.758	4.299	8
9	2.357	2.773	3.517	4.435	5.159	9
10	2.593	3.105	4.145	5.233	6.191	10
11	2.853	3.478	4.652	6.175	7.430	11
12	3.138	3.895	5.350	7.287	8.916	12
13	3.452	4.363	6.152	8.599	10.699	13
14	3.797	4.887	7.075	10.147	12.839	14
15	4.177	5.473	8.137	11.973	15.407	15
16	4.594	6.130	9.357	14.149	18.488	16
17	5.054	6.866	10.751	16.672	22.186	17
18	5.559	7.689	12.375	19.673	26.623	18
19	6.115	8.612	14.231	23.214	31.948	19
20	6.727	9.646	16.366	27.393	38.337	20
25	10.834	17.000	32.918	62.668	95.396	25
30	17.449	29.959	66.211	143.370	237.376	30

INDEX

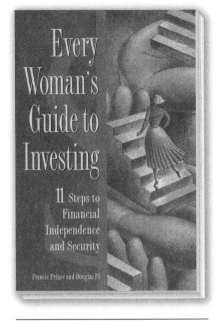

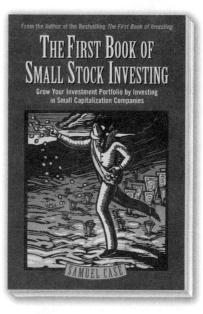

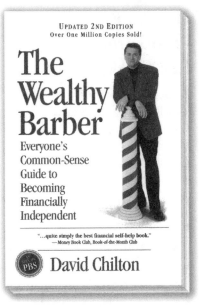

To Order Books

Please send me the following items:

Quantity	Title	Unit Price	Total
_____	**Every Woman's Guide to Investing**	$ 14.95	$ _____
_____	**The First Book of Small Stock Investing**	$ 12.95	$ _____
_____	**Successful Investing with Fidelity Funds,**	$ 18.00	$ _____
_____	**Revised and Expanded 3rd Edition**	$ _____	$ _____
_____	**The Wealthy Barber**	$ 12.95	$ _____

<table>
<tr><td colspan="2">*Shipping and Handling depend on Subtotal.</td></tr>
<tr><td>Subtotal</td><td>Shipping/Handling</td></tr>
<tr><td>$0.00–$29.99</td><td>$4.00</td></tr>
<tr><td>$30.00–$49.99</td><td>$6.00</td></tr>
<tr><td>$50.00–$99.99</td><td>$10.00</td></tr>
<tr><td>$100.00–$199.99</td><td>$13.50</td></tr>
<tr><td>$200.00+</td><td>Call for Quote</td></tr>
</table>

Foreign and all Priority Request orders:
Call Order Entry department
for price quote at 916-632-4400

This chart represents the total retail price of books only
(before applicable discounts are taken).

Subtotal	$ _____
Deduct 10% when ordering 3–5 books	$ _____
7.25% Sales Tax (CA only)	$ _____
8.25% Sales Tax (TN only)	$ _____
5% Sales Tax (MD and IN only)	$ _____
7% G.S.T. Tax (Canada only)	$ _____
Shipping and Handling*	$ _____
Total Order	$ _____

By Telephone: With American Express, MC or Visa,
call 800-632-8676 or 916-632-4400.   Mon–Fri, 8:30–4:30.
WWW: http://www.primapublishing.com

By Internet E-mail: sales@primapub.com
By Mail: Just fill out the information below and send with your remittance to:

Prima Publishing
P.O. Box 1260BK
Rocklin, CA 95677

Name _____

Address_____

City _____ State _____ ZIP_____

American Express/MC/Visa# _____ Exp. _____

Check/money order enclosed for $_____ Payable to Prima Publishing

Daytime telephone _____

Signature _____